THE COMPLETE GUIDE TO

Drying and Preserving Flowers

THE COMPLETE GUIDE TO

Drying and Preserving Flowers

Lesley Gordon and Jean Lorimer

Bloomsbury Books
London

Frontispiece: an arrangement of astrantia,
borage and young ash leaves on a pale background.

Published in Great Britain 1982 by
Webb & Bower (Publishers) Limited
9 Colleton Crescent, Exeter, Devon EX2 4BY

Designed by Vic Giolitto

Copyright © Webb & Bower (Publishers) Limited 1982

This edition published 1992 by
Bloomsbury Books, an imprint of
Godfrey Cave Associates,
42 Bloomsbury Street, London WC1B 3QJ,
under licence from Webb & Bower Ltd 1992.

ISBN 1–85471–054–0

Typeset in Great Britain by Keyspools Limited, Golborne, Lancashire

Printed and bound in Great Britain by
BPCC Hazells Ltd
Member of BPCC Ltd

CONTENTS

Introduction

Lesley Gordon

On 5 November, 1665, on the Lord's Day, Samuel Pepys visited his friend Mr John Evelyn and, among other 'very pretty things', was shown his *hortus hyemalis* or winter garden, otherwise known as *hortus siccus*, a dried garden. In his diary Pepys described with enthusiasm these 'leaves laid up in a book of several plants kept dry, which preserve colour, however, and look very finely, better than any Herball', although he could not forbear to note of his host that 'a most excellent person he is, and must be allowed a little for a little conceitedness'.

This *hortus siccus* was not a new hobby for Evelyn; indeed, he had started it twenty years earlier when visiting the Botanic Gardens at Padua, and it was compiled for its scientific rather than its artistic value.

The earliest known *hortus siccus* is that of John Tradescant the Elder. Both he and his son, John Tradescant the Younger, were gardeners and plant collectors to Charles I and Charles II. The elder John sent his flowers from Virginia 'lay'd Betwin paper leaves in a Book dried'. The Tradescant *hortus siccus* is now in the Bodleian Library, Oxford. After three hundred years it remains in marvellously good condition, thanks, it is believed, to the glue which was used to fasten down the specimens. If anyone cares to try it, here is his secret formula: '$\frac{1}{4}$ lb of Isinglas $\frac{1}{4}$ of a threepenny stick of mouth glue put them in an earthen vessell and cover it over with water, or ale, or claret, or sack, or aquavita (this latter is stronger and still the better). Let them stand so in infusion 3 days. Set them after upon the embers or gentle fire that they may only dissolve, and so wheresoever you use it, lay it on with a sharp pencill.'

It was probably not until the reign of Queen Victoria, when the interest in natural history penetrated every well-bred home, that young families, conducted back with glowing cheeks from an afternoon in the country, laid out their specimens of ragged Robin (*Lychnis flos-cuculi*), tufted vetch (*Viccia cracca*) and meadow cranesbill (*Geranium pratense*), and listened to papa expatiating upon the remarkable ingenuities of root,

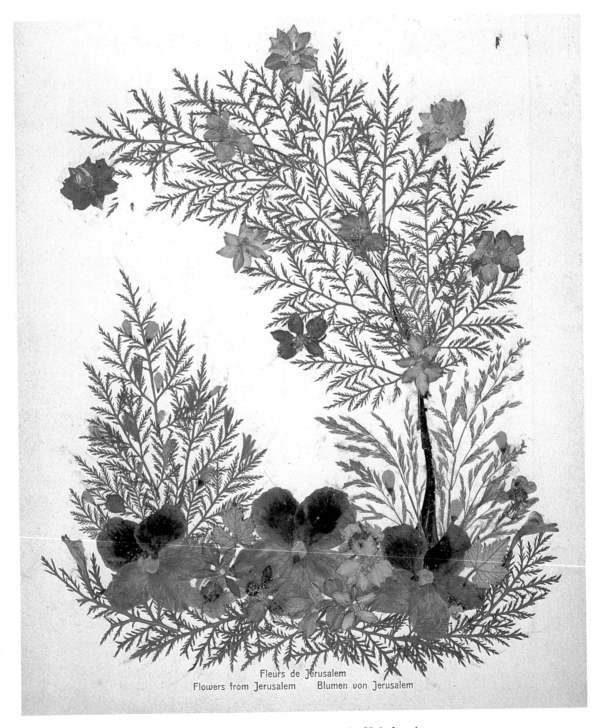

Fleurs de Jérusalem
Flowers from Jerusalem   Blumen von Jerusalem

Flowers from Jerusalem. An arrangement of pressed flowers from the Holy Land, taken from a magnificent book bound in olive wood, a Victorian tourist trophy still in excellent condition. Among the flowers are Love in the mist (*Nigella damascena*), which in the biblical language of flowers of that period symbolized perplexity.

Buttercup from 'Wild Flowers and their Teachings', 1848. This charming little book contains pressed wild flowers, each accompanied by suitable and improving verses, and a botanical description such as this: 'Ranunculus bulbosus – bulbous crowfoot, or buttercup. Named from rana, a frog; from the plants delighting to grow where frogs abound.'

Above right: Lavender bags and pot-pourri – some practical uses of dried flowers.

tendril and calyx, and the goodness of God who provided them.

Although some specimens, such as cuckoo pint and the man orchid, were left in the wild as being unsuitable for tender eyes and ears, most were carefully dried and neatly spread out on the pages of specially provided albums, anchored with small strips of paper and named and divided into tribes more numerous than the tribes of Israel. Books for wild flower collectors could be obtained with illustrations and descriptions, and with blank spaces waiting to be filled; after more than a century, many of the spaces remain blank, proving human frailty as predictable as botanical desiccation.

It must have been mama who realized the artistic possibilities of these researches and, dispensing with paper strips and tribal nomenclature, assisted her daughters in the making of flower pictures, while her sons were occupied with the intricacies of Greek translation or indulging in manly sports in the garden with papa.

Owing to the ravages of insects and the toll taken by light on fugitive colours few of these charming pictures remain, but there still exist some rare wild flower books that were issued with each page containing an actual specimen of a wild flower accompanied by a religious verse. Although they were the work of a parson in St Albans they were published in Bath, at twenty-five shillings, a considerable sum at that time. They were destined to be the treasured gifts from husband to wife or parent to child, and as such have been handed down as heirlooms; in some, the specimens are almost perfect after more than 135 years. *Lychnis flos-cuculi*, for example, still shows a muted pink over the information that its name signifies *a lamp*, 'the thick cottony substance of the leaves of some species, having been employed as wicks to lamps'. An accompanying verse describes the lychnis as 'blushing like the newborn day', making clear that there is more to life than pure science.

Many books issued with pressed flower illustrations were brought from the Holy Land, some as simple tourists' gifts, and others of great magnificence, with covers of carved and polished olive wood and elaborately mounted flower pictures. Some contain views of Jerusalem and are captioned in French, German and English. Because the pages within a book were only rarely exposed to the light, the flowers have kept their colours remarkably well. A Reverend Harvey Green spent three springs in gathering and pressing the flowers of Palestine with the assistance of native helpers, buoyed by the unusual prospect of combining business with religion, and his small books and cards were accompanied by a declaration by British and US Consuls that, prior to publication in 1899, these flowers were indeed growing in the Holy Land. Pressed flowers framed in olive wood from the Mount of Olives also reached the walls and mantelpieces of the Victorian devout. Other travellers in foreign countries sent home pressed flowers for scientific as well as romantic reasons, although few of these would have been used for artistic purposes.

Sometimes we may find small dried flowers in a locket beside a ghostly photograph. Occasionally some faded petals will drop from the pages of an old book or we will discover a crumpled rose from a wedding bouquet, or a sprig of white heather or a four-leaved clover for luck. Scented flowers were often pressed in bibles and, in some of these, the perfume, although faint, has lasted through the years. More touching are the forget-me-nots, the heartsease pansies or the poppies sent to loved ones from the battlefield – still cherished however wrinkled or faded. On 4 September, 1918, Private Ralph Turner of the 12th Suffolk Regiment sent a page of little pressed heartsease pansies to his wife from somewhere in France, their stems neatly slotted in and out of cuts in the paper. The petals are now rather the worse for wear, some missing altogether, but the rest still lovingly kept by his family more than sixty years later. 'Pansies for thoughts,' Private Turner had written in pencil.

From Normandy, in 1944, Rex Whistler managed to send a leathery sprig of mistletoe, the plant whose magic caused enemies to be reconciled, in a last letter to his mother. The magic failed. Two days later he was killed by enemy action.

Three and a half centuries earlier, in *Delights for Ladies*, published in 1594, Sir Hugh Platt described the drying of 'red rose leaves, pansies, stock gilliflowers, or other single flowers' in sand. 'This secret,' he added, 'is very requisite for a good simplifier' (a gatherer of simples, or herbalist) 'because he may dry the leafe of any herb in this manner: and lay it, being dry, in his Herbal with the simple which it representeth, whereby he may easily learne to know the names of all simples which he desireth.'

Sir Hugh's secret was evidently either handed down or forgotten and later revived, for an excerpt from *The American Gardener's Monthly*, reprinted in *The Florist* of April, 1860, under the heading, 'How to Preserve Flowers in their Natural Forms and Colours', describes a

Preserved beech leaves and
chrysanthemums make an
ideal autumn arrangement.

similar treatment. Perhaps, although well known in the still-rooms of the
past, this was the first time that flowers were thus dried commercially, for
the writer says that 'of late an entirely new article of trade has arisen in
Germany, in the shape of dried flowers. Erfurt, the city of nurserymen
and florists, excels in manufacturing bouquets, wreaths, floral decorations for rooms, dinner tables, etc., made of such flowers. We are glad
therefore that we are enabled to lay before our readers the *modus operandi*,
by translating for them the following article from the *Deutsches Magazin
für Garten und Blumenkunde*.'

He goes on to describe the sand-drying treatment which has in turn led
to the use of modern desiccants described by Jean Lorimer on pages 188–9
in her section on 'Preserving and Using Unpressed Flowers and Foliage'.
The method has changed little over the years, but the use of silica gel or
borax is far kinder to delicate petals than the sharp-grained sand once
was.

The desire to preserve flowers either pressed or unpressed is increasing
and Jean has much to contribute, with her own personal recipes for pot-
pourri and her method of candle decoration. Perhaps most tempting of all

A colourful arrangement of mixed seed-heads, perpetuelles, dried grasses and honesty.

to try are her crystallized flowers and attractive flower sugars.

Discovering a talent for making pressed flower pictures and all the small and delightful objects that can be devised for home decoration may lead to the realization of the artistic possibilities of dried flower arrangement, as suggested by Jean Lorimer.

In a little travel book published some thirty years ago, Ray Dorien wrote, 'There is something to be said for the old Victorian fashion of pressing flowers. The square page of a notebook, small enough to be carried in a handbag, holds a dried flower, pressed quickly between the covers, and a pencilled date. And from the paper-thin, wine-dark shape, and that pencil mark, rises a vivid red poppy, just one of the spots of colour growing in the wild grass on the Acropolis at Athens.'

From such simple beginnings a creative art may grow that will give pleasure to the maker when flowers are few in the winter world outside. It is in this belief that designs for pressed flowers and dried flower arrangements have been brought together in this book, in the hope that some new and exciting ideas may result.

1 Pressing and Preparing the Materials

The equipment necessary for the art or, more modestly, the craft of pressed flower pictures is neither very expensive nor is it hard to come by. The materials will be listed later but quite as vital as any of these is the possession of a pair of eyes not only on the look-out for the obvious, such as the poppies, the pansies and the buttercups, but alert to the veining on the back of a leaf, the beaked profile of a woody nightshade flower or the golden semicircle that succeeds the bloom of the willowherb. This pleasurable search is not all. At odd moments of each day, whether in town or country, the picture-maker should look out for suitable patterns into which flowers will fit. Wallpapers, curtains, carpets, tiles, china and glass: all these may have patterns that can be used for pressed flower pictures. The list is endless.

The enthusiastic flower presser would not agree with the attitude of Wordsworth's Peter Bell:

> A primrose by the river's brim
> A simple primrose was to him
> And it was nothing more.

If a simple primrose does not say more to you than that, then perhaps you should seek another craft but, if you can enjoy the revival of the 'I spy with my little eye' game we played on long railway journeys of the past, then the marrying of form and colour, of flower and textile, will give you endless pleasure.

Lucky people with gardens or week-end cottages have advantages over townsfolk but we must not envy them. Those without such desirable properties may find the trophies of the chase even more exciting. A hole in a wall may shelter a fern; a crack in the pavement may produce a daisy. Sometimes a tiny, starved town daisy will fit more snugly into a design than a buxom country daisy will. A walk at the week-end or a day by the sea will provide all sorts of treasures in the way of grasses and the ferny fronds of seaweed. There is also the commendable habit that many garden plants and shrubs have of diving under their owner's fence and coming up on a patch of waste ground outside, where they seem to flourish even better in unwonted freedom and may be taken without fear or favour. Known as 'garden escapes' to the botanists, these adventurers will not enjoy their freedom for long before they are spotted by some passing flower presser. Spirited youngsters in the form of cow parsley or herb Robert have been known to push up through newly asphalted paths. After accomplishing this fantastic feat, they remain looking deceptively frail (or defiant, or smug, as it strikes one) until disaster in the form of a suburban flower presser overtakes them. Roadside verges contain all kinds of treasures; probably the most valuable is an occasional haul of silverweed (*Potentilla anserina*).

A few potted plants on a balcony may provide a desirable leaf or two. Perhaps in spring an annual extravagance might be a single branch of mimosa. We may not all be Voltaires and cultivate our gardens but at least we may cultivate our friends who have gardens and repay them with a picture that they will cherish.

Material for pressing should be picked if possible on a dry day about noon, when sun and wind have dried the morning dew. The sooner the pressing is done, the better, to avoid wrinkling or withering, which occur more rapidly with some flowers than others, according to their texture. If the flowers are taken straight from the garden, this presents no problem but flower pressers should adopt the scouts' motto: 'Be Prepared.' Do not venture out walking, visiting or even shopping without a folded newspaper, a magazine or a plastic bag in which to carry home safely a few leaves or flowers encountered on the way. Many of the pictures illustrated here owe vital parts of their composition to lucky encounters in unlikely places: miniature horse chestnut leaves sprouting at the base of their trees in spring; leaves of common wayside plants turned scarlet or purple in late summer; skeleton leaves blown into the hedges in winter and there lodged. Once I found a colony of blackberries, nettles and other hedgerow plants, all suffering from some soil deficiency or the effects of a weed-killer spray, magically turned to pink and apricot and cream, out-beautifying nature.

Pressing

It is at the time of pressing your plant material that the craft shows the first signs of becoming an art. The imagination begins to stir; indeed, it must stir, or the resulting picture will be just another bunch of flowers, and not a design *with* flowers.

The specimens you have picked will usually need thinning out, so that the leaves do not lie across the stems or over one another, making unsightly bulk. If thinning is left until after pressing, some parts will be permanently marked. The prunings of buds and seeds, as well as the flowers, may be pressed separately and, if not used at the time, can be kept for stock.

Cup-shaped and rayed flowers are best pressed face downwards. Have a mental picture before you start and coax stems, flowers and tendrils to follow the lines of the picture you see in your mind, for, once they are dried, no alterations are possible. Thicknesses of calyx which are difficult

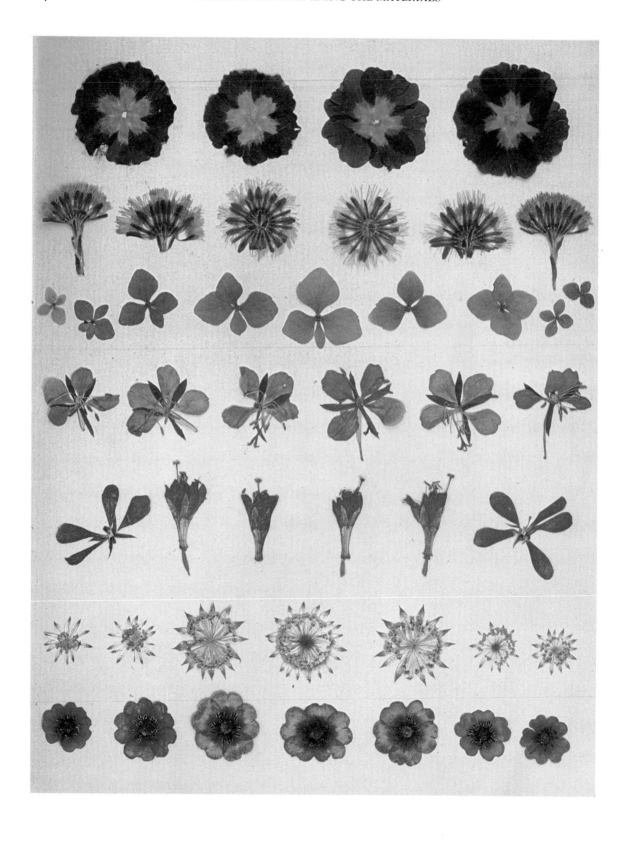

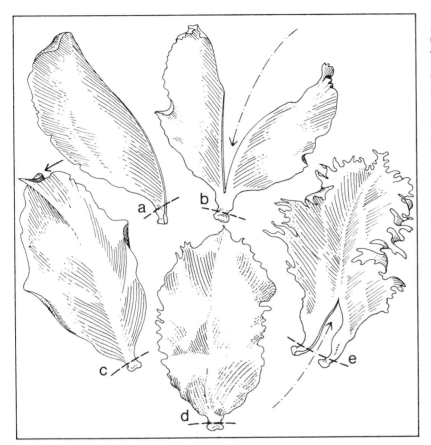

Fig. 1 : *Cutting and pressing tulip petals.*
(a) Petal halved and cut to curve. Thick growing point removed.
(b) To flatten cup-shaped petals, split down to near base and remove growing point before pressing.
(c) Cup-shaped petal can be pleated and pressed flat.
(d) Semi-cup-shaped petal may be smoothed and carefully adjusted for pressing, after removing the growing point.
(e) Parrot-type petals may be split from the bottom upwards.

Opposite: *A Page From a Specimen Book.* A useful method of presenting at a glance a small number of flowers and leaves which act as a reminder of what is available in store, which can be replenished and kept up to date as the material is used.

to press may be cautiously pared down with advantage but not too much or the flower will drop to pieces. Twiggy and too sturdy stems may also be pared down from behind, so that the spray may set more easily.

The thick growing point of tulip petals is full of sap and should be removed before pressing. The petal will then be less likely to adhere to the paper and the chances of it tearing when it is dry will be reduced. It will be found that in many tulips there are three petals that will press flat without difficulty and three alternate petals which are cup-shaped. If the cup-shaped petals are slightly split and the points removed in a double curve (fig. 1), the problems of wrinkling and sticking can be successfully dealt with. Hollyhocks and other similar petals can be treated in the same way, since these points will need removing also.

Methods of pressing vary. Some people iron the flowers under paper, immediately before storing in books or presses, but it would be impossible to treat tiny flowers in that way. The most usual method is to press the flowers between sheets of newspaper folded into four and neatly stacked in piles of not more than a dozen folded sheets. These should be placed on a board or some flat surface, on a shelf or in an airing cupboard, with a large book on top and two bricks or a flat-iron to weight the book. Another method is to dry the flowers between tissues in old telephone directories; one directory for leaves only, one for flowers and single petals and one for stems, tendrils, stamens and centres. These, too, should be weighted down. Quick drying between sheets of blotting paper before final storage may be satisfactory but blotting paper is expensive and quickly becomes stained and unusable; in any case, frail petals are inclined to stick to the slightly woolly surface, with disastrous consequences. Glossy magazines should never be used, for a slightly absorbent paper is necessary for flowers to dry properly. Absorbent paper can absorb too much exterior damp if kept too long in an airless cupboard or a damp room, occasional exposure to a current of air is advisable.

Flower presses are useful and you may find the results more satisfactory but if you are taking up this craft seriously you will need more than one press, since promising material is apt to present itself in large quantities in summer and early autumn and the opportunity may not occur again. Two or three children's presses, available at most art- or toy-shops, will prove most useful during the rapidly changing flower season, especially for the frailer petals and flower-heads. With larger presses it will be found more difficult to manipulate the greater number of items and to hold down the curving stems while screwing down the press. Old tie-presses are useful but trouser-presses are too large and clumsy to be suitable. Slow-drying and heavy-textured materials such as stems, centres and autumn leaves must be kept together and not pressed with delicate petals and small flowers, which will take far less time to dry and may also be damaged with impressions of heavy veins and centres.

Flower presses are fitted with corrugated cardboard inter-leaves for ventilation, which must be thickly padded with newspaper or blotting paper cut to size. If this is not done, fragile silken petals will be deeply and permanently striped with the corrugations.

It is a simple matter to make, or to have made up, a flower press of a reasonable size, not so large as to be difficult to manipulate but not so small as to be inadequate and time-wasting. Plywood of about $\frac{3}{8}$ in. (9·5 mm) thick and 14×16 in. (35×40 cm) in surface measurement would be serviceable and adequate for most requirements. This can be supplied and cut at any DIY shop, which will also furnish nuts and bolts of a suitable size. If business is quiet, they may also be persuaded to make the necessary holes to accommodate the bolts, leaving you only the small job of rubbing down the rough edges and corners of the wood. However, business is seldom quiet in these hives of activity. If you have not got the necessary tool, it should not be too difficult to ask the assistance of a friend or neighbour, who may welcome the offer of a small picture or some greetings cards as payment in kind.

Some books state that, while drying, the specimens should not be disturbed for periods of between five days and six months, according to the nature of the plant but experience proves that examination at reasonable intervals is important. This gives an opportunity to throw out any flowers showing signs of mildew or bad discoloration which may spread and to smooth any creased or wrinkled petals with a soft brush or a gentle finger-tip.

Press stems and sprays with a curve wherever possible, for straight lines do exist in nature, whatever may have been said to the contrary, and

A page showing foliage from a specimen book

they are not attractive in flower design. Small flowers pressed in profile are valuable, since a design composed of all forward-facing flowers gives an uncomfortable suggestion of a regimental photograph, unless perhaps in an abstract design. In the case of leaves having silver backs or with some contrast in reverse, a few should be coaxed to fold in pressing, where this is possible, so that both sides may be seen and an effect of light and shade obtained.

It may be better to dismember some flowers, pressing the parts separately and building them up again when desired, since the petals may be fragile or perhaps doubled and the centres thick. The different thicknesses cannot possibly press well together. Better still, is to choose what parts you need to create flowers of your own designing. Study the superb patterns of William Morris, Charles Voysey and Walter Crane and the work of the modern textile designers, and notice the numbers of flowers that they have freely adapted and made anew. Nothing can give greater satisfaction than the making of a flower that never existed before you thought of it: flowers entirely composed of leaves, birds made of columbines or dianthus petals, moths of sycamore seeds, butterflies of hollyhock petals, fish of tulips; exotic blooms and strange creatures that never were on land or sea. Suggestions for making some of these will come later but they may have a bearing on what you press and the way you press it. Turning one flower into another, or a catkin and a skeleton leaf into a bee, has a magic not to be missed.

When all parts of a plant feel dry to the touch, they may finally be stored in bags measuring 10×12 in. (25×30 cm), which have a paper backing and a cellophane front, allowing a small degree of porosity but enabling plants to be identified without any further handling. Final storing by this method, instead of in books, does away with tiresome labelling. If you have a number of fragile flowers of similar varieties, they should be laid side by side but not overlapping on sheets of thin paper (typing paper will fit these bags) and stored one over another inside a single bag. Do not mix types or thicknesses of material. Ensure that they are stacked firmly and tightly, with a weight on top, or in a suitcase or drawer, or all your good work may be wasted.

At the end of the season, if no more pictures are planned for a time, it is advisable to check the material and remove any that may be torn or mildewed. Pack the rest between fresh dry paper and see-through bags, between sheets of cardboard, strapped together or tied with string. Piled on one another, they should then remain in perfect condition until required.

To make a picture: tools and materials

The necessary equipment is very simple:

1 Curved scissors, two sizes if possible: small straight scissors and large scissors.
2 Pointed tweezers. Avoid square ends.
3 One small and one medium paintbrush, for smoothing and dusting off small fragments.
4 Adhesive, preferably Pritt New Cream or PVA, but one which is colourless when dry.
5 A shallow lid or dish to hold the adhesive and a cocktail stick to apply it.
6 Tissues or clean rag.
7 A retractable Stanley knife, a scapel and a small craft knife.
8 Mounting board or paper.
9 Pencil, rubber and ruler (steel if possible).
10 A needle for picking up small particles.
11 A frame, with glass and backing, panel pins and gummed strip for sealing.
12 A large drawing board or piece of hardboard is desirable and a clear working space essential.

Artemisia Vase, an Art Nouveau design, simple in itself, but valuable as an exercise in the control and economy of material.

It is advisable and cheaper to design your picture to your frame, so that you may work comfortably within the bounds of the frame and use the glass for covering the picture between working sessions. Flowers soon begin to curl or wrinkle if left uncovered for long. You can also use the glass as a template when cutting the mounting paper or board. If the picture is large or intricate, the glass can be useful to rest your hand on while working on a small, tightly packed area.

You can make a good and orderly start by arranging the outlying leaves and flowers and perhaps one or two others of importance within the design. It is vital at this point to remember to leave a fair margin so that the picture will not look too crowded; that is, unless yours is a repeat design which will necessarily run off the edges of the paper. Formal

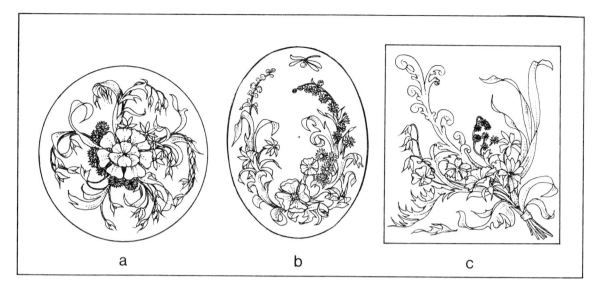

a b c

Fig. 2: *Designing to the shape of the frame.*
(a) A round frame is the most difficult to fill gracefully, and the density should usually be central, thinning towards the perimeter.
(b) The more popular oval designs usually follow the contour of the frame from a point at the base, which may be central or to one side, lightening in weight towards the top.
(c) Square pictures may be designed from the centre or the base, or even from the corners, according to whether the pattern is formal or informal. (c) is an informal treatment.

designs such as those used in textiles and wallpapers must have an observable pattern and a controlled balance, even though the two sides can never be identical, because of the material you are using.

An attractive exercise in pattern-making is to cut from a good quality art paper the simple shape of a vase and to decorate it with pressed flowers or leaves in a suitable design. The colour contrasts of mounting paper and vase are important. Adhesive should be applied sparingly at the top of the vase only, to avoid any buckling of the paper when the flower material is laid down. Before this is done, a highlight of white chalk may be applied with a pad of cotton wool or the tip of the finger to indicate the contours of the vase. This is an improvement but not entirely necessary; it is better that it should be ignored than overdone.

The *Artemisia Vase* (page 19) is made with the grey undersides of the leaves of mugwort (*Artemisia vulgaris*). Ensure that the leaves follow the roundness of the column and do not let them overlap. The symmetry of this pattern is all important. Mounted on grey paper and framed in narrow black and gold, this will make an attractive picture.

When designing a bouquet or a large vase of flowers, the weight of colour and texture is usually at the bottom of the flower group, to avoid a top-heavy appearance. However, with a spray or crescent, the largest flower may be in the centre. Flowers may arch outwards from a point in the middle or towards one side or, following the outline of the frame, both sides can curve towards the centre to form an oval (fig. 2).

Combinations of large and small, rounded and slender, light and dark are usual in most designs, although there may be exceptions to this rule, as with the *Moonrose* picture (page 138), which is restricted to two colours, dark blue and silver, with little variety of shape and size of the seed-vessels used.

Handle the plants with tweezers wherever possible and pick up seeds and small particles with a needle. It is easy to bruise and damage the texture and delicate patina of the petals. For a deep design, such as

Tribute to Arcimboldo or *Comedy and Tragedy* (pages 140 and 141), it is necessary to fix the back and outline petals first, adding details such as features when you are certain of your basic shape. This type of picture allows no space between the petals, although overlapping is to be avoided wherever possible.

In most other designs, space is as important as the solid shape, to give lightness and life. Before you start, have ready all the tools and materials you will need and allow no other clutter on your working surface. Spread the leaves, flowers and stems that you have chosen on a clean sheet of white paper or, better still, white card, so that you can see each item at a glance. Tiny fronds and seeds are easily mislaid or blown away. Do not start until you are certain that you have time to fix the outlines and the most important features of the picture without interruption. After that, leave the telephone bell to ring unanswered. Petals left around uncovered may rapidly deteriorate.

If an idea is not yet clear in your mind, choose a design from this book that appeals to you and for which you have the right sort of material. You can also study the shapes in fig. 2 and work from one of those, remembering that shape and colour are equally important. If this is your first large picture, keep it simple. Later on you will find pleasure in exploring ovals, circles, diagonals, diamonds or the lovely sweeping 'S' curves, from corner to corner, that look so professional.

Once the picture is outlined, you can stick down these leaves and flowers or leave them free, as you choose, and then gently cover them with glass, checking that the edges are flush with the edges of the mounting paper. By this means, you will have freedom to slide the rest of the material over the surface of the glass without disturbing your basic shape, until you find a pattern that satisfies you. This may come about almost immediately, or it may take a day or two. Do not hurry, for the decisions taken now are the lasting ones. When you are completely certain that the picture can not be improved, lift the glass gently to one side, leaving the design undisturbed on the surface. If you have not already done so, stick down your basic outline and then transfer the material from the glass on to the background paper, sticking each piece down, working from top to bottom or from back to front according to the nature of the pattern. It may help to make a few faint pencil dots to indicate where the most important plants should go. If you have no suitable glass or frame available, arrange the complete design loosely and, when satisfied, mark the positions of flower centres and outlying features before you begin to stick them down.

You will need only a small quantity of adhesive squeezed out ready into the container, since it dries quickly and a larger amount would be wasted. Pick up each item with tweezers and examine front and back carefully before you decide which is the most attractive. Often the calyx showing at the back of a daisy or a potentilla has a more interesting pattern then the front. Having made a decision, turn the flower to the angle which best fits your design and make a mental note of exactly where it must be returned. Then hold it with the tweezers in your left hand, apply tiny spots of adhesive along the back of stems and veins and centres and transfer it to

A flower sampler to be kept at hand as a reference. A guide to the colour relationship between flower and background.

your right hand. Place the flower down firmly and do not try to slide it about if you discover it is wrongly sited. If this happens, remove it at once and find another flower that will fit. Centres, stamens and so on should be left to the last. When sticking down tiny stamens or flowers, it may be more convenient and it is certainly quicker to put a minute spot of adhesive on the paper where the flower is to go and then gently and accurately to press the flower down. If the petals drop off during this process, they can easily be fitted in with a spot of adhesive at the growing point.

All this takes far longer to describe than to accomplish. It will not be long before you become adept. Most important, use only a minimum of adhesive and clean your tools frequently with tissue or rag. A smeary picture is *not* a lovesome thing.

Backgrounds: colour and texture

So far we have not discussed mounting card or paper, although this is of the greatest importance. Bearing in mind that the colours of the picture will be muted, for pressed flowers are seldom very bright, a white background is not often satisfactory. There are exceptions to this rule, of course, and one such may be seen in the *Wedding Fan* (page 129). The background colour should complement but not compete with the design. Do not waste your good work on cheap paper. Sugar paper and other cheap papers are made in a range of attractive colours, but they will certainly fade. Good papers, such as Ingres and Canson, prove less expensive than you may think when you buy them, for you can get two large or four small pictures from one sheet. Off-cuts can be joined to make two-coloured backgrounds, which can be very effective. If you are able to stock up with a few good papers and some well-designed wrapping papers for borders, cut-out vases and other collages, you will be able to produce a satisfying number of large and small panels and pictures.

A suggested list of coloured papers

Black	Midnight blue
Dark grey	Soft dark green
Dark red	Pale grey-blue
Cream	Straw yellow
Pale green	Warm mid-brown

You can buy one or two sheets at a time and add to them, if you have a good art shop or a printer's near by. Store them flat if possible. Rolled papers may crack and are difficult to control.

Chinese and Japanese papers as a background to pressed flower pictures reflect a delight in and sympathy with plant forms and are perhaps the best of all for the purpose. The Japanese make a bark paper that resembles the living wood and may be obtained in two shades of brown, two golden straw colours, two greens and, most effective of all, silver birch.

It is a useful exercise to cut several panels of different coloured papers

and to try the plants you want to use against each in turn. The changing effects are surprising. If your picture is designed for a particular room, special care must be taken in the choice of coloured backgrounds.

There are advantages in using a Daler board, in which there is a splendid colour range. They are, however, more difficult to cut to size and the plant material is inclined to lie on the hard surface, instead of sinking comfortably into a soft paper, which must be backed with board when framed. Sometimes a picture framer's gilt board can be used with exciting results. Let no one persuade you to use a cut mount round a pressed flower picture, although you may sometimes see them on sale or pictured in a book. The air let in between glass and flowers will certainly cause wrinkles and deterioration before very long.

A 'sampler' or a sheet of small shapes of variously coloured papers with designs of tiny leaves, buds and flowers, is useful to keep as a reference guide for larger and more ambitious work; like other samplers, it has a certain charm in its own right (page 23). The handling of the smallest possible fragment of fern and leaf and petal, like the neat and perfect stitches of a sampler worked long ago, is a skill worth cultivating and it will be found useful later on in the designing of miniatures and small articles such as pendants and the lids of pill boxes and powder compacts. A framed pressed flower sampler hanging on the wall above your work-table can act as a source of inspiration for larger pictures, as well as a decoration for your room. Hung on a reasonably sunny wall, it can also act as a colour guide and a test of the reliability of particular flowers over a period of time. Tiny buds and leaflets must be used to scale and a suitable space left between the design and the edges of the picture. The amount of adhesive used is correspondingly minute. The small and delicate particles must be handled only by narrow pointed tweezers or a needle. A number 0 or 1 water-colour paintbrush is useful for smoothing refractory petals and tendrils. The work needs to be done with the precision of a jeweller or a watchmaker and the search for suitable material requires the eyes of a hawk. It is, however, a fascinating occupation. From a picture measuring $1\frac{1}{2} \times 2$ in. (4×5 cm), a design of small flowers can be extended to much larger pictures such as the *Patchwork Quilt* (page 102) and the *Paisley Shawl* (page 104), if you have the patience!

Whether your picture is large or small, frame it as soon as possible to exclude the air, although it would be as well not to fix all the panel pins in finally until you have placed it on view for a day or two. Delicate additions or subtractions may still be made before it is too late, or a fallen petal be removed that might have escaped notice. Pack up the back with card as well as hardboard if there is room, and seal the edges with gummed paper strip. If the picture is to be professionally framed, it might be worth enquiring into the matter of heat-sealing, which is used by some artists. Metal frames, box-lids and trays have their own special fittings, some with pins and some with self-sealing backs.

Every picture needs a title as a means of identification. It also lends an interest and an atmosphere, a sense of importance to your work. A title will sometimes present itself in an odd moment, even before the material is available to give it body and presence. A song title, a line of poetry, a

A Victorian Garland.
Flowers picked in this year's
garden may recall, in their
soft colouring, the warmth
and sunshine of a garden
long ago.

chance remark will act as a fingerpost. It is haunting, irritating,
impossible to dismiss and yet months may pass before the flowers and
mosses may be found that you know you must have for the picture that is
half-formed in your mind. Write down that title and leave it where it can
be seen among your materials. It is a game requiring patience but it is well
worth while.

You may make a picture first and then have to wait for a title but a title
you must have to make the picture valid. Label all pictures on the back
with title, date and, perhaps, the area from which the flowers were
gathered, from a friend's garden or a holiday in the country. Add your

name and address. It may be useful for an exhibition catalogue or simply as a family record. If your handwriting is good or if you are capable of neat lettering, your work can, of course, be signed on the front but do not spoil an otherwise charming picture with an untidy signature. Modesty is the best policy in this case.

Plant colour and colour changes

Some flowers are completely useless for pressing. It is as well to discover which they are, to avoid disappointment and disenchantment with the craft as a whole.

Sweet peas, for example, can never be captured and kept, for their frail and lovely petals will go brown and spotted within two days. Small pea-flowers, such as gorse and broom, will go dark brown or black but they have an interesting profile (a front view is impossible) and you may like to use them. The purple pea-flowers, the vetches, keep their colour reasonably well but most of them are too small when separated to be useful, although the tufted vetch is desirable for its neatly paired leaves and the small tendril it wears like a topknot on its head.

Orchids and many other sappy flowers, however rich their colouring, should be avoided; so should nearly all roses, except for single and semi-single varieties. If you are content to work with cream and light brown roses, avoid the deadening effect of a white background; try a peach, apricot or a dull green paper or board. The garland in *A Victorian Garland* (page 25) is made of Japanese windflowers (*Anemone japonica*), which changed considerably in pressing and will probably go on changing, but the peach-coloured background, the brown-red and green of the leaves and the addition of extra centres to build up slightly damaged or inconspicuous centres have given them a new beauty which may last for a long time. The dragonflies' wings are made from the silky reverse of white African daisy (*Dimorphotheca*), petals.

Parrot tulip petals, ragged of line and splashed and slashed with bright colours, and some varieties of bi-coloured carnations and picotees, although they are likely to become softer in colour, give life and drama to a design. Indeed, most striped, spotted and strangely mottled or jagged petals are worth while, as you can see in *Tulipomania* (page 119), but the lovely crimson-splashed Rosa Mundi, traditionally named for the mistress of Henry II, Fair Rosamond, who was poisoned by his jealous Queen, is sheer disaster. It should have been expected. So bright and beautiful in the garden, she cannot be saved. Her petals become brown and stained, even when each one is separately pressed.

Do not let such disappointments depress you, however, for many pleasant surprises await. Hollyhock petals dry with a silken sheen and their heavy veining gives them strength and character. Some varieties improve and grow brighter with drying, except for the palest pinks, which are apt to become drab, but these are still useful for such floral jokes as *Tribute to Arcimboldo* (page 140) and *Comedy and Tragedy* (page 141). If caricatures do not appeal, such is the versatility of these many-coloured petals that they can be used for butterflies or reassembled in

Designs for Four Seasons: Summer. A few petals, some catkins and stamens, and a handful of grasses, are enough to create an atmosphere of eternal summer.

Blue Medallion. Formal
designs such as this may be
derived from a host of
household articles; boxes,
vases, carved frames, drawer
handles, door knockers and
garden urns. Choose some
nearby object that will give
you the basis for a pattern
that makes the best use of the
flowers at your disposal,
leaving them in their natural
colours, or spraying them
with gold or silver.

their own form. The butterfly panel, *Summer* (page 27), is intended as one in a set of the *Four Seasons*. It is mounted on silver birch Japanese bark paper, measuring 11 × 30 in. (28 × 76 cm), and is a simple arrangement of grasses with the hollyhock petals and small pieces of willow catkins for butterfly bodies. The picture may not necessarily be cut as a panel but it must be large to accommodate the hollyhocks. Smaller silken petals will make smaller butterflies but it would be hard to find a flower so suitable both in shape and colours as a hollyhock.

Having worked out the proportions of *Summer*, why not try the other three seasons, made to the same dimensions? Autumn, with its wide choice of red and russet leaves on a gold-coloured Japanese bark paper, presents no great difficulty. Spring, with willow catkins, grass and crocuses, with perhaps a scattering of daisies, would be simple. Winter, however, presents problems but what a challenge!

On a silver bark background, lay some evergreens such as cedars, firs and ivy, with a light spray of white on the upper leaves and another waft of white in the foreground. Those who have had the forethought to press holly leaves when they were young and malleable, could use their black silhouettes with stunning effect for this picture. Perhaps a few shed leaves in the foreground? It is worth a try.

There are still more pleasantly surprising colour changes yet to be found in dried flowers. Salmon pink opium poppies change rapidly to a soft pinkish-purple; their ragged petals with dark purple splashes take on the texture of fine silk and the colour then lasts well. They can sometimes be pressed whole but this is a less safe method; separately pressed petals can be used for such insects of unknown species as those in the Chinese design (page 151).

Nasturtium petals press well, retaining their interesting guidelines, although their colours lose their brilliance and they cannot satisfactorily be reassembled in a true nasturtium form. Half-opened flowers may be pressed in profile, showing their characteristic horn.

Most daisy shapes, both large and small, press better if the backs are pared down a little, but it is important not to cut too much away, or the petals will drop out. With the large marguerites and rudbeckias, their thick centres make it necessary to press the petals separately and to reassemble them.

Hydrangeas of any variety are reliable, although subject to interesting colour changes. All such changes are unpredictable, depending largely on climate and local conditions. The white florets of the Japanese climbing hydrangea (*Hydrangea petiolaris*) are uniformly cream when pressed but their curious shapes make the most appealing little families of mice for children's greeting cards, with the addition of a seed eye and a tendril tail (page 69).

Blue is usually regarded as a fugitive colour, yet lobelias, larkspurs and delphiniums may be relied on to keep an excellent colour. An example of the use of blues is in the circular pattern, *Blue Medallion* (opposite), adapted from the design on a silver salver. A line was drawn round the salver on a dark blue paper and seven circles drawn round the base of a wine glass on pale blue, which were then cut out with pinking shears. The

large circle was lightly pasted on to a background of silver wrapping paper and the seven small circles stuck down accurately into place. After this, it was a simple matter to fix six flowers of masterwort (*Astrantia major*), on to the six points which divide the perimeter of the circle. Silverweed, showing alternately front and reverse sides, divides the pale blue circles, with delphinium blooms between and a pale blue delphinium placed centrally. A large masterwort flower on top of this fixes the central point. A touch of soft pink by means of an unidentified rockery plant is fastened to the centre of each pale blue circle; these circles are finally linked by a chain of florets from a head of Queen Anne's lace. This design could equally well be carried out in pink and blue larkspurs.

Deep purple is a long-lasting colour, although in time some clematis varieties will turn soft grey and fawn. Nellie Moser, a rosy pink when growing, produces more interesting patterns on the reverse side. This can be seen in *Memory of Summer Past* (opposite), which, after seven or eight years, has settled down to a soft range of colours from silver to dull purple. The brown of the Japanese bark paper, 15 × 20 in. (38 × 51 cm), is a good foil for the silver-grey leaves, mostly on reverse. They are raspberry, buddleia, *Cineraria maritima*, silverweed, *Alchemilla alpina* and *Artemisia*. The soft pink is supplied by nerine lilies and the centres of the clematis are each accented by a floret of Queen Anne's lace.

Autumn leaves, having already achieved the colour changes ordained by nature, are usually reliable, although some have grown rather leathery and intractable. Japanese maples look marvellous on a background of golden bark paper.

Beetlemania (above) is an amusing exercise in inventiveness and the use of colour. With the exception of one green honesty seed and one blue delphinium petal, the insect bodies are each composed of an autumn leaf. A few have decorations imposed, as in the case of the large purple beetle,

Above: *Beetlemania*. A lively party of Chafers Anonymous, coleopterous insects, whose upper wings have been converted into hard cases that protect the lower and true wings, like a violin case over a delicate instrument. Blake wrote that 'He who torments the Chafer's Sprite/Weaves a bower of endless Night'.

Left: *Memory of Summer Past*. An example of the gentle fading of our memories of summer in a garden long ago. Some objects remain as clear as if it were yesterday, like the grey and silver leaves that encompass the design. Others have softened and grown dim in the twilight of the past, like flowers in the warm dusk of evening.

second on the top left, where a single purple and white dahlia petal gives an extra dimension and an appearance of shine to an otherwise dark body. It is fascinating to find suitable minute oddments for feelers, legs and eyes, so that no two insects are alike. A few of these lively looking creatures, front legs meeting in a 'Here we go round the mulberry bush' circle, would make a good picture for a child's playroom, or a decoration for a toy-box lid, covered with a protective film.

Green leaves are subject to all kinds of change, some lighter, some darker; the new leaves of holly and plane and the delicate young greens of *Eccremocarpus scaber*, with its orange tubular flower, will turn almost black.

Silver-grey, grey-green and silver-backed leaves for drying

Ballota A garden perennial with curious flowers like white and purple pompoms, spaced at intervals on tall stems. Grey and white woolly leaves. Requires well-drained soil and sun.

Carnation (*Dianthus*) Many of these beautiful flowers have spear-like, grassy, silver-grey leaves, which should not be overlooked because they are so familiar.

Chrysanthemum haradjanii Rock perennial, forming a mat of silvery-white, finely divided, fern-like leaves. Short-stemmed orange flowers but usually grown for its attractive leaves. A little choosy and enjoys sun.

Cineraria maritima One of the most useful plants for pressed flower pictures. It has leaves that are attractively cut and near-white on both sides. Treat as a half-hardy annual.

Cotton lavender (*Santolina*) A bushy ever-grey shrub, with stems covered in a white felt. Like so many grey-leaved plants, it has yellow flowers in midsummer. There is a valuable dwarf form, 'Nana'.

Lady's mantle (*Alchemilla alpina*) This attractive and unusual plant has undistinguished yellow flowers and solid green leaves with bright silver reverses. It requires a well-drained soil and a sunny position.

Lamb's ears (*Stachys lanata*) This plant is also known as Saviour's flannel. A border plant of great appeal to children, for its silvery-white furry leaves. No well-equipped rabbit can do without a pair. It has red flowers in summer, borne on an erect stem. It likes a well-drained soil in sun or light shade. There is a form, 'Silver Carpet', which rarely flowers (no great loss) and is a useful ground-cover plant.

Pearl everlasting (*Anaphalis margaritacea*) Grey foliage with heads of small white papery flowers, which can be dried for winter arrangements or pressed for pictures. It requires sunshine.

Poplar, black (*Populus nigra*) The buds of both black and white poplar are perfumed in the spring and, when pressed between the fingers, yield a balsamic resin. The flowers of both, it has been said, have little attraction except for the bee and the botanist. The leaves of the black poplar, however, are of great dramatic value to the pressed flower artist, for their grey-black, slightly powdered surface lined with thick white felt.

Rue (*Ruta graveolens*) An evergreen shrub with small yellow flowers and attractive blue-green leaves. It is the Herb of Grace and was used for sprinkling holy water; it was carried as an antiseptic during the Great Plague. Useful against the evil eye, as well as for pressed flower pictures.

Scabious (*Scabiosa caucasica*) A small and charming form, with small lavender blue flowers, and silvery grass-like leaves. It reaches $1\frac{1}{2}$–2 ft (45–60 cm).

Senecio greyii A hardy shrub with thick grey leaves, felted with white underneath. It has yellow, daisy-like flowers and appreciates a sunny position. It needs firm control by pruning, to avoid straggliness.

Silverweed (*Potentilla anserina*) This graceful weed may be found in local colonies in damp grassy places, especially along hedgerows. It has attractive yellow flowers from May to August but its value lies in its curving stems and toothed leaves, sometimes silvery on both sides, sometimes on the underside only and sometimes only a dull green.

Silver willow-leaved pear (*Pyrus salicifolia pendula*) A fairy-like tree, having white flowers in spring and willowy leaves covered in silvery down. Hardy.

Snow-on-the mountain (*Lepadina marginata*) An annual which should be better known in Britain. It has green leaves and petal-less flowers, but its great attraction lies in its snowy green and white-margined bracts. Although these fade in pressing, they are none the less desirable, and can be grown from seed. It prefers a dry soil, and is widely cultivated in the USA, where it frequently escapes into waste land. Unfortunately, it has no such characteristic when grown in Britain. A member of the spurge family, *Euphorbiaceae*.

Southernwood (*Artemisia abrotanum*) Another useful member of the wormwood family. It has a haunting perfume and is also known by the contradictory names of old man and lad's love. Its finely divided, grey-green leaves make it a satisfactory plant for infilling in flower designs. Perennial.

Wormwood (*Artemisia absinthium*) Named after the goddess Artemis, and believed to have sprung from the trail of the serpent as it dragged its way out of the Garden of Eden. There are many varieties, of which 'Lambrook Silver' is the most attractive. It flourishes on poor soils.

Most grey-green and silver-backed plants may be relied on to remain unchanged for years, although a few such as *Alchemilla alpina*, backed with shiny silvery hairs, may dull a little with time.

Marina (page 34) is an example of the use of a silvery plant. It is seldom that a design can be composed of a single variety of leaf, but the adaptable silverweed proves that it is not impossible. Varying sizes and angles of nine pairs of leaflets give an impression of seagulls in a stiff breeze. (This constitutes fewer leaflets than usually go to compose a single silverweed

Marina, an exercise in
economy. A small piece of
blue paper, a handful of
silver-grey leaflets, and we
have wind and sea, and
weather-tossed birds.

leaf.) In other words, take apart a fair-sized pinnate leaf and you may have the material for a panel measuring $7\frac{1}{4} \times 11\frac{3}{4}$ in. (18 × 30 cm). The only bit of cheating is a small piece of yellow stamen from a passion flower, chopped into fragments for beaks and claw; an improvement but not essential to the design.

So many other leaves are good for pressing that it is scarcely necessary to list them. Those with a natural sense of design will treasure small top sprays of passion flower, clematis and bryony, as well as the separate leaves of maple, acanthus and most ferns, as well as tiny, neatly paired leaves. The size will govern the choice. Many leaves are too large for any but the biggest pictures but wild plants should not be overlooked for the delicate shapes they have to offer.

Garden Flowers and the Results of Pressing

For those wishing to build a stock of garden flowers for picture making, the following are given 'As Found', as the auctioneers say, thereby saving themselves a lot of trouble when things go wrong. Many of these have been tried over a period of eight or nine years, some for a shorter time, and no results can be absolutely assured. Most of them can be seen in this book.

African Daisy (*Dimorphotheca*) Half-hardy perennials. The flowers are pink, orange, yellow and white. It is unusual for white flowers to press well but these are recommended. The white will disappear entirely, leaving grey-blue lines and shadows on silken daisy petals. Seen at their best in the design for a lampshade (page 87). The complete flower-head may be pressed and separate petals are useful for dragonflies. Handle with extreme care.

Baby's breath (*Gypsophila paniculata*) Hardy annual and perennial. Can be grown in several colours and is useful in miniatures and as an infiller for larger pictures. Likes sun and chalk.

Californian fuschia (*Zauschneria*) A perennial rock plant, blooming in late summer. It is sheer flattery to call it any kind of a fuschia, although it has one advantage over that lovely and graceful plant, that of grey foliage and scarlet tubular flowers that keep their colour. Since it is a tender plant, cuttings should be overwintered in a greenhouse.

Candytuft (*Iberis* spp.) Hardy annuals, perennials and rock plants. Easy to grow and easy to press. Colours last well.

Christmas rose (*Helleborus niger*) Our most beautiful winter flower, disappointing only in its habit of turning to old parchment when dried. It and its near relatives *H. corsicus* and *H. orientalis*, are all worth pressing, however. See *Marquetry* (page 127).

Clary (*Salvia sclarea*) Hardy biennial. Splendid, long-lasting, coloured bracts, purple, green and shocking pink. There is a white variety, veined with green. The only thing lacking in this admirable plant is grace. Easily grown from seed.

Clematis Deciduous and evergreen climbers, of which the most useful are the commonest. Press Jackmanii, Nelly Moser and Ville de Lyon but avoid all the large pale and double varieties.

Coreopsis grandiflora The bright gold flowers which appear in summer are satisfactory for colour fastness; if picked a little too late, they turn brown pleasantly. The petals are best separately pressed and later reunited to their centres to avoid wrinkles. Sow seed in April or propagate in spring. Perennial.

Cosmea (*Cosmos*) A half-hardy annual that blooms from midsummer until the autumn. The crimson and pink varieties are recommended. Press the whole flower.

Crocus (*Crocus susianus*) Grow the small *C. susianus* and other miniature striped crocuses. They press like fine silk and, when the colour fades, the glossy texture and the mahogany stripes outside remain.

Daisy (*Bellis perennis*) Lawn daisies are better than cultivated varieties for pressing. Pick only in dry sunshine before mowing, for otherwise they refuse to open fully. Choose the pink-tipped ones for preference and a range of sizes from the tiniest to the largest.

Delphinium (*Delphinium ajacis*) and **Larkspur (*Delphinium consolida*)** Of the many varieties of the perennial plant, the dark blue are perhaps the most satisfactory. Among the annual larkspurs, the pinks keep their colour better than almost any other pink flowers. Delphiniums need a good rich soil.

Dianthus The pinks, carnations and sweet williams which are included in this genus are disappointing for our purpose. Only single petals can be pressed and, with the exception of the striped carnations, these will fade. A few fringed petals can be used for birds' or moths' wings; the leaves, if you need grassy leaves, are always reliable.

Eccremocarpus scaber A fast growing tendrilled climber, to be treated as an annual or grown as a perennial greenhouse plant. The whole plant, including the tubular orange flower will turn black when it is pressed but it is charming and decorative used as a silhouette.

Fennel (*Foeniculum vulgaris*) A useful herb, which can be pressed in either its green or bronze form. The small yellow flowers are particularly useful in miniature designs.

Forget-me-not (*Myosotis*) The blue will slowly fade but the little curled scorpion tails, which gave them their early name of scorpion plant, will still be pretty in small pictures. Excellent for greetings cards, etc.

Fuchsia When successful, fuchsias are graceful in design but they are unreliable and prone to discoloration. Their pink stamens are useful for fantasy flowers.

Golden rod (*Solidago*) Perennial, blooming in late summer and autumn. Trouble-free plants in several varieties, which press well and keep their colour.

Heather (*Erica*) The ericas are reliable for colour stability but the small leaves are bad droppers when dry. They are not very good for mixing with other flowers.

Hebe, Veronica Tender shrubs which grow well by the sea. The spired flowers press into graceful shapes and thus are useful in spite of the fact that they are inclined to go brown. They are better pressed in bud, particularly the small white varieties.

Himalayan honeysuckle (*Leycesteria*) An interesting deciduous shrub. Only the purple and green bracts can be used for pressing. These are of a strange shape and will give character to many designs. See *Random Flight* (page 101).

Honeysuckle (*Lonicera*) All varieties of honeysuckle, both deciduous and evergreen, may be used, although scarlet trumpet varieties are best. None keep their colour after pressing but the pleasant curves of buds and flowers are good for borders and infilling. Buds that have turned brown, when arranged round an attractive card, look like an old-fashioned carved wooden frame. See *Bookmark* (page 76). Press each blossom separately.

Hydrangea Colour results are unpredictable but interesting. Whatever they achieve, they will last indefinitely. Easy to grow, especially by the sea. Prune hard, but not until the spring. (See skeletonizing, page 46.)

Kaffir lily (*Schizostylis*) Red or pink star-like lilies with self-coloured stamens, about 2 in. (5 cm) across. These autumn-blooming flowers press like sheer silk and, though rather fragile to handle, are useful among larger flowers in pressed bouquets. They appreciate damp soil but they need sun.

Knapweed (*Centaurea nigra*) A hardy annual with many varieties but only the deepest blue are useful for their arrow-like petals. Unpredictable in their behaviour, some fade and others do not, but they do make admirable paws for mice!

Lobelia erinus A half-hardy annual, one of the best dark blue flowers for keeping its colour.

Marigold (*Calendula officinalis*) Hardy annual, the commonest and least petalled varieties being the best for pressing.

Masterwort (*Astrantia major*) Flowers white and green, or pinkish, in small dry wheels, reminiscent of the Victorian craft of tatting. A completely unfussy perennial, propagated by division in autumn and spring, or by seeds sown immediately after harvesting.

Meadow foam (*Limnanthes douglasii*) This bright little hardy annual blooms in late spring and early summer; its yellow centred white flowers are popular with flower pressers. It may be grown from seed sown in March and April in a sunny position in almost any soil. Press flower-heads only.

Monarch of the Veldt (*Venidium*) Half-hardy annual orange daisy. Its purple-black zone and black centre make it a suitable subject to press, face down and stem removed. Sow in a cool greenhouse and plant out in late May or June.

Montbretia, garden (*Crocosmia*) Valuable late-flowering corms. The flowers press well and keep their bright orange colour. The buds are valuable for miniature arrangements.

Nasturtium (*Tropeoleum majus*) Hardy annual. Press single varieties in scarlet and mahogany in preference to those with paler colour; the buds and young flowers in profile and fully opened nasturtiums with separate petals. Although the colours lose their brilliance, the honey guide-lines remain to give interest to the design.

Nerine bowdenii These graceful pink lilies are not reliable for pressing but their shape, and the lines of their stamens remain beautiful. The stamens may also be used for other flowers. They bloom in autumn, and are best grown against a south-facing wall.

Pansy (*Viola*) Perennial and biennial. Most colours will press well, though the smaller varieties are the most attractive. A few buds pressed in profile will soften the bold stares of too many front-faced pansies. Keep plants dead-headed.

Passion flower (*Passiflora*) A fast-growing climber with handsome leaves and tendrils, slightly tender. The remarkable flowers should be taken apart for pressing. They are more attractive when used in a simplified form, without their many parts to clutter the design. The 'crown of thorns' is valuable for many purposes.

Penstemon barbatus Perennial. Thrives in light loam. The rosy-purple flowers sometimes turn brownish, but pressed in profile they are still worth using.

Phlox Only the *Phlox drummondii*, Cuspidata 'Twinkle', is worth pressing. These many-coloured stars will make any small picture attractive. Seed packets of *Phlox drummondii* 'Twinkle' have been hard to obtain in recent years but they are worth searching for.

Plume poppy (*Bocconia*) A tall and handsome perennial, with roundish, lobed, grey-green leaves, lighter beneath. The erect plume-like flowers are a pale yellowish-pink and should be pressed while still in bud; the leaves should be pressed separately.

Poppy (*Papaver*) The opium poppies, *Papaver somniferum*, are probably the most satisfactory, although it is worth experimenting with Iceland poppies (*P. nudicaule*). Cut out the seed-head with a scalpel and remove the stem. Remove the fluted head of the poppy, which can be dried but not pressed. These can be used as a surround for small pictures (page 45). Press the complete head of petals without the seed, if they are not too fully petalled, and reserve a number of ragged and purple-splashed petals for separate pressing.

Primula and **Auricula** Very satisfactory flowers for pressing singly. Primroses are at their best when they are pressed front-faced, or in profile on their own stems. Press only the heads of primulas and auriculas. None have good leaves for pressing.

Rock rose (*Helianthemum*) Plant in full sun on rockery or in the front of the border. Look out for 'Fire Dragon', an orange-red variety. Use only the brightest colours and keep the sepals for making flies and other insects.

Salpiglossis sinuata A half-hardy annual, a difficult plant to germinate but very well worth while. The trumpet flowers may be crimson, scarlet, gold, mauve or violet, with strange dark veins. Not entirely reliable but their beautiful markings will last. Sown in a warm greenhouse in March, they should not be planted out before the end of May and then with your fingers crossed.

Saxifrage (*Saxifraga*) Of this large family only a few are recommended for pressing. Of these, London pride, St Patrick's cabbage, is the best. It is charming in miniatures with forget-me-nots, particularly for those patient enough to press the separate little flowers. The red freckles on the small pink faces of these little Londoners (the Irish have them too) are most appealing. The slightly leathery, rounded leaves, with their pinked edges, also press well, particularly in their autumn colouring, but should not be used in the same pictures as their flowers. The flowers are valuable for miniatures but the leaves are thick and sturdy and need space.

Snowflake (*Leucojum*) Resembling a tall and graceful snowdrop, this flower is considerably better than the snowdrop for pressing. There are spring, summer and autumn varieties.

Sunflower (*Helianthus* spp.) Hardy annuals and perennials which are good for lasting colour. Press petals separately.

Tobacco Plant (*Nicotiana alata*) A half-hardy annual, valuable for the shape of its flowers. Not entirely reliable. White blooms should be avoided, lime green ones press well but the violet-black are better. Even these are variable and all should be picked in the driest possible conditions.

Tulip (*Tulipa*) So many tulips are worth pressing that it is difficult to make a choice. For small flowers, which can be pressed complete after stem and stamens are removed, try the early flowering *T. turkestanica*, with narrow creamy-white petals, having yellow base and cream reverse. 'Viridiflora Artist', 'Greenland' and 'Praecox' are flushed with bright green on pink and yellow petals. 'Bybloemen', 'Bizarre' and 'Rembrandt' are streaked with strong colours, which even when muted are splendid for large Dutch-looking pressed flower groups. Parrot tulips are heavily fringed and twisted, in a variety of dark and splendid colours. When pressing, cup-shaped petals will need to be split or even cut in half to make them lie flat.

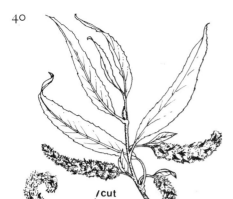

/cut

Above: Fig. 3: *Willow-chrysanthemum*. Take the young tip of a willow cut in May while the catkins are fresh. Press and store until required. Remove catkins and keep the remainder for other pictures. The smaller catkins may be curled inwards and the longer ones outwards to form a chrysanthemum flower. Arrange these willow-chrysanthemum flowers with genuine chrysanthemum leaves.

Right: *Willow-chrysanthemums*. A simple arrangement of chrysanthemum leaves picked and dried in late summer, and willow catkins pressed in spring. The catkins will darken with age, and turn from chrysanthemum-yellow to a soft grey-brown, giving the picture a second life and a distinctly Japanese appearnace.

Below: *Cool Silver, Pale Gold*. An arrangement that should last for many years, and a gentle colour-range that will suit many different surroundings.

Catkins, seed-heads and skeleton leaves

The pressed flower artist's palette is not all leaves and petals. The calyx of a flower , as we have seen, is often more interesting than the flower itself; a bract can be more colourful than a petal; catkins, seed-heads and skeleton leaves may all at some time be a point of interest in a pattern.

Soft fluffy catkins of whatever size are always worth pressing, although at times they may be too hard to be useful. Since they are composed of tiny hanging flowers, they become very fragile when dried but a gentle blow when a picture is finished, or perhaps the application of a soft dry paint-brush, will be enough to remove all the excess pollen and tiny pieces they shed. If you do your own framing, however, be sure no little fragments are adhering to the inside of the glass or loose on the surface of the paper before you imprison them, when they will be a reproach for ever more.

The joy of long willow catkins is that they may be cut to any length or curled to any shape. Although the colour changes a little, they are fairly dependable. Among other talents they possess is one of looking more like a chrysanthemum than a chrysanthemum does when it is pressed. Willow catkins make excellent dull yellow chrysanthemums on bark paper or on unframed hessian-type wallpaper (opposite and fig. 3).

Quite a number of seed-heads are very ornamental; perhaps the best are from some but not all of the clematis varieties. The silvery mop of the yellow *Clematis tangutica* is enchanting, and this can be seen in *Cool Silver, Pale Gold* (opposite), an arrangement of mixed varieties after full development. Here silverweed and artichoke leaves are seen in reverse against a dull green board. It is advisable to use mounting board for plant material of extra bulk, to avoid the possible buckling and creasing of a light-weight paper.

The early stages of clematis seeds, when they resemble a maze of gold wire, are extremely beautiful, perhaps even more so than when they reach the silken fluffy stage, but so far they have presented insuperable difficulties. Pressed under heavy books, bricks and flat-irons (what you will), they still insist on developing into feathery parachutes, each one carrying a seed; no weight of books, bricks, and flat-irons is going to stop them. They have even been known to continue developing after they have been framed.

Michael Tyler Whittle, in his delightful and most un-common book, *Common or Garden*, mentions other plants with a strong disinclination to lie down and die. He cites charlock, wild cabbage, treacle mustard, pennywort, houseleek, roseroot and wall pepper among these floral stout hearts, although surely it is optimism personified to imagine that one could get the better of a houseleek? However, he states that after a minute or so in boiling water these plants will give up the unequal struggle and resign themselves to the press.

Our method with the clematis seed-head is less mediaeval, although equally effective. Recently, clear varnish spray has been found quite successful but a polyurethane spray will tarnish their lovely metallic glint.

Some decorative clematis seed-heads

C. alpina Spring flowers produce fluffy seed-heads which are pretty in summer. 8–10 ft (2·5–3 m). The soft blue flowers appear in April and May, with often a second blooming in the autumn.

C. aristata Small white flowers in spring. Plumose seed-heads. Only hardy in sheltered gardens in the spring.

C. flammula The fragrant Virgin's bower. 12–15 ft (3·5–4·5 m). Small flowers with centres of crowded white stamens, giving a sweet hawthorn-like scent. Silky plumose seed-heads. Vigorous.

C. fusca 8 ft (2·5 m). Solitary flowers, reddish-brown and hairy on the outside, violet inside in June, followed by thick round heads of plumose seeds.

C. glauca 10 ft (3 m). Glaucous leaves and orange-yellow flowers in late summer and autumn. Silvery seed-heads.

C. grata Best grown in trees, as it can reach 20–30 ft (6–9 m). Creamy-white flowers and silky seed-heads.

C. orientalis The yellow Indian Virgin's bower. A vigorous climber reaching 20 ft (6 m). Glaucous leaves and yellow, scented, star-like flowers in August and September, followed by silky heads of feathered seeds.

C. paniculata Japanese Virgin's bower. Very vigorous. 20–40 ft (6–12 m). Hawthorn-scented white flowers in September and October, followed by masses of feathery seed-heads. Requires a warm and sunny position.

C. quinquefoliolata 20 ft (6 m). It produces white flowers in August and September, and long silky seed-heads. Needs a sheltered wall.

C. stanleyi A semi-woody shrub which can grow to 6–8 ft (2–2·5 m). Hanging flowers of ribbed pink to purple in August and September, followed by silvery-white seed-heads. Greenhouse.

C. tangutica Graceful nodding yellow flowers from August – September, followed by shining silvery seed-heads. 10 ft (3 m). The 'Gravetye' variety is recommended.

The clematis has been used in *Swan Lake, a Fragment* (page 44). A fragile *corps de ballet*, fusion of spring and autumn. The slender arms of an unfolding fern is a moment captured, like the memory of the arms of a ballet dancer on a darkened stage. The newly burst seed of a wild clematis, (*C. vitalba*), is as light as the tutu of a dancer.

Tomorrow the outstretched arms of the young ferns will thicken and develop into leaves. In a few months the white down of the clematis will be blown away on the wind or it will be soaked with rain and cling miserably grey to shabby trees, earning it the name of old man's beard.

To capture this fleeting magic, however, will take from Easter to Michaelmas; to be precise, from the unfolding of the first young ferns in

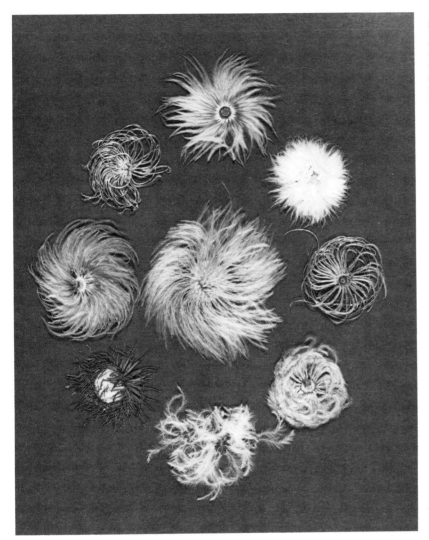

Decorative Seed-heads.
These should be pressed in
different stages of their
development. To hold them
in their golden, wiry stage,
spray with clear varnish. For
feathery heads, spraying is
unnecessary.

the spring, to the bursting of the wild clematis seed in the autumn and yet all it takes to set the scene are five heads of fern and five heads of clematis seed.

The wide-flung arms dictate the choreography and all that is necessary is to display the tutus with customary grace, a more difficult feat than may be imagined. Enough adhesive will hold them down but a fraction more will turn them into grey flannel petticoats. It may be found easier to stroke in a few spots of adhesive where the tutus should come and there to settle the clematis heads gently down.

The frail gold semicircles that contain the seeds of willowherb are other wonders of the world that, if captured young enough, may beautify a pressed flower picture for many years. A day, an hour, perhaps a minute, and you will be too late, for, like the clematis, the willowherb will release its fluffy seeds even if it is under pressure or behind glass. But since its golden semicircles appear singly, not in a tangled maze like the clematis,

Above: *Swan Lake, a Fragment*. Balletomanes may enjoy an exercise in floral choreography with this simple material. Single figures are useful for greetings cards and notelets.

Opposite: *Prince Philippe, Count of Flanders*, in a poppy-head frame, as delicately carved as a miniature Grinling Gibbons. Common to every garden and usually ignored, the fluted tops of poppy-heads make a charmingly simple surround to portraits and pictures of childhood.

Fig. 4: *Removing the fluted rose from a poppy-head*. Cut closely under the fluted rose at the top of the poppy-head with a sharp craft knife, and discard the remainder.

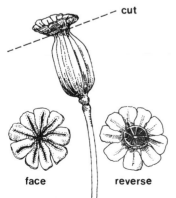

cut

face   reverse

it is possible to catch it and keep it; if you are successful, the glint of gold will remain.

Many tiny wild flower seed-heads, including grasses, make delicate silhouettes and present no problems. There are not so many garden plants that produce seed-heads that will press well. Honesty seeds have many uses, both in their green and in their silver states, and these may be seen in *Moonrose*, (page 138) and in *Pricksong-wort* (page 146).

The fluted ends of poppy-heads, especially small varieties, make most satisfactory little carved wooden roses, when cut off with a scalpel or craft knife and left to dry but not pressed (fig. 4). They dry in various shades of cream and brown, with sometimes a touch of green, and can be used in graduated sizes as a charming surround to an old print, if framed without glass, or in a box frame. Opposite, you see them mixed with the pinkish-cream buds of bocconia.

The winged seeds of sycamore and various maples perform miracles when bleached in a solution of one tablespoonful of bleach to about one pint or litre of water. The length of time to immerse them depends on the age of the seeds: when green they will take longer than when brown and dry. Their response to bleaching also seems to be affected by the weather conditions in which the seeds matured. Since results are unpredictable, it is useful to prepare a number from which to choose. Some will bleach to a uniform cream but others, after turning a dark brown, will burst their outer skins and emerge with mottled wings like new-born moths, for which purpose they seem to have been designed. A successful pair may be seen hovering in the top left corner of *Cool Silver, Pale Gold* (page 40). To make these moths, it is necessary to clip away the thick seeds of the sycamores, using only the wing parts, matching each pair as best you can, for no two will be absolutely alike, (page 46 and fig. 5).

The seed-heads of the cape gooseberry (*Physalis*) are too wrinkled to press well, even when opened out like flowers and with the berry

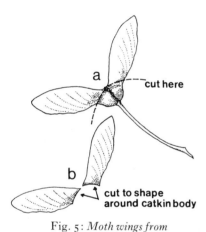

Fig. 5: *Moth wings from sycamore seeds.*
(a) After bleaching, cut off the dried wings from the thick seeds, which are discarded.
(b) The wings should be shaped to fit the catkin bodies, and a smaller pair of under-wings added slightly below the top wings.

Top: *Moth-wings.* An accidental discovery when endeavouring to bleach sycamore seeds white. Some of the winged seeds will bleach to cream or pale green but the majority produce these marvellous mottled effects, perfect for moths and of far greater interest than their plain colours.

removed. They will, however, make splendid lace flowers if left in the garden all the winter to skeletonize. Immersion in bleach will whiten them but do not leave them in too long or they will disintegrate.

There are not many flowers that are suitable for skeletonizing; hydrangeas seem to be the most successful. If the flower-heads are left on the plant all through the winter, they will not only protect next year's growth from frost but many individual flowers, and in rarer cases complete heads, will be found to have become skeletonized, or nearly so, by the time the plant needs pruning. All that is then necessary is a very short immersion in bleach of the same strength as that used for cape gooseberries and sycamore seeds, and delicate white lace flowers will result. See *Bouquet for a White Witch* (page 155).

Hedgerow harvesting will produce many skeleton leaves but do not postpone the hunt too long after the leaves have fallen, or they will be ragged and torn. Holly skeletons may often be found intact. Only tough and leathery leaves will skeletonize successfully and, of these, camellias seem to be the best. You can hasten their progress by leaving them in a bucket of water for several weeks, but the water should not be changed, and the smell is not agreeable. When the water becomes slimy, take a trial leaf and wash it under the tap, gently rubbing away the pulpy material. You will not want to do many.

A quicker method is to boil a few strong and perfect specimens in an old saucepan containing 4 oz (113 g) of soda crystals to 2 pt (1 l) water; if preferred, the same quantity of blue detergent can be used instead of soda. Simmer until pulpy and then with tweezers lay one or two leaves on a sheet of newspaper, leaving the others still soaking. Gently scrape away the tissue, wash them in cold water, and press between sheets of blotting paper. The rest can be treated in the same way, as and when they are ready, but treat them with care, for they have suffered and will have little strength left. Leaves that are slightly damaged can be cut into bees' wings with good effect. See *The Passion Flower and the Bee* (opposite).

The Passion Flower and the Bee. A single flower in full bloom attracts a passing bee. His body, a part of a catkin pressed in May, is borne on wings cut from a section of skeletonized Cape gooseberry, a product of the autumn.

It is possible to capture and to keep a dandelion puffball in an oval frame with a convex glass. There are two methods of doing this. One is to spray the puffball with hair-spray. The day must be still and the puffball expanding. Only the gentlest spray is necessary, or you will blow the feathered seeds off their little white leather cushion. It should then be carried with the greatest care and fixed on to the background, which has already been prepared with a thin patch of adhesive on which to set it down.

Another method is to pick a bunch of dandelions in bud and keep them in water in the house until they are beginning to expand. Spray them lightly and choose the best one for mounting. A background of grasses should be ready to receive the puffball, for few leaves would survive the air contained under a convex glass without wrinkling.

This experiment lasted quite successfully for a few months, until the frame was needed for another purpose, and so it is not known how long this charming picture would have survived. The convex glass had necessarily to be quite deep and it seems likely that groundsel or some other of the downy-headed seeds would have a greater chance of success and perhaps a longer life, for they are easier to handle and will fit under a shallower glass, with less air to upset the background material. The back of the frame must fit tightly without panel pins, to avoid hammering (page 50 and fig. 6).

Grasses press easily, although they are prone to drop seeds. They are naturally graceful, forming their own designs, and require only the smallest amount of adhesive. Although they mix well with other materials, they are of most value in the decoration of lampshades, waste-paper bins and other designs where height is an advantage. When seen against the light, as in a lampshade, their patterns are fantastically beautiful, with the added advantage of being proof against fading (see opposite).

Wild grasses for pressing

Common cat's-tail grass (*Phleum pratense*) Also called timothy grass, after Timothy Hansen, who cultivated it extensively in America. Green and white panicles in June. 1–2 ft (30–60 cm).

Common quaking grass (*Briza media*) Its botanic name is taken from a Greek verb meaning 'to vibrate' and this is exactly what it does. It likes poor ground, and has shining spikelets of purplish-brown and white in June. 1–1$\frac{1}{2}$ ft (30–45 cm).

Fine bent grass (*Agrostis vulgaris*) One of the most attractive, as well as the most common of all the grasses. It grows in meadows and pastures and at the base of walls and other dry places. Flowers June and July in clusters of purplish spikelets, in hair-like branches which quiver in every breeze. 1$\frac{1}{2}$ ft (45 cm).

Meadow foxtail grass (*Alopecurus pratensis*) Common in Britain, flowering in May and June, with a yellowish-green erect panicle. Useful for making animal pictures but less graceful and adaptable than most

A Pattern of Common Grasses. The delicacy and beauty of grasses, alone, or with a few field flowers such as buttercups, meadow vetchling, bird's foot trefoil and scentless mayweed, needs little skill in arranging. Perhaps they will be better alone, with only petal butterflies and insect life for company, since the wild flowers will lose their colours long before the grasses show signs of deterioration.

others listed here. *A. agrestis* flowers a little later, in June and July; sea-green tipped with purple.

Panicle grass (*Panicum violaceum*) Hardy annual, having clouds of small purple flowers.

Taper field brome grass (*Bromus arvensis*) There are many varieties of brome grass, both annual and perennial. In one form the spikelets are smooth and shining; in another they are downy; *B. sterilis*, one of the commonest, is pale green in early growth and sometimes tinted with purple, later becoming greyish-green and then brown. Flowers in June, by the wayside and on waste ground. 2 ft (60 cm).

Wild oat grass (*Avena fatua*) Presumably sown in one's youth but should be reaped later on for its decorative value. Farmers, however, do not welcome its appearance in their fields. Pale green spikelets, striped with darker green in July and August. May reach a height of 3 ft (90 cm).

Wind grass (*Apera spica-venti*) Large panicles of green and purple awns. 2–3 ft (60–90 cm). Common amongst corn.

Captured Groundsel Puffballs. The smaller the downy head, the less the resistance to currents of air. The groundsel is easier to imprison than a dandelion clock, but a box-frame about $7\frac{1}{2} \times 8\frac{1}{2} \times 1\frac{3}{4}$ in. ($19 \times 21.5 \times 4.5$ cm) will give room for its accommodation and the result will be considerably more surprising and exciting. A dandelion stalk can be split and pressed in advance, ready to take its place among the grasses that form the background.

Fig. 6: *Framing puff-balls.*
(a) Remove frame
(b) Lift oval mount and press back.
(c) Remove convex glass. Prepare background grasses, leaving adequate space for puff-balls. When assembled, replace glass, mount and frame. Seal carefully with adhesive tape but do not nail.

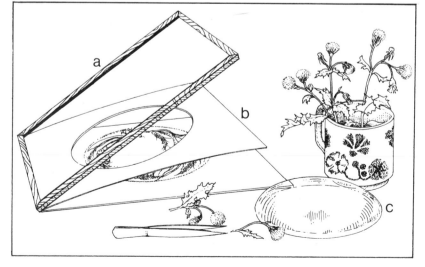

Cultivated grasses for pressing

Bent grass (*Agrostis nebulosa*) Known also as cloud grass, this is a fine cultivated variety. Hardy annual. $1\frac{1}{2}$ ft (45 cm).

Hair-grass (*Aira capillaris*) All the members of this large family are suitable for picture-making, being light, flaky and glistening. Blooming in midsummer, they may be grey, green, greenish-brown, silver, yellow or purplish-green. Collect a good range of these grasses.

Hare's-tail grass (*Lagurus ovatus*) Has a soft white bloom resembling a rabbit's or a hare's tail, and therefore invaluable for making children's pictures. Grows best in a warm place. $1-1\frac{1}{2}$ ft (30–45 cm). Hardy annual.

Pampas grass (*Cordateria argentea*) A giant among grasses but included for its feathery flowers, suitable, when divided and cut, for pictures but unsuitable for small gardens. 9–10 ft (2·7–3 m). There are two smaller varieties, *C.a. carminea rendatleri*, rosy pink, and *C.a. pumila*, which do not exceed 3–4 ft (90–120 cm).

Quaking grass (*Briza maxima*) A very attractive hardy annual. Pendant and nodding, with heart-shaped pearly flowers, which give it the name of pearl grass. One of the most striking grasses in pressed flower pictures. Likes poor soil. 1–2 ft (30–60 cm).

Sheep's fescue (*Festuca ovina*) Leaves grey-blue, slender, and purplish flowers in panicles in late spring to midsummer. Perennial. The variety 'Glauca' has bluer leaves. Height variable.

Aquarium. The underwater aristocracy, where life glides by with the grace of a valeta, except at mealtimes, when a sudden loss of dignity is displayed. The autumn leaves and bright colours suitable to *Beetlemania*, are here exchanged for silken petals and soft colours.

Squirrel-tail grass (*Hordeum jubatum*) Hardy annual, with feathery silver-grey to brown seed-heads. $1-1\frac{1}{2}$ ft (30–45 cm). Likes dry soil.

Most of the ornamental grasses are sown in April. A few of the more hardy varieties may be sown in the autumn. The seedlings need to be well thinned out.

Many of the materials and techniques we have described are brought together in *Aquarium* (page 51), which uses leaves, seeds and flowers.

Rupert Brooke wrote of the cool and silent fish world:

> form and line and solid follow
> Solid and line and form.

It is a world as inviting to the pressed flower artist as is the sky with its birds and butterflies and bees by day, the glimmering of moths by night or the silent communities of insects under a stone. Only the birds make audible comments on the sunshine and rain and the heat and hunger of their daily lives. The rest of the world of wings and fins is silent.

Since we have tried to imitate with leaves and petals the ways of birds and bees, of butterflies and moths, let us now attempt to reproduce Rupert Brooke's world of

> myriad hues that lie between
> Darkness and darkness.

Just as autumn leaves formed the basis of all the varying insect designs (page 31) and just as the many-patterned moths (page 46) were all made of sycamore seeds, so in *Aquarium* the variously shaped and larger fish have, without exception, bodies made of tulip petals. The smaller fish, however, herrings and mackerel, sardines and such small fry, were each composed of a single daisy-type petal of rudbeckia or dimorphotheca. Flower buds, petals and seeds supplied the tails and fins of all varieties and small flowers and seeds supplied the eyes. Their sinuous underwater movement depends solely upon the careful joining of tail to body, steering the fish to right or left, upwards or downwards, according to the angle at which the tail is set.

So far, all these have been only exercises in observation, imagination and, of course, exaggeration: the mystery and the fun of turning one natural object into the likeness of another. Since we are unable to make a single one of these ourselves, not even a petal, this odd translation is a kind of magic. Those who enjoy the exercise will want to use their skill in picture making, using patterns of birds and insects and fish.

There seemed little hope of capturing and keeping the actual fabric of a flower, when, towards the end of the sixteenth century, John Donne wrote,

> Little think'st thou, poore flower,
> Whom I have watch'd sixe or seaven dayes,
> And seene thy birth, and seene what every houre

Gave to thy growth, thee to this height to raise
  Little think'st thou
That it will freeze anon, and that I shall
Tomorrow find thee falne, or not at all.

With civilization, men had begun tentatively to recapture, in paint and cloth and clay, the shapes and colours that they accepted would disappear with every season. Flower and leaf patterns were woven into the clothes they wore; they were trodden underfoot in patterns of tile and carpet; they decorated walls and ceilings and they were carved in wood and hewn in stone in their places of worship, but it was reluctantly agreed that the grass withereth and the flower fadeth and no efforts were made to hold them back.

Even when their medicinal properties were explored, and the very essence of a flower, its fragrance, had been distilled and bottled by alchemists, and herbalists began to dry and press plants to further their researches, it occurred to no one to conserve them for their beauty of line and form.

Now there is a happier prospect before us. We are learning, slowly and uncertainly as yet, how rapidly colour may fade and what is left of value when it has gone. When colour changes, is it necessarily for the worse? If, by the magic of chemistry, we may one day be able to preserve colour entirely and indefinitely, would we gain so much? Accepting and understanding that the old must make way for the new, meantime we can explore the pleasure, not only of painting flowers but of painting with flowers; if we can add a little to their short lives and add to our small experience it is surely worth while.

Wild flowers and the pressed flower artist

When gathering wild flowers for pressing, it should be remembered that no plant is common everywhere and that, where wild flowers do not grow plentifully, few should be picked and a number must be left to produce seed.

The Conservation of Wild Creatures and Wild Plants Act 1975 gave protection for the first time. Twenty-one rare flowers and ferns are totally protected: digging up and picking are illegal. It is now an offence to remove any wild plant without the permission of the owner or occupier of the land, but flowers growing on roadside verges or along the edges of cultivated fields and waste ground and all plants that would otherwise be cut down or ploughed up may be picked. Those growing on any Nature Trail, Nature Reserve or National Trust property are protected.

The twenty-one listed Protected Plants are shown on pages 54–5 and are listed at the top of page 56.

More than twenty British wild flower species have disappeared since recording began in the seventeenth century and at least a dozen have been lost in the present century. Wild flowers of meadow, marsh and bog have been destroyed by ploughing and drainage, while herbicides have accounted for many species of arable weeds.

Endangered plants protected by law

Wild Gladiolus
Gladiolus illyricus

Alpine Sow-thistle
Cicerbita alpina

Red Helleborine
Cephalanthera rubra

Drooping Saxifrage
Saxifraga cernua

Alpine Gentian
Gentiana nivalis

Snowdon Lily
Lloydia serotina

Lady's-slipper
Cypripedium calceolus

Spring Gentian
Gentiana verna

Teesdale Sandwort
Minuartia stricta

Tufted Saxifrage
Saxifraga cespitosa

Military Orchid
Orchis militaris

Killarney Fern
Trichomanes speciosum

Mezereon
Daphne mezereum

Cheddar Pink
Dianthus gratianopolitanus

Monkey Orchid
Orchis simia

Spiked Speedwell
Veronica spicata

Ghost Orchid
Epipogium aphyllum

Oblong Woodsia
Woodsia ilvensis

Blue Heath
Phyllodoce caerulea

Diapensia
Diapensia lapponica

Alpine Woodsia
Woodsia alpina

Schedule 2 Species of Protected Plants

Common Name	Botanical Name	Common Name	Botanical Name
Alpine gentian	*Gentiana nivalis*	Military orchid	*Orchis militaris*
Alpine sow-thistle	*Cicerbita alpina*	Monkey orchid	*Orchis simia*
Alpine woodsia	*Woodsia alpina*	Oblong woodsia	*Woodsia ilvensis*
Blue heath	*Phyllodoce caerulea*	Red helleborine	*Cephalanthera rubra*
Cheddar pink	*Dianthus gratianopolitanus*	Snowdon lily	*Lloydia serotina*
Diapensia	*Diapensia lapponica*	Spiked speedwell	*Veronica spicata*
Drooping saxifrage	*Saxifraga cernua*	Spring gentian	*Gentiana verna*
Ghost orchid	*Epipogium aphyllum*	Teesdale sandwort	*Minuartia stricta*
Killarney fern	*Trichomanes speciosum*	Tufted saxifrage	*Saxifraga cespitosa*
Lady's slipper	*Cypripedium calceolus*	Wild gladiolus	*Gladiolus illyricus*
Mezereon	*Daphne mezereum*		

Valuable sites of rare and threatened species have been acquired by the Nature Conservancy Council and the nature Conservation Trusts and it is now possible to visit nature reserves in Britain where the military orchid, the monkey orchid and the fritillary may be seen. In the Royal Botanic Gardens at Kew a seed bank of endangered British plants is being developed.

In most gardens outside the big cities, wild flowers such as buttercups, daisies, dandelions, speedwell, willowherb and ground elder appear uninvited but, when in doubt, it may be as well to pick only on your own property. Many people are raising wild flowers from seed packeted by reputable seedsmen. A great number of wild plants, flowers or leaves are unsuitable for pressing but the following are attractive for picture-making and may be picked, provided they are not uprooted. Use scissors, tread with care, and take only separate leaves or flowers, not entire plants. Press leaves and flowers carefully between the folded sheets of a newspaper, or carry them loosely in a plastic bag, sealed at the top and sheltered from the cold winds or hot sun.

Wild Plants Suitable For Collecting and Pressing

Bracken (*Pteridium aquilinum*) Perennial and pestilential but of value for its curled tips and fronds, pressed while green. When russet brown, it becomes rather stiff and intractable. At this point it is better as a garden mulch!

Coltsfoot (*Tussilago farfara*) Perennial found on waste land. Still used for making herbal tobacco and cough lozenges. Golden flowers appear in spring before the leaves and are excellent for pressing when folded in half for a side view or used in reverse.

Comfrey (*Symphytum*) Perennial, frequenting dry waysides and waste places. An ancient wound herb, used for poultices. Flowers throughout the summer. Pick only curved flower-heads, for their attractive scorpion-tail buds.

Common knapweed (*Centaurea nigra*) Perennial, blooms from July to September in grassy places. The purple rays may be pulled from the thick flower-heads for use for paws and hands for small flower creatures.

Common mallow (*Malva sylvestris*) A perennial once used to make poultices and ointments. The pressed flowers turn into pinkish-mauve silk but the purple honey guide-lines remain to give them character. Flowers July to August in hedges and on waste ground.

Cow parsley (*Anthriscus sylvestris*) Perennial or biennial. Essential to flower pressers. The earliest and most beautiful of the larger umbellifers. Fortunately there is no shortage of this decorative wayside plant. Flowers April and May.

Daisy (*Bellis perennis*) and **oxeye daisy (*Leucanthemum vulgare*)** Both retain their whiteness and are excellent for pressing.

Hawthorn (*Crataegus oxyacanthus*) Its fragrant white flowers, which open from May to June, turn cream after pressing but the darkened stamens keep it usable and attractive. The pink and red garden varieties, both single and double, are valuable.

Heartsease (*Viola tricolor*) This most appealing of all wild flowers is more often to be seen in small gardens than in the countryside from where it came. Annual or biennial, it blooms obligingly from April to November. It presses easily and retains its colours, as well as its expression of a worried kitten. It has to be said that it wrinkles easily too, so do not leave it uncovered.

Heather (*Calluna vulgaris*) Flowers from August onwards and keeps its colour, although it is inclined to shed its evergreen leaves when dried. Bell heather (*Erica cinerea*), flowers June to September, and has much the same characteristics.

Ivy (*Hedera helix*) Variously lobed leaves, which should be pressed in different sizes. Evergreen and excellent as a filler for large pictures.

Japanese knotweed (*Reynoutria japonica*) Tall, vigorous perennial shrub, found on waste land as a garden escape. Small white flowers in branched spikes in August and September, which turn brown when pressed. They are useful, especially when sprayed.

Lesser celandine (*Ranunculus ficaria*) Wordsworth's flower. Perennial, March to May, on bare, damp ground. Both its glossy green leaves and its shining gold flowers, which eventually turn to shining white, are valuable, though common, in pressed flower pictures. If introduced into the garden, it is a terrible spreader.

Mugwort (*Artemisia vulgaris*) Bushy perennial, of value only for its leaves, which are dark green and grey-white beneath. Once used for garlands and hung on St John's Eve as a protection against the Evil Eye.

Oxford ragwort (*Senecio squalidus*) Annual or short-lived perennial. Blooms April to October on waste ground and railway embankments. Heads of yellow daisy flowers, which should be separately pressed.

Rosebay willowherb (*Epilobium augustifolium*) Perennial. Flowers from July to September. Tall, with pinkish-purple spires, that arrived unheralded to beautify the bomb sites of London. Elegant and charmingly shaped flowers, that should be pressed separately. Press the tip of the spire, tightly budded, as well. Also useful for its slim seed-pods, curved and gilded, but apt to shed its white fluffy seeds even under glass, not that that matters perhaps.

Silverweed (*Potentilla anserina*) Perennial. Flowers from May to August in damp grassy places. This plant is the pressed flower artist's best friend.

Sow thistle (*Sonchus arvensis*) Perennial. Flowers on marshes, dunes and roadsides. Yellow dandelion-like blooms from July to October, which give place to small puffballs, suitable for capturing and keeping under convex glass.

Tufted vetch (*Viciacracca*) There are many uses for its paired leaves and its curly topknot and purple flower-heads. Flowers June to August in hedges and bushy places.

White bryony (*Bryonia cretica*) Climbing perennial, found in hedges. Small greenish flowers with darker veins, May to September. Invaluable for its handsome leaves, gracefully curved stems and tendrils, and neat flowers that keep their colour.

A flower presser's calendar

January Weather permitting, this is the month to start searching for skeleton leaves, before they become ragged and torn. A few flowers, such as hydrangeas and the seed vessels of the cape gooseberry, may not yet be ready; it is worth pressing their heads down into surrounding leaves and bushes, so that, in a state of almost permanent dampness and bewilderment, the fleshy material will rot away to leave their beautiful skeletons. Details for treating these will be found on page 46.

February Spring cleaning time in the flower pressing world. Old, faded and wrinkled stock can safely be dispensed with, telephone directories shaken out of the window and stained pages removed. Only material of the highest quality should be kept now, for are we not on the threshold of spring? Probably not, but do not be discouraged. Consult the new seed catalogues and make lists of seeds and plants that you will need for next season's pictures.

March Almost unawares, we begin to find the lesser celandine, a few primroses, the invaluable coltsfoot and, in the garden, crocuses and some of the early daffodils. Now you will be glad of those cleaned and emptied telephone directories and smooth, cut and folded sheets of clean newspaper that await them. There is not a moment to be wasted.

April We now enter the lilliputian world of the new leaf. Immature oaks, fledgling sycamores, tiny holly leaves, with prickles soft as a baby's eyelashes, are all there for the finding. Take several strands of a small-leaved ivy and you will discover, nestling under each mature leaf, a tiny, glossy and pinkish-green infant, so soft and delicate that it would be unrecognizable but for its inherited features. Even evergreens must renew themselves sometimes, so, disregarding all your finer feelings, press both parent and child. You will be glad one day, when you plan to make a miniature.

May An *embarras de richesses du jardin*. Now you can afford to be choosy. The collection is building up faster than you can use it and too much material defeats its own ends. Delicate petals become damaged with frequent handling, so press only the best, the most suitable or those with which you want to experiment. This is taking the optimistic view, of course. If it has been a cold, wet spring and May is no better, there won't be any *richesses*.

June The rose month but not for flower pressers, who are more interested in delphiniums, larkspurs, cosmos, clary, coreopsis, potentillas, candytuft and the leaves of *Senecio maritima*, acanthus, southernwood, rue, fennel and maidenhair fern.

July Burgeoning as the July garden is, it is less rich in flowers that are good for pressing. It is, however, an excellent time for finding tendrils and stamens, small buds and all the little oddments that give grace to a design. Many flowers that fade and lose their charm when pressed have stamens to offer instead; these may be long, pink and silky, or short, sturdy and golden. They will willingly adapt themselves to another flower which may be a little lacking in those charms.

August Is it fancy or is it fact that the flowers of August open directly from bud into maturity? Textures seem less youthful, colours more middle-aged. Even the rosebuds have lost their *ingénue* look by August. The vibrant colours of the dahlias know nothing of youth, nor do those of the sophisticated zinnias. The flat faces of the michaelmas daisies seem to have seen it all before.

Flower pressers have little to worry about yet, however. For those who are successful in growing it, the lovely trumpeted annual, salpiglossis, with its subtle colours and tracery of dark veins, has great value. The pink *Anemone japonica*, the so-called Japanese windflower that originated in China, when dried and seen in reverse, has petals of a beautiful satiny sheen, like an eighteenth-century petticoat. The arctotis, another slightly difficult beauty, is well worth the effort.

September 'Season of mists and mellow fruitfulness, / Close-bosom friend of the maturing sun,' but no friend to the flower presser. There are still late flowers to be found. *Hibiscus syriacus*, the shrubby althea, gives us red, rose-coloured, lilac and blue petals, blotched darker at the base, and the kaffir lily, with rose-pink or bright red blooms that grow in spikes gladiolus-like will successfully press like silk, complete with their elegant stamens. Most dependable of all, the little-known *Zauschneria cana*, with grey foliage and scarlet tube-like flowers, retains its bright colour better than the others, unless frost lays it low. Many plants continue putting out late flowers but the enemy of these obliging blooms proves to be those very September mists that Keats admired. Leaves and spider webs spangled with dew, flowering branches ghostly until the sun breaks through, warn us that it is time to give up.

October Yet there is a reprieve. As compensation for the dwindling blossoms, the flower presser is now treated to a new surge of colour, which must be captured without delay, before leaves turn leathery and unbiddable. Seldom now can stems be gently curved and leaflets coaxed to fold becomingly. They have become set in their ways, like the rest of us.

Now, a walk through the woods or a turn round the park will furnish us free of charge with all the gold we need; it is unnecessary to compile lists of desirable plants. Even the damp of autumn dew on the leaves is no serious matter, for their sap is already dried and only a gentle mopping-up operation is needed before they are laid between their newspaper sheets. True, their colours will go on changing and some leaves may acquire a few brown spots but there are no great problems and we can now look forward to a long-earned rest.

November Or we could, if Christmas was not just round the corner, with all those Christmas cards to be made. Out come the small pressed holly leaves and those red and brown autumn leaves so good for making robins. The primulas, forget-me-nots and daisies must be arranged in nosegays to send through the post the memories of summer so lately past or the promise of summer so soon to come again. There is not a moment to spare.

December Canon Ellacombe said of his Gloucestershire garden in 1895, 'In almost every season I can pick flowers in December from the white variety of the heath of Southern Europe all through the winter.' Laurestinus, jasmine and, of course, the Christmas rose, can also be found in many gardens.

But there are other, may we say even more pressing, matters to be attended to, as Thomas Tusser, who farmed in Essex in the sixteenth century, wrote,

O dirtie December
For Christmas remember.

2 The Practical Uses of Pressed Flower Design

The art of dried flower arrangement and that of pressed flower pictures runs parallel and requires similar skills, although methods of preserving and preparation differ. For garden lovers, it is possible to combine these arts, from the sowing of the seed to the harvesting and final use of the flowers and leaves, with the added pleasure, perhaps, of a bowl or two of sweet scented pot-pourri, to hold fast to summer through the long winter days.

Within the last decade, interest in these sister crafts has grown rapidly, with the classes and competitions that are taking place in towns and villages all over the country. The fund-raising potential for the many never before so needy, good causes has been discovered and has stimulated the desire to help in this pleasurable and interesting way.

Pressed flower greetings cards and gift tags will sell as quickly as they can be made. Small gifts for friends or for bazaars and larger ones for fund-raising raffles are always appreciated. Horizons are widening with the introduction of well-made and reasonable products for pressed flower decoration, such as handbag mirrors, powder compacts, pocket ashtrays, pill-boxes, scarf rings and pendants with chain or brooch attachments.

Frames and other available settings

Oval and circular frames, fitted with either flat or convex glass, can be obtained in gilt or silver-plated finish or in wood, with flat glass only. Glass-topped trays and dressing table sets comprising brush and comb, mirror and clothes brush, ready to be decorated, for wedding presents and other suitable occasions, are now available; so are christening gifts in the form of a baby brush and comb set. A few of these decorated articles can be seen on page 77. In fig. 7 you can see the assembly of an oval pendant; most of the other items can be put together in the same way.

Into the empty frame (a) put the acetate (b). The finished design (c), done on your own choice of paper or material or on an oval card supplied, is now laid in place. An oval sponge (d), which is supplied, may not be

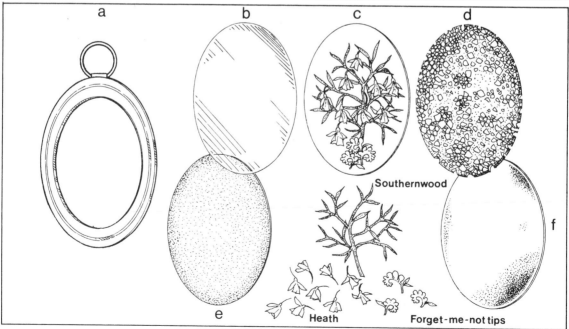

a

b

c

d

Southernwood

e

Heath

Forget-me-not tips

f

Opposite above: (left) Flock-backed circular frame, 6″ (15 cm) in diameter, with *Senecio maritima* and *Senecio greyii, Polygonum bistorta*, lavender and hedge parsley, on a grey-blue background.
(top right) Circular frame with a watch-top hanger, 3″ (7·5 cm) in diameter, with a formal arrangement of cream elderflowers and the leaflets of a canary bird rose.
(bottom right) Handbag mirror, 3″ (7·5 cm) in diameter. On the reverse side it has a pattern of young oak leaves, primulas and tufted vetch. It is supplied with a dark blue pouchette.

Opposite below: Fig. 7: *Assembly of an oval pendant.*
(a) the empty frame.
(b) acetate shield.
(c) the finished design.
(d) the oval sponge to go behind the design is not always necessary.
(e) flocked card for backing.
(f) alternative gilt metal backing.
Plant material used: southernwood, forget-me-not tips and heath.

Below: (top) Pill box, 1½″ (3·7 cm) in diameter, lined with scarlet. It has a design of montbretia and groundsel. (bottom left) Handbag ashtray, 1½″ (3·7 cm) in diameter, with an extending cigarette rest. It has a pattern of montbretia buds and bracken.
(bottom right) Circular frame with a watch-top hanger. A minature metal-backed frame, 1½″ (3·7 cm) in diameter, decorated with calluna blossoms and eccremocarpus leaves on a white ground.

required. Flocked card oval (e) is now inserted. A gilt metal backing (f), which may be obtained extra, makes a more suitable finish if it is to be worn as a pendant. The plant material used was southernwood, forget-me-not-tips and tiny pink florets from a variety of heath.

The smallest of the miniature articles is a polished gilt $1\frac{1}{2}$ in. ($3\cdot8$ cm) circular frame, furnished with a watch-top hanger and ring. A gilt chain or a gilt bow brooch can also be obtained on which to hang it. Considerable skill is required in the handling and choice of the tiny leaves, buds and flowers that are needed to make these miniature designs but the results can be charming, especially if silk is used as a background. Unfortunately, for technical reasons, these tiny frames are fitted with acetate instead of glass, which scarcely does justice to the delicate work of the designer, but it is hoped that the difficulties of cutting glass in such tiny circles and ovals may be overcome.

A selection of miniature articles is shown on pages 62 and 63 including a personal ash-tray, a pill box and a handbag mirror.

The personal ash-tray, is fitted with a movable gilt cigarette rest. A cut-out lid $1\frac{1}{2}$ in. ($3\cdot8$ cm) in diameter contains a minute frond of bracken, montbretia buds and a single yellow helichrysum.

The scarlet-lined, $\frac{3}{4}$ in. (2 cm) deep pill box, with a $1\frac{1}{2}$ in. ($3\cdot8$ cm) cut-out lid, has a design composed of groundsel, montbretia buds, artemisia leaves and Queen Anne's lace, sprayed black.

The handbag mirror, page 62, has a circular frame on the back, designed with young oak leaves, primulas, tufted vetch, a white bryony flower, pink clary and the calyx of a potentilla on a peach-coloured background. It is fitted with a blue pouchette.

A 3 in. ($7\cdot6$ cm) circular frame with a watch top and ring is decorated with elderflowers and the leaves of the canary bird rose.

A 6 in. (15 cm) circular frame fitted with a watch-top hanger is fitted with glass. The design, on a soft blue-grey background, is composed of *Senecio greyii*, *Senecio maritima*, *Polygonum bistorta*, lavender and the pinkish buds of an umbelliferous plant, probably hedge parsley. (Page 62.)

The glass-topped tray, opposite, measures 12×8 in (30×20 cm). It has a neat gilt rim, secured by brass nails, and a plywood base on four feet. This has, of course, greater scope for the designer; as a dressing-table tray or a small occasional drinks tray, it would make a charming wedding present when decorated. The tray illustrated is designed with the fan-shaped leaves of the tree lupin and the wonderfully decorative flowers of rosebay willowherb.

A most practical and charming sewing kit containing folding scissors, thimble, needle and threads, can be obtained for decoration, as well as silver-plated frames and trinket boxes and oval walnut frames.

Greetings cards and envelopes, etc

Several varieties of greetings cards, some plate-sunk and others decorated and already prepared for pressed flower designs, can be obtained and there is an excellent colour range of good quality plain cards with matching envelopes which are suitable for the purpose.

In the cheaper range, pastel-coloured deckle-edged note-paper, once folded, can be used with matching envelopes, to decorate for notelets. It is still cheaper to make your own from off-cuts. A matching envelope for a home-made card can be contrived by cutting a strip from the same paper. For a single card measuring 4×4 in. (10×10 cm), or a double one sized 4×8 in. (10×20 cm) and folded in half, cut a piece from the same paper measuring $9\frac{1}{2} \times 4\frac{3}{4}$ in. (24×12 cm). Fold this 3 in. ($7 \cdot 6$ cm) up from the bottom, keeping the sides in line. Run a line of paste along the inside edges on both sides, with the applicator, the nozzle of the tube or the tip of your finger. Press the sides together (fig. 8). Check with the card to make certain that your measurements are correct. Make as many of these as you require and leave them to press in a heavy book. When dry, fold the flaps over $2\frac{1}{2}$ in. ($5 \cdot 7$ cm) from the top. These envelopes can be made for all cards that are not of a standard size. It is advisable to address all envelopes before enclosing the cards, to avoid damaging the flowers.

Once the card is finished and written on, slip it in your home-made and ready-addressed envelope and paste down the flap. When making

Glass-topped tray. Small glass-topped trays may be designed in soft pale colours for dressing tables, or in brighter shades on a dark background as a drinks tray.

Fig. 8: *Home-made envelope for card or notelet, measuring 4″ by 4″ (10 × 10 cm).*
(a) Cut matching paper 9½″ × 4¾″ (24 × 12 cm).
(b) Fold this 3″ (7·5 cm) up from the bottom, keeping sides accurately together.
(c) Run a line of adhesive inside both edges up to 3″ (7·5 cm) and press together. Check with card for size and leave to press.
(d) Insert card, folding over flap and crease neatly before opening again. Run a thin line of adhesive under the edge of the flap, refold and press.

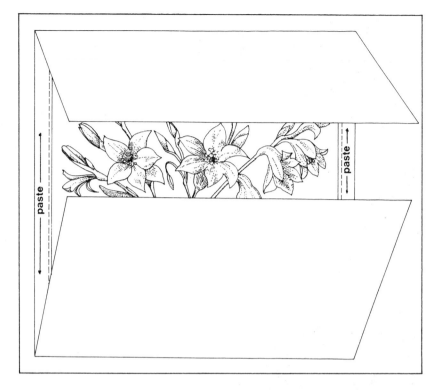

numbers of cards, you will be surprised how quickly these envelopes can be made, particularly if you cut them out two or three at a time. The result, made in good quality art paper or note-paper, can look smart and expensive. This method is, of course, suitable for private use only. Cards for sale must be designed to fit standard envelopes.

Self-adhesive film can be used for the protection of flower-cards. It may be obtained in rolls of shiny or matt finished film. Cut the film on its backing a little larger than the card and gently peel away the backing at one corner. Holding the film directly over the card, roll down the backing, a little at a time, and attach the film accurately along the top of the card. Gently lower the rest until the card is completely covered. This must be done with the greatest care (and confidence!) to avoid leaving air bubbles or wrinkling the film. Smooth it over with a tissue, pressing out any air bubbles there may be. There is a danger, when lowering the film, that loose petals may leap up and attach themselves to the film before it is accurately sited, and then chaos ensues. If the design is a small one, it may be easier to cover the flowers only and not the whole card. A little practice on odd pieces of paper will give the necessary expertise.

When done to your satisfaction, shear off the surplus from the edges of the card. It may be considered simpler and more attractive to protect your cards with a small piece of white tissue paper but there are times when the use of adhesive film is a necessity. For objects that are frequently handled or need to be protected from dirt, such as waste-paper bins, box-lids, match-box covers and book-marks, it is indispensable, so it might be useful to practise on a few greetings cards to gain the necessary skill.

If you plan to design greetings cards for sale, either for pocket money or for charitable causes, the following list will remind you of all the possibilities of this profitable business.

Greetings cards for all occasions

Christmas, New Year, Easter, Birthdays.
Special age and Relative cards.
Engagements and Weddings.
Anniversaries, Wedding, Silver and Golden.
Valentines. Coming of Age.
Good luck. Bon Voyage.
Get Better Soon. Thank you.
I'm sorry I forgot. Exams, and
general Congratulations.

Here are more than twenty varieties of 'occasion' cards, not to mention blank all-purpose cards and notelets, gift tags, menus and place cards: all could be decorated with pressed flowers.

A quick and effective design, cutting down on detailed work, is to make a template of a vase in thin card (fig. 9). The shape can then be rapidly outlined on coloured paper, or on a small-patterned wrapping paper or wallpaper, and cut out. Prepare a number of coloured cards and lay out a sheet of small pressed flowers and grasses. Having cut out several different shaped vases, paste one on each card, either centrally or in one lower corner. Paste sparingly round the edges of the vase, for too much damp produces cockling. Prepare about six cards at a time. Leave these in a heavy book to dry. If you are planning to make a considerable number, you can proceed with the next six, while the first are drying. Use different colours and patterns for each one. Customers like to think they are buying a 'one off' and the work will be more interesting to do. A vase cut out of adhesive film only will give the appearance of glass, especially if an indication of highlights and contours is made on the background before sticking down the film.

When all the vases are ready, choose from your stock a single spray for a Japanese vase, or a country bunch for a round-shaped pot, and stick them down. See that your flowers are in proportion to the vase. It is flower arranging on a small scale, a little different from the usual flower cards and interesting for the designer, the customer and the eventual recipient. If the cards are variously coloured and the vases differently shaped, you could fill a corner of a stall in quite a short time and they will all be sold by the end of the day.

For your own personal cards at Christmas, except for the special few that you wish to give more time to, it is best to work to a theme each year. Each card will still be different but, if the materials are prepared for autumn leaf robins or tulip petal mice or vases of flowers, you will get twice as many done in half the time.

If your lettering is good enough for a two or three word message, it can go either on the front or the inside of the card. If not, then the use of

Fig. 9: *Vase Templates.*
Trace vase on to the back of
gold, silver or patterned
paper, and cut out. Paste on
to a suitable background
card. Choose pressed plant
material to blend well with
the vase, arrange and stick
down.

Letraset in gold or black letters is a good substitute, although more time
consuming. As a rule, friends like to see familiar handwriting on the cards
they receive; a card printed throughout lacks warmth. Cards made for
sale, however, are better for a two or three word message.

A Christmas card (see opposite) illustrates the use of the vase, cut from
wrapping paper, combined with skeletonized hydrangeas (see page 46)
and young holly leaves. In early spring, small holly leaves can be found on
the tips of all holly branches; often, complete little immature holly trees
are found growing uninvited beneath the parent tree or in nearby hedges.
There is no harm in removing these unwanted babies, nor in careful

pruning of the larger bushes, and a useful stock should be pressed at this time for use later on. For a short period the leaves are malleable and easy to fold and the prickles a mere promise of what is to come, but disappointment lies ahead in the discovery that the dried leaf, so elegantly convoluted, is completely lacking in its characteristic gloss. In the illustrated card, the leaves were placed face downwards on a piece of glossy film, and carefully cut out, although spraying with clear varnish serves as well and with less trouble. Nature's gloss on a holly leaf can never be equalled, but there is a certain satisfaction in an attempt at imitation, however feeble. The newly grown miniature trees retain their green but the bronzy tips of mature trees dry almost black, making a marvellous silhouette. Some of these, given a thin white spray and superimposed over the black ones, make an interesting pattern (see *The Thousand Flowers*, page 149).

Children's cards are amusing to make. The ones illustrated above, are from a series featuring small mice, in every case composed of the white

Greetings cards. A Christmas card using a cut out paper vase on a festive red background, with holly and skeletonized hydrangeas (bottom centre). Children's cards, two of a series of six cards featuring mice made of the petals of *Hydrangea petiolaris* (top). Notelet with ballerina figure, made of a young fern tip and the leaf of a zonal pelargonium (bottom left). Card containing a pot-pourri sachet (bottom right).

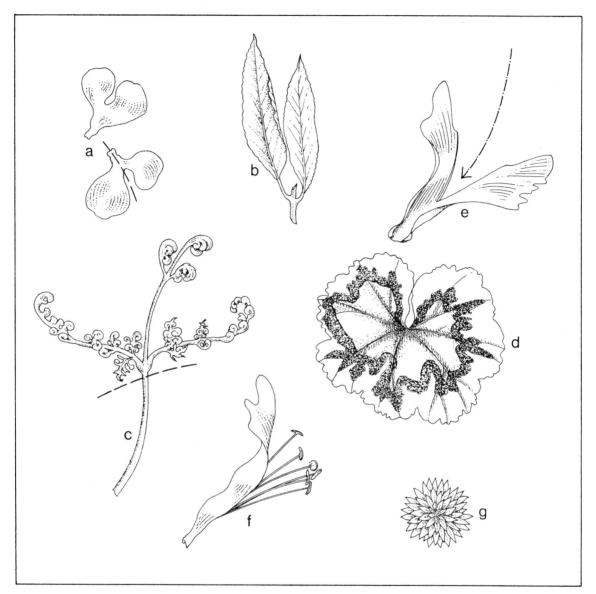

Fig. 10: *Mouse heads.*
(a) Miniature mouse, head and body. White *Hydrangea petiolaris*. Use one complete petal for head, and remove the smaller lobe from a second petal, using the larger lobe for the body.
(b) A larger mouse head. Take the tip of a young shoot of grey sage and remove all but the two tallest leaves. Use with any suitable leaf or petal for body. Paws and feet can be made of *Cineraria maritima*.

Ballerina.
(c) A young unexpanded tip of fern forms body and arms.
(d) A single leaf of a zonal pelargonium or geranium is lodged under the open arms.
(e) Cut geranium or zauchneria petals to make ballet shoes, cap ribbons and skirt trimmings.
(f) The feather duster can be formed of stamens.
(g) The mob cap is made from an anaphalis bloom.

petals of *Hydrangea petiolaris* which dry a uniform cream. The head, with its two upstanding ears, is made of a single petal and the body of a half petal, cut from a larger floret (fig. 10).

In the same figure can be seen the simple assembly of a ballerina, from a single leaf of a zonal pelargonium, slotted through with a just-unfolded tip of a fern. The mob-cap is an anaphalis flower and the feather duster is the anther of a red epiphyllum, a cactus plant. Ballet shoe, cap ribbons and skirt trimmings are cut from two scarlet flowers of zauscheria. It is used as a design for a notelet.

The *Valentine Nosegay* (page 72), requires little explanation. The tightly packed bunch of heartsease pansies and daisies, surrounding a single flower of *Limnanthes douglasii*, is encircled by a lace border of skeletonized cape gooseberry seed-heads (see page 46) and small ferny leaves. The twisted ribbon bow is made from cut hydrangea petals, some halves used in reverse, to give a suggestion of light and shade. The gold border is obtainable from an address given at the end of the book.

Unusually pretty gift cards can be made to frame a pot-pourri sachet. To make an oval opening in the card, it is best to cut a template, which can then be used for any number of cards. Since oval shapes are not very easy to measure accurately, it is quicker and more convenient to trace one from a small photograph mount, or perhaps a greeting card. Packets of tights and stockings frequently display their wares through an oval opening of suitable size; by looking round the house it is not difficult to find a shape that can be used for your purpose. Circular openings can be drawn round glasses or cups and oblongs present no difficulties, although they are less attractive. Cards with flower-decorated openings can equally happily be used for family snapshots to send to friends.

Having solved this minor problem and cut the opening in the front of the card with a sharp craft knife or scalpel, make as many similar cards as you require and arrange your design of pressed flowers to frame the shape, then stick them down.

Slim pot-pourri sachets made of fine muslin or net, of the right proportions to fill the opening, may have been prepared in advance, or they can now be done (fig. 11). The edges of the sachet should be cut a little larger than the sachet, with pinking shears if possible, and the two sides fastened together with running stitches or by machine, leaving an opening for filling. At this point, test your sachet for size, by placing it at the back of the opening, as you would a photograph, and make sure that your stitches are not visible from the front.

Fill the sachet with a small quantity of pot-pourri, avoiding unseemly bulges, and stitch up. Open out the card, run a thin line of adhesive round the back of the opening, and press down the sachet. Put the open card under a weight to dry. Do not close the card until the adhesive is set, in case you find that you have successfully stuck it together. The card can be neatened with paper cut to size to hide the back of the sachet, or the sachet itself can be backed with an oval of paper, but since, no doubt, it will very soon be removed from the card, that extra work is hardly necessary if it has been neatly done.

A simple pot-pourri filling, mostly gathered from garden and kitchen,

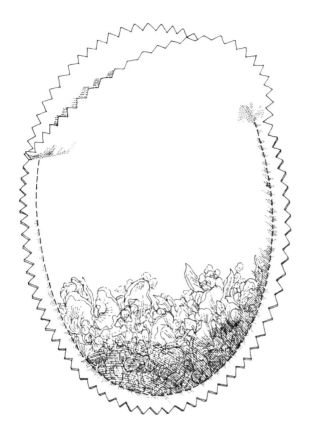

Left: Fig. 11: *Pot-pourri sachet*.
(a) Cut oval or round opening in front of double card.
(b) Cut two pieces of net a little larger than the opening. Stitch together by hand or machine, leaving an opening for frilling.
(c) Part fill sachet with small quantity of pot-pourri. Stitch up and neaten edges, preferably with pinking shears.
(d) Open card, run line of adhesive round the inside of opening and press down sachet inside. Put open card under weight to dry.

can be mixed for this purpose using one of Jean Lorimer's recipes on pages 200–203, or it can be bought already prepared from herbalists.

Another pleasant use for small pot-pourri sachets is to scent a gift box of pressed flower decorated notepaper. Even a small number of hand-decorated sheets with matching envelopes and a sachet, sealed in a plastic bag, is regarded as a luxury and gives great pleasure.

Calendars can be made from off-cuts of card or paper, perhaps combining two colours, with paper mounted on card. Printed dates for every year can be bought in the shops from September onwards, in various shapes and sizes in cream or brown, and these may be suspended by ribbons or pasted directly below the design. Use a matching loop for hanging.

Opposite: *Valentine Nosegay*. Tightly clustered small flowers of any kind can be used for a Valentine or birthday nosegay, and skeletonized hydrangea petals could replace the cape gooseberry skeletons here representing the paper lace frill so popular with the Victorians.

Decorative borders for cards, book-marks and table match-boxes

How often we buy a card to send away and then, because we cannot bear to part with it, it is put in a drawer and forgotten. Each year there are Christmas cards and birthday cards too beautiful to throw away but bound for the same drawer. How seldom we look at them again!

Cards, even the well-printed reproductions of old masters, never seem

The transformation of a
picture postcard into a
subject worthy of a frame.
Both the mount and the
material chosen as a
surround should be related
to the subject, and if possible
the edges of the card should
be masked in places, so that
the familiar postcard shape is
forgotten.

quite suitable for framing, and this may partly relate to their shape and
size. They just look like postcards.

A border of pressed flowers or leaves, or even seaweed, sometimes
makes all the difference but the border must bear some relation to the
card. A picture of a Victorian child looking out of a jasmine-surrounded
window was enlarged and greatly enhanced by mounting it and then
extending the flowers with pressed jasmine and its leaves to a width of
about $8\frac{1}{2} \times 10\frac{1}{2}$ in. (21×27 cm). Framed in a gilded frame of the period, it
made a charmingly nostalgic vignette.

The postcard reproduction above of an illustration from *Dombey and
Son* shows the faithful Florence sitting beside her little brother Paul,
at the moment when the dying boy says, 'The sea, Floy; what is it that it
keeps on saying?' It makes a sentimental little picture, and not perhaps a
great work of art, but it was a familiar scene to lovers of Dickens. The blue
mount, measuring $7\frac{3}{4} \times 10$ in. (20×25 cm), with its border of cream
seaweed, repeats the colours of the painting. It seems to be no longer just
a picture postcard but a pathetic scene that brought tears to the eyes of
many a Victorian family in a typical Victorian setting; for decorating with
seaweed was a popular pastime when little Paul looked his last upon the
sad sea waves. A typical Victorian child, no doubt, would have told us that
this cream border was no seaweed, for papa had told them that it was a

common zoophyte, probably *Flustra foliacea*, which was lending verisimilitude to the picture.

Whether animal or vegetable, this dried material is tough and needs the application of rather more adhesive than is usually necessary.

For the making of book-marks, ready cut lengths of pastel coloured ribbon reinforced with card can be obtained. These are the most convenient to use, although stiffened ribbons of suitable width and in a good range of colours can also be bought by the metre. To cut and make your own, a ribbon of about $1\frac{1}{4}$ in. (3 cm) wide and about 12 in. (30 cm) long is needed. The design must be stuck down much more firmly than usual, partly to withstand frequent handling but also because it is essential that the book-mark should be covered with adhesive film, glossy or matt according to taste. Although the flowers require firm sticking, it is also important to do this with a minimum of adhesive, to avoid unsightly stains on the reverse. The film should be cut a fraction longer and wider than the ribbon and applied deftly in one operation from top to bottom. Smooth down firmly but gently, reverse the ribbon and cut off the surplus film with sharp scissors, carefully avoiding the bound edges at either side. The ends can be cut in points, or with pinking shears, or a good silk ribbon can be fringed. If fringing is intended as a finish, extra allowance should be made when cutting and both design and film confined to a smaller space in the centre of the panel.

Simple and efficient book-marks can also be made with a strip of paper 12 in. (30 cm) long and 2 in. (5 cm) wide, folded in half, so that it measures 6 in. (15 cm) when doubled. The design is then arranged on the upper side, and the place may be marked by slipping the page between the two sides of the book-mark.

On page 76, the book-mark made on Japanese silver birch paper mounted on a darker grey has a frame of honeysuckle buds resembling wood-carving. Within the panel there are three purple solanum florets and five calices of potentillas.

The daisy book-mark is cut so that the rounded head hooks on to the top of the page, and so can never slide down and disappear. Keep the material as thin and flat as possible, for no raised or lumpy parts must be allowed to make indentations on the pages of the book.

Large table boxes of matches covered top and bottom and attractively decorated, make useful small gifts. Cut two pieces of paper, $4\frac{3}{4} \times 2\frac{3}{4}$ in. (12 × 7 cm), which allows for a slight turn over at the edges. Remove the tray of matches and stick the paper on the top and the bottom of the box keeping the sides clear for striking. Arrange your design on the top only (fig. 12). Make a few pencil indications for placing the flowers accurately and stick them down. Measure two pieces of film, each a little larger than the box, and cover the bottom first. Neaten the edges with large sharp scissors. The least sign of bluntness and you will only succeed in bending the film. Lastly, cover the decorated top of the box with the film, avoiding air bubbles and pressing gently and firmly round the flowers. Rosebay willowherb and the fronds of ferns have been used in this design. Cut off the excess film round the edges and replace the match tray – preferably the right way up!

Designs for Bookmarks. A formal design framed in honeysuckle buds on Japanese silver bark paper gives a suggestion of wood carving (left). A hook-on bookmark decorated with pink-tipped daisies is designed so that the top daisy peers over the edge of the page (right).

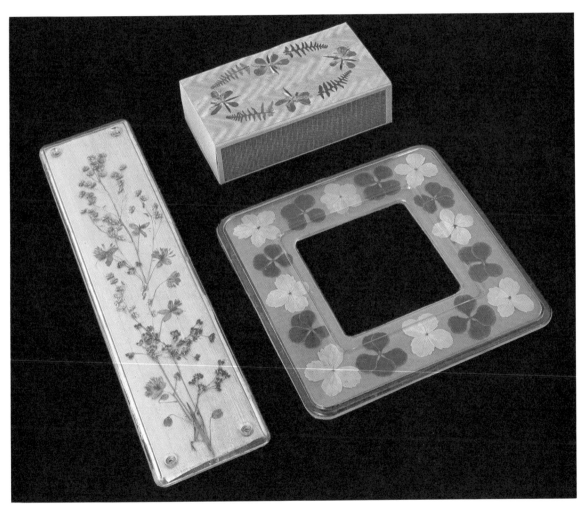

Match-box Cover. A design of fern leaves and rosebay willowherb on a soft green paper covered with transparent film, makes a table match-box into a useful and attractive gift.
Switch-plate. A simple but striking design of clover leaves and white hydrangeas in a recessed plastic surround. Suitable for use on a plain wallpaper or colour wash only.
Finger-plate. Enclosed in recessed clear plastic, this finger-plate or door-plate can be designed in colours suitable for its surroundings. A light Japanese bark paper makes an attractive background.

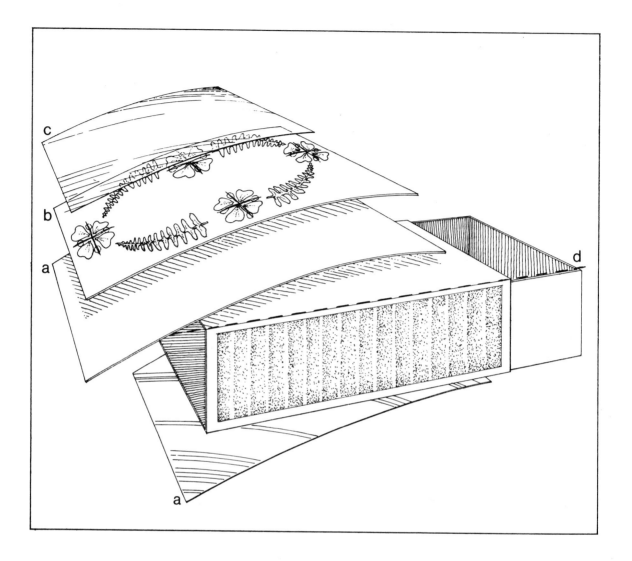

Fig. 12: *Table match-box.*
(a) Cut two pieces of paper, $4\frac{3}{4}'' \times 2\frac{3}{4}''$ (12×7 cm). Remove match tray. Cover bottom of case with paper. Next cover top of case, keeping the sides clear.
(b) Decorate top with pressed flowers and stick down.
(c) Cut two pieces of protective film, $4\frac{3}{8}'' \times 2\frac{3}{4}''$ (11×7 cm). Cover top first, and then bottom.
(d) Neaten edges with large sharp scissors.

Finger plates and switch plates

Varying sizes of clear plastic plates can be obtained from decorators and DIY shops, for finger plates, or door plates. They are usually sold in pairs, some slightly recessed and others to be screwed flush with the door. Door plates designed with a particular room in mind can look very attractive but switch plates decorated with pressed flowers are not suitable for use on flowered wallpapers. If door plate and switch plate are to be used in the same room, design them to match, so that they can be regarded as a pair.

A good firm backing paper is needed for all types of plates. Japanese bark paper is very effective on light coloured doors but it is light-weight and thin and will require a second, firmer backing paper to reinforce it. The design is pressed into the recessed plates, or laid against the flat ones, and it can then be held in position with two small pieces of sticky tape until the plate is screwed to the door; after that, any surplus can be cut off.

The switch plate should be laid on the background paper and held there with one or two pieces of sticky tape. Steadying this with the left hand, carefully cut round the inner line of the plate with a sharp knife. Now cut round the outside. Take this paper frame and try it inside the plate. Since switch plates are usually recessed, you may have to pare the paper down until it fits neatly inside. Remove the paper, arrange your design on it, leaving a sufficient margin; stick the flowers down and then return the paper to the inside of the plate. No further sticking will be necessary. There is no screwing required, as the plate is held in position by the surround of the switch, but if you are fixing it yourself, remember to turn the electricity off before unscrewing the switch.

Paperweights

Perhaps the most popular of all pressed flower decorated gifts are paperweights. These can be obtained in several shapes and sizes: oval, square, circular, domed and as a dish. The domed variety magnifies the material and has a pleasantly mysterious effect. All of them, if left on a desk in a sunny window, will cause the flowers to lose their colour. Although the designs can be renewed easily enough, it is best to keep paperweights out of the sun.

On the whole, because of the confined space and rigid shape, a formal design will suit them best. Sometimes a single large flower, completely filling a circular paperweight, can be quite effective. A large white marguerite or a scarlet anemone on a black background, is simple to arrange and very striking. Dark flowers and leaves in almost black silhouette on a gold background have an almost jewel-like quality. The flowers can also be mounted on thin but firm material such as silk or satin. Recent models are fitted with a design card which can be covered with your own material; they also have a self-adhesive base disc and some have a presentation box, useful either for posting or in sales presentation. For older models, it will be necessary to cut your own design card, by drawing round the paperweight and cutting inside your line, so that the shape is smaller than the glass. Some are narrowly rimmed underneath; in this case, the card must be cut to fit the inner rim. These models will require a backing of felt, baize or leather fastened on with glue. Self-adhesive green Contact is very useful for this purpose, clean, and easy to apply.

An oval paperweight is perhaps the most satisfactory from the designer's point of view, as it gives scope for a free arrangement. On page 80, the oval contains a few tiny, undeveloped ash leaves, delicately silhouetted on a stone-coloured paper. This colour makes a perfect foil for muted shades as well as a good background for bright red, orange and green. The small ash leaves used here are also ideal for the purpose; the younger they are when they are pressed, the more quickly will they darken, until within a week or two they will be almost jet black. The two daisy-like items are the calices and centres of marigolds, with the petals

Paperweights. The unusual arrangement of stone-colour and black shown in the oval paperweight is less likely to deteriorate than brighter colours, and the oval shape gives more freedom to the designer. The gold mount of the large domed paperweight makes a splendid foil for almost any colour. Here it is used with dark comfrey heads and small helichrysum flowers, which are unlikely to fade for a long time. The small dome is most suitable for one single flower. More unusual is the dish-shaped weight, and the reverse sides of hawkweed flowers make a fascinating pattern.

removed, with a scattering of elderflowers, which will turn from white to deep cream when pressed, in a matter of days. Among the many hundreds of tiny flowers used in miniature work, these are among the most reliable and easy to press, separately or in small sprays.

The pattern of the large dome is an arrangement of the undeveloped heads of comfrey flowers, a larger version of the scorpion tails of the wild forget-me-nots, to which they are related. They are mounted on gold paper, with an infilling of tiny yellow helichrysum flowers.

The smaller dome contains a single flower of the canary bird rose. This is mounted on dark green paper, although almost nothing can be seen of the mount. A thin circle of foam padding helps to keep the rose pressed close against the glass.

The dish-shaped weight, a handy container for paper clips and other oddments that clutter a desk, makes an unusual and attractive gift. It needs to be designed with care, owing to the various thicknesses of the glass, which can enlarge or diminish accordingly. In this, the reverse sides of one of the hawkweeds, and four others in profile, are pressed as close as possible to the glass, on their background of turquoise paper, having a layer of foam padding to ensure good contact. This formal and almost geometric pattern may keep the recipient guessing as to what it really *is*, as the darkened scorpion tails of the comfrey in the larger dome may do. Both of these, as well as the oval, can be obtained with the necessary fittings and a presentation box.

Cork pictures, tile pictures, waste-paper bins and mirrors

Quite durable pictures can be made on cork backgrounds. Sturdy materials such as ivy leaves, if finished with a polyurethane spray, have a long life, and posies of tiny alder cones, poppy heads and other small natural objects, even longer. Cork or wooden mats and coasters decorated in this way are easy to make and are attractive presents. A set of wood-framed cork coasters can sometimes be found in tourist shops, which require only a screw-in picture ring fastened to the top to supply you with professional-looking little pictures at small cost. Half a hazelnut, nicely polished, makes a good vase for these arrangements of seed-heads and those with squirrel-infested gardens will find them neatly and accurately halved free of charge. Without the skilled assistance of squirrels (about the only good deed in their naughty world), patience is required but Nature herself will oblige when the root is ready to emerge. Nutcrackers are clumsy instruments.

The personal touch is always appreciated by children, from a very early age to the time when childhood has almost passed. A flower-decorated initial in a neat little frame, whether C stands for Christopher or Caroline, makes a very special gift, particularly if the initial is cut out in *gold*. Initials can be traced from headlines in magazines, book jackets, and so on; or library books on lettering can be consulted. To trace out a complete alphabet, about $1\frac{1}{2}$–2 in. (3·8–5 cm) in height, to keep for reference, would

A Cork and Wood Coaster Picture. Half a nutshell, the fluted heads of ten small poppies and a few bracken leaflets, make a miniature that requires no glass, and only a picture-ring for hanging.

be a useful way to fill an odd moment, for personalized birthday cards, book-marks, boxes and all kinds of small gifts.

A gold wrapping paper looks quite well if neatly cut, or Letraset Pantone is a good firm paper obtainable in a dull gold. This has been used on page 84. If the initial does not show up enough, use a felt tip pen of a darker colour to outline it. The leaves and flowers must be in proportion to the initial, so that they can be satisfactorily integrated. Montbretia buds and the tiny paired leaflets of the canary bird rose form the pattern on page 84.

When tracing off an initial it is better to do this in reverse on the back of the gold paper, to avoid pencil marks that would be difficult to erase. Cut

it out with small sharp scissors from the back of the paper or, if the letter is a straight-sided one, such as L or H, it might be easier to use a scalpel and a ruler. Some letters are more difficult than others to cut neatly and a little practice on odd pieces of paper may be helpful.

The same sort of design can be done on a tile for a child's bedroom door. It can be fastened on quite safely with Sticky Fixers. Initial tiles for doors must be covered with film, preferably matt surface. The smooth exterior of a tile makes the trapping of air bubbles only too easy, and great care must be taken to avoid this.

Small square pressed flower pictures without initials make a pleasant decoration for an older girl's room. Many modern tiles are beautifully

Tile Picture in the Style of William De Morgan. A study of Victorian and Edwardian tiles will produce many ideas for attractive small pictures. Economical in materials and inexpensive to frame, they also take only a short time to make. Suitable for gifts and for sale.

Personal Tile Picture. Trace the letter in reverse on the back of black, brown or gold paper. Choose bright, small flowers and tiny leaves in proportion. Place initial accurately in lower left corner, weaving the pressed plant material under and over to reach the outer edges of the square.

designed and will be found as excellent sources of ideas. This is useful practice before embarking on larger pictures. Colourful patterns can be produced with small quantities of pressed flower material. These tile pictures have the added advantage of being inexpensive to frame.

The work of William de Morgan will be mentioned again later but his colour range is unique. The illustration on page 83 is greatly influenced by his strong blues and vivid yellows, giving great strength of character to a small design. Eight autumn-tinted chrysanthemum leaves, six yellow daisies and a single rudbeckia bloom fill a space of 6 sq. in. (38 sq. cm) to great effect.

Waste-paper bins of painted metal or leatherette are both decorative and useful. For oval and round metal bins, a small spray of flowers on one side, or perhaps both sides, can be covered with a square or circular piece of film, just big enough to cover the design. Flat-sided leatherette bins can be differently treated, with tall grasses reaching from bottom to top and perhaps a butterfly or two to introduce colour. In this case, the film, preferably matt surface, should completely cover each side and be pressed down over stems and seed-heads as closely as possible. Smooth out air bubbles downwards as you lower the film, remembering that it cannot be lifted without irreparable damage once it is down. A small amount of air trapped round the grasses is impossible to avoid (page 86).

Eighteenth-century wall mirrors were sometimes surrounded with satin frames, embroidered with flowers and leaves, worked in silver thread and silks and lightly sequined. Victorian mirrors might have flower-painted surrounds. The illustration on page 86 shows a mirror bordered with silverweed and clematis seed-heads. An oval photograph mount is placed over a mirror, which can be cut to the size of both mount and frame by any glass supplier.

A central pencil dot at top and bottom of the mount is helpful to make this formal design. The golden silverweed was found growing on reddish sand, which may account for its unusual colour, and the silver and gold is linked by three metallic-looking clematis seed-heads. A few odd leaflets have been introduced to create balance. This sturdy material, if fastened more firmly than usual, with thin adhesive at all the leaf-edges to avoid curling, may be framed without glass. In this case, spray the decorated mount with clear varnish before assembling. Do not use polyurethane spray or the clematis seeds will tarnish. If a pattern of more fragile flowers and leaves is preferred, glass will be necessary to avoid wrinkling.

Lampshades

Pressed flower decorated lampshades can be covered with silk, parchment or buckram. They are made in all simple shapes and sizes. Most popular at present are the table cylinders, trimmed with autumn leaves and sometimes honesty seed-heads, covering the entire surface. Delicate grasses make lovely patterns against the light, and the proportions are right for these large lampshades. They are difficult for a beginner to tackle, however, for transparent film is necessary to protect the shades; it is not easy to get this down over fragile materials in a large size.

Beginners would do well to start on a small bedside lamp or even to renovate an old lampshade. Unpicking this carefully will give you a pattern from which a new one can be made, or you can buy an undecorated lampshade on which to practice.

To make a completely new shade, you will need to buy a wire shape, which must be bound with lampshade tape if it is to be covered in silk or painted white or a matching colour for a parchment or buckram covering. Pin a sheet of greaseproof paper round the wire shade if it is a simple cylinder and cut round top and bottom, making a small overlap for a single join. You will then have a paper pattern to fit the curve. Other shapes will have to be cut in panels to fit the wire and will need several joins. It is therefore advisable to begin with parchment or buckram in a simple cylinder and gain experience before you try anything more advanced.

The small bedside lamp illustrated on page 87 has a smooth white buckram shade, fitted to a white painted shape. It was cut from the discarded shape of a previous shade and has only one join. The buckram shape was then fastened to the wire by means of a few stitches top and bottom to hold it into place (fig. 13). The old shape was then laid out flat on the table and a pattern of blue-grey African daisies and small pieces of

Framed Mirror. A formal arrangement of silverweed leaves and clematis seed-heads, shading from silver to old gold on a brown mount, relating the silver mirror with the antique gold frame.

Folding Waste-paper Bin. This white leatherette bin, which may be folded flat for postage, has two large panels and two small ones, each with an arrangement of grasses and the buds and flowers of the plume poppy, *bocconia*. The four narrow corner panels are undecorated.

Above right: *A Pressed Flower Trimmed Lampshade*. A lampshade can be decorated for a new lamp or renovated for an old one. This small bedside lamp of Art Nouveau period must have had many shades in its time, but probably this is the first to be trimmed with real flowers.

Fig. 13: *Lampshade*. Cut out lampshade, joining a to a and b to b with narrow overlap. Stitch shade to wire top and bottom. Arrange design on flat pattern, and then transfer flowers to shade one at a time. Cover with net and neaten with braid top and bottom.

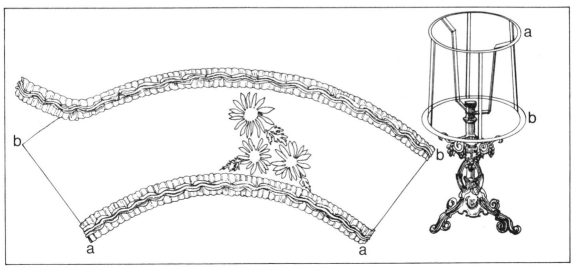

ferny leaf was arranged on this as a preliminary. This gave a clear idea of how many flowers were needed and their approximate position on the shade. The daisies were then lifted one by one, the adhesive applied to centres and outer tips of each separate petal, and then the whole flower was pressed gently into place. The first flower was arranged with its petals covering the join of the buckram. A good margin was left top and bottom, to accommodate the soft greenish braid which was applied later.

When sticking down the plant material, hold the lampshade either before you on the table, on the lamp-stand itself, or on your lap, whichever seems most convenient, twisting it slowly round as the pattern builds up. Ensure in advance that you will have an adequate space to fit the last flower in without over-crowding; if possible, the tips of the petals

The White Rabbit. Alice's White Rabbit shows an awareness of his University background. He is past his first youth, anxious, fussy and slightly irritable. Careful of his appearance, he wouldn't be seen in the same hole with any of the common cotton-tails of the surrounding countryside.

should just cover the join and meet the flower you started with. The in-filling with small pieces of ferny leaf will hold the design together; the silhouette of flowers and leaves against the light will be delicate and pretty.

The lampshade must now be covered. This is usually done with adhesive film. In this case, a fine white net was chosen for its daintiness. Since net is stretchable, it is also a great deal easier to apply and, although less durable, it is softer and more pleasant to look at. It is a matter of choice. Film can only be used to completely cover a shade when the sides are straight, as they are in the tall table cylinder-type shades. Otherwise, it can only be used in small pieces to cover separate sprays, a not very satisfactory answer to the problem. Net gives a lampshade a more feminine appearance and is therefore not very suitable for use on a desk or in a study. When used, it should be stitched top and bottom and the surplus cut off when this is done; the net should then be neatly tucked in at the join, without stitching. Lastly, the braid is applied with adhesive only, its main object being to cover stitches and rough edges of buckram and net. It also does much to enhance the colour scheme of the whole.

Pictures for children and pictures by children

Children love to have pressed flower pictures in their own rooms, particularly animal pictures, and it is usually animals that they will make, when they are first invited to try their hands at the craft. The pictures on

The Cheshire Cat. 'It vanished quite slowly, beginning with the end of the tail and ending with a grin.'

pages 88–91 have been chosen because they are characters familiar to all children and for which there seems to be no age limit.

Animals at times can make all of us laugh but what can there possibly be about tulip petals and autumn leaves to raise a smile? The White Rabbit, the Cheshire Cat, and indeed all the other strange creatures from Alice's Wonderland never fail to amuse us. Although some are beyond our scope in this present craft, there are others, such as the March Hare, the Dodo, or perhaps a diminuendo of Oysters, which you may find will pose for a pressed flower portrait with remarkable civility. *The White Rabbit*, who opens Alice's fantastic chronicle, is looking anxiously at his watch, a masterpiece of horological ingenuity in the form of a single small astrantia blossom, safely attached to its owner by a silvered tendril. 'Oh dear! Oh dear! I shall be too late,' says the anxious animal, always known formally as The White Rabbit, never familiarly as Flopsy, or Long ears, or Bunny, or any other childish diminutive. But before he disappears down the rabbit hole, we had better describe him, while he is still to be seen.

Mounted on a black card, $6\frac{3}{4} \times 12\frac{3}{4}$ in. (17×32 cm), he pauses, the better to show off his alert and furry ears, two leaves of *Stachys lanata*; his whiskers, the product of a nearby hedgerow; and his head and body, contrived of the reverse sides of two raspberry leaflets, small and sensitively pointed for the head, larger for the body.

He is posing for his portrait, wearing his best black velvet jacket, a folded leaf from a black poplar tree, his familiar everyday check jacket having presented insoluble problems. The one chequered flower known to us, the lovely drooping fritillary, being entirely unsuitable for a brisk and active gentleman's summer suiting; in any case, the fritillary is now a Protected Wild Flower and it should not be cut even for such a world-famous character.

His paws and feet are supplied by *Cineraria maritima* and his tail by hare's tail cotton grass. His eye is a seed of unknown origin. Two small raspberry leaves supply his starched collar and a rather arty necktie comes from the reverse of an *Alchemilla alpina* leaf (page 88).

These details being thus achieved, with one further anxious look at his astrantia watch, he disappears down a rabbit hole, a White Rabbit hole, of course.

The Cheshire Cat is shown characteristically (and conveniently for the flower presser) in the act of disappearing. He is on the way out, as we would say, although Alice would have been quick to observe that he was out already and could not well be more so. She would also have pointed out, no doubt, that his grin is coming from the wrong tree; for it was a chestnut tree in the Deanery garden in Christchurch, Oxford, where the original Alice grew up, that Dinah, the cat with the smile at least as famous, if less enigmatic than that of the Mona Lisa, was to occupy over those historic years. If chestnut trees had not such large leaves, this important matter would have been attended to, but surely a cedar is as good as a chestnut to harbour a grin – and the author himself never once mentions the name of the tree.

Eight tulip petals compose the feline head and the grin is by courtesy of four folded florets of silverweed and a single montbretia petal.

Lobsters' Pas de Deux. An economy version of Lewis Carroll's immortal frolic, *The Lobsters' Quadrille*.

Umbelliferous whiskers, greenish eyes of potentilla calices and spurge bracts complete what is left of one of the world's most famous felines.

Three nearly black parrot tulip petals should be arranged with their shaggy edges outwards, to give a furry outline to the top of the head. Choose a long, veined petal to reach from the top of the head to the nose. One petal at either side, with their ends meeting under the nose, come next. Two petals forming cheeks meet a third placed centrally, their points joining at the chin. These will need shaping with curved scissors for a smooth outline. When the shape seems satisfactory, stick these petals down with tiny spots of adhesive at the edges, leaving a convenient space still free into which to slip the ears when the rest of the head is firm.

Pointed and folded cream and red tulip petals make the pricked ears. Slip them into the spaces you have left for them and, if you are lucky enough to find two petals for the inner ears (in this case, two dahlia petals), slip them down over the others. This is a refinement and not a necessity. When they are all arranged to your satisfaction, remove the two pairs of petals, apply the adhesive, and gently slip them back into place.

The four silverweed leaflets that compose the grin are already folded and pressed into shape. They are arranged in curves that meet at the corners and the centre of the mouth; a montbretia petal slipped in sideways supplies the tongue. Three greenish bracts of spurge are cut to shape for the eyes and stuck into place. Two potentilla calices make the pupils of the eyes and a flattened brown seed forms a nose. The whiskers

My Shy Friend. He crouches
among the young ferns,
silent and distrustful. A
movement from us and he
will swiftly vanish, returning
to the small heap of dried
petals and leaves from which
he emerged.

are prepared from the dried umbelliferous head of a cow parsley bloom, with the flowers removed. Two sections of this were carefully cut at the base so that they still adhered and could be more easily stuck into place. And now, only the greenery remains to be done. The picture measures $8\frac{1}{2} \times 9\frac{1}{2}$ in. (21×24 cm) (page 89).

The Lobster Quadrille, that joyous occasion, involves altogether too many jointed legs and claws for any but the most dedicated floral interpreter and so we have settled for an economical *Lobster Pas de Deux*. Made up entirely of autumn leaves and leaflets, with the exception of four bulging honesty seed eyes and a flourish of hydroids to provide extra gaiety to the scene, this picture is not difficult to furnish.

Start by choosing two autumn leaves of a becoming lobster red, cooked lobster providing a more lively and realistic effect than the more natural ocean grey. Place these at a suitable distance from each other; that is, near enough to hold claws but leaving space for four pairs each of jointed legs. The curved tails are made from rose leaflets in diminishing sizes, alternately yellow and green, and ending in an aristocratic strawberry leaf. Strawberry leaves, by the way, should be inspected at intervals during the summer, for they may produce a rare splash of colour at any time, for no better reason than that they feel like it.

The jointed claws are formed of Japanese maple leaflets in their fashionable autumn shades, and the legs are conveniently provided by the evergreen palmate leaves of stinking hellebore, folded over to simulate joints. The feelers are slender sections of Japanese maple. Add the bulging seed-eyes and the frivolous wisps of hydroids if you have them in stock; if not, a feather of pampas grass or any bit of nonsense will do to finish: 'Will you, won't you, will you, won't you, will you join the dance?' (page 91).

My Shy Friend – the picture that made itself (opposite). It was the ears that conjured this up. One split dried tulip petal could scarcely belong anywhere else than half hidden among ferns, pricked ears listening, timid and alone. One autumn leaf became a body, of what small beast it is still uncertain. Two large and luminous eyes came from seeds of doubtful origin, a rounded seed provided an inquisitive nose, and whiskers were cut from an umbel of Queen Anne's lace. Two honeysuckle buds produced paws and a tail came from a young bracken stalk; more ferns made shelter. Pictures do not often come as easily as that.

Children can learn to make flower pictures almost as easily as can adults and usually their first attempts bear a strong resemblance to the pictures that otherwise they might have painted or drawn with crayons or felt-tip pens.

Lucy and Piers Atkinson, aged eight and nine-and-threequarters, chose both colour and dimensions of mounting paper, as well as the flowers they felt were necessary, and no instructions were given, except the basic one of applying the adhesive.

Lucy's characters stand in a straight row, like pantomime people taking a final curtain, and are described by herself as Fat Man, Thin Man, Lady with Umbrella, A Large Lady, the Lady's Dog and Another lady. A butterfly of massive proportions swoops down from above, guided by a

Piers Atkinson
age 9

Design by Piers Atkinson.
Title: *Two Rabbits Playing*
Chase in the Grass. The back
legs of the leaping rabbit are
cleverly jointed, both
whiskers and grasses cleanly
and neatly applied, and the
eyes skilfully directed.

Design by Rebecca Salmon.
Rebecca's flowers are well-placed and show a natural gift for design and colour.

Design by Lucy Atkinson. The masculinity of the two figures, left, and a dog worthy of Crufts, show a strong sense of character, while the well-developed profile view of the lady wearing a feather boa (?), right, and the frilly skirts of all three ladies, are charmingly suggestive of Toulouse-Lautrec and the *fin-de-siècle.*

small fly between three wind-tossed clouds. The sun, in the shape of a yellow viola, surveys the scene impassively. The picture measures $16\frac{1}{2} \times 12$ in. (42×30 cm).

Piers has made a small but lively scene of rabbits at play. The foremost rabbit, with ears swept back and bucking legs, glances back at his would-be captor. The picture is well designed to the proportions of the paper, $8 \times 8\frac{1}{2}$ in. ($20 \times 21 \cdot 5$ cm).

Rebecca Salmon's picture, a mature design for a child of nine, was placed centrally on a huge sheet of paper, which had to be cut down for reproduction. Considering the vast pot of glue with which she had equipped herself, she has avoided disaster reasonably well, and the soft colours and balanced composition show considerable promise.

3 Designing Larger Pictures

Textile designs – Chintz, 1830

Textiles probably provide the most useful source of design when making pressed flower pictures. They have an age-long and world-wide history, originating in the fundamental art of weaving. Like most crafts, weaving developed from a basic human need, the need for warmth and shelter; like other crafts, it was conditioned by climate and the raw materials available. Gradually the need for shelter was overtaken by a natural desire for beauty; from the simple manipulation of thread, a world of colour and shape, simple and intricate, has evolved.

Before the introduction of man-made fibres, the four materials most valuable to the clothing and decorating of man and his habitation were wool, silk, linen and cotton. Of these, wool and silk were derived from animal sources and linen and cotton from vegetable sources. Whatever the provenance of the material, artists and craftsmen have always borrowed heavily from the world of flowers for their inspiration. Now man may borrow from what man has made and the student of design has the choice of going direct to nature or of developing a new style from those that have preceded him.

Multi-coloured tapestries were being woven under the pharoahs and ancient Egyptian wall-paintings depicting the weaving of textiles may still be seen. Roman garments were often interwoven with gold, which, being virtually indestructible, outlasted the material in which it was originally the decorative part.

Brocade was a fabric which was woven originally with raised patterns of gold and silver but, by the sixteenth century, it was being made in many colours and floral patterns were usual. Another ancient material was velvet, which could be cut into piles of varying depths; designs could also be made of uncut pile on a voided background.

The name 'chintz' was derived from the Hindu word for white calico with a painted design, usually of flowers. By 1660, chintz was immensely popular in England but its boom period was terminated by the Act of 1707, which imposed limitations on the import of Indian fabrics. Even as

Chintz, 1830. A typical textile design of the period, which seems never to have become old-fashioned. The clean and practical value of glazed chintz, as well as its porcelain-like appearance, has made it a permanent addition to the range of furnishing textiles.

contraband, their exotic floral patterns and durable colours continued to be worn in fashionable European circles during most of the eighteenth century. Glazed chintz, with its shiny and dirt-resistant surface giving the appearance of china, retained its popularity for furnishing throughout the 1920s, '30s and '40s and is of particular interest to the pressed flower artist.

Lutestring, a shiny silk and ribbon fabric, was known in the fifteenth century and was also usually woven with flowers. Mrs Delany, describing the dress she intended to wear at the royal wedding, wrote on 16 March, 1734, 'I have got my wedding garment ready; 'tis a brocade lutestring, white ground, with great ramping flowers, in shades of purples, reds and greens. I gave thirteen shillings a yard; it looks better than it describes.'

Textile printing was introduced into Europe at the end of the seventeenth century. Block printing had been known in the Middle Ages in Italy but the designs were printed in oil colours and were not washable. The fast-dyed, highly coloured, hand-painted Indian cottons were imported into Europe during the early seventeenth century but attempts to imitate these in France, Holland and England were not successful until after the 1670s.

William Sherwin, an engraver, took out a patent in England in 1670 and textile printing became a well established industry in areas around the rivers near London. In 1721, in order to protect the wool and silk trade, cottons printed in England were prohibited and London printers were forced to work for export. The prohibition lasted until 1774 but the very heavy excise duties were not withdrawn until 1831.

Printing from engraved copper plates made possible much larger repeat patterns. The new technique was successfully carried out in England in 1756. Patterns were at first printed in monochrome and the extra colours added by wood block. The designs were printed in purple, red and sepia, all derived from madder, or in deep indigo blue. By 1765, several firms had started work in the north, near the weaving centres of Carlisle and Lancashire.

From then on, textile designing was to become a highly skilled craft, which reached its peak at the end of the nineteenth century and into the twentieth, with the Art Nouveau period. A study of the textile designs of William Morris, Walter Crane, Arthur Silver and the brilliant artists who worked for the Silver Studio between 1880 and 1963 will be of the greatest value to students of pressed flower art today. Arthur Silver died at the height of his career at the age of forty-three but his sons, Rex and Harry, carried on with the business of designing which made the Silver Studios one of the most influential centres of its kind in the world. Many of the artists worked anonymously and it is only in recent years that their names have become known. The contents of the Silver Studio of Design were presented to the Hornsey College of Art, which is now part of Middlesex Polytechnic. Here, in the archive and research library, these designs and the records of their artists may be studied. If a visit is not possible, a copy of their splendidly illustrated catalogue (see Bibliography) would be an invaluable guide for pressed flower artists.

The design opposite is adapted from a chintz, c. 1830. Poppies, clematis, tulip, nicotiana and hydrangeas form the main part of the picture. They are fringed with kaffir lilies, larkspur, delphinium, primula, primrose, convolvulus, mallow and leycesteria, on a base of ivy leaves. The colours of these flowers may fade or change with time but the balance of light and dark on a pale blue paper will remain attractive for years.

This is a straightforward design to reproduce, with no particular problems, either in the availability of the materials or in their arrangement. It can be adapted to almost any reliable garden flowers and the background can be chosen to reflect the colour scheme as a whole. The weight and depth of colour lie at the bottom of this typical chintz pattern and, when arranging the material, it would be best to work from the bottom upwards.

After the design is loosely set out on the background, mark the positions of the outlying petals and leaves. To stick them down, cover the lower half of the picture with a small sheet of glass or, failing that, paper, on which to rest your hand. Work from the top downwards.

Random Flight

Random Flight may accurately be described as a patch-up job but as such it constitutes a minor triumph over the vagaries of the British climate and might in future years point the way to triumph over the climates as temperamentally and intemperately inclined.

In the district where a small body of tenderly nurtured parrot tulips awaited decapitation in the interests of art, not unlike turkeys facing doom before Christmas, the skies that did not drop relentless rain from dawn to dusk, on alternate days were curtained with heavy moisture-laden clouds. Not a ray of sunshine heartened this ragged regiment and yet it thrived.

One would think that these beautiful fringed petals, their rich purple-black shining with moisture, only needed a gentle application of blotting-paper or a soft tissue or towel before pressing and all would be well but this was not so.

In other years, they had survived the sunshine and showers that every springtime is supposed to bring and the subsequent drying and pressing treatment meted out to them, not with flying colours but with colours that did not fly and there are pictures to prove it. This year was a disaster. On opening up the presses came the moment of truth, a sorry harvest of brown spotted petals. Only a miracle saved them from ignominy on the compost heap. Blemishes and all, they were still too beautiful in their ragged outlines for destruction.

They were too solid to spray and any other application of paint on such dark colours had no chance of success. But it was possible that waterproof coloured inks might work. A translucent wash of viridian, cobalt and carmine, quick drying and random, has given them the iridescence of a blackbird's wing or a beetle's carapace. It also mystifies the uninformed.

On a lime green background, these happy survivors are mixed with other untreated petals of a previous year, with which they may be

Random Flight. Damp-spotted tulip petals, rejuvenated with a quick brush-over with waterproof ink in blue, green and carmine, give a beetle-shard iridescence. Large oval frames are difficult to find, although they still turn up, battered but not beyond repair, on market days. A design such as this can be adapted to any shape.

compared. The bracts of *Leycesteria formosa*, a sprinkle of heuchera flowers to supply a glimpse of red and one or two small leaves whirl with the tulips in a snowstorm of Queen Anne's lace, like some strange bird-insects or insect-birds, travellers in outer space celebrating their metamorphosis.

It must be said that only the dark-coloured tulips can be treated in this way. The case for *pale* damp-stained petals is hopeless.

A patchwork picture

Just as the making of a patchwork quilt began as an economical way of using up small pieces of contrasting material, so a patchwork picture may be made of off-cuts from other pictures and both have similar charm. Tiny sprays and buds and leaflets too small and insignificant for use elsewhere may be just what is needed to represent this old-world craft. A patchwork picture for a teenage bedroom would be much appreciated, especially if it is in key with the colours of the room.

Templates of various shapes (square, hexagon or honeycomb, octagon and diamond) can be bought from any needlework shop; or they are not too difficult to cut at home from thin card. A square $1\frac{1}{2} \times 1\frac{1}{2}$ in. (4×4 cm), with the corners accurately cut off (fig. 14), can be made into either hexagon or octagon shapes; it is a simple matter to draw and then cut round these on the coloured papers.

Whichever shape is chosen, it must be mounted with thin paste or wallpaper adhesive on to a firm backing sheet, with the pieces accurately fitted together and pressed under a heavy book for twenty-four hours to prevent buckling later on when the flowers are applied. Colours may be used at random or in a formal design, as is the way with patchwork quilts.

Unlike other pressed flower pictures, whose size is dictated by the size of the leaves and flowers used, a patchwork picture may be of any size, from the very small square to a large panel, and can be enchanting at either extreme. Brightness can also be achieved, for the colours that may be lacking in the flowers can be introduced in the many-coloured shapes of paper used.

For the sentimentally inclined, patchwork pieces, even in the old 'crazy' quilts, can be cut out of scraps of favourite materials, from a first party dress or a bridal dress to a ball gown of the past, still smelling of camphor. Just as sentimental might be the choice of tiny flowers in a patchwork picture: alpine flowers from a Swiss holiday; flowers from a birthday posy; memories of a country lane or a cliff-walk by the sea. Always the eye returns to one special patch with affection.

Some old patchwork quilts are furnished with documented pedigrees and it might be well to do the same with a patchwork picture, if the flowers are of any sentimental or romantic interest. Dated and pasted on the back of the picture, a label should give the source of the flowers or the occasion the patch commemorates; this, too, might become an heirloom one day, or a delightful house-warming present.

Simple to make, it is also a good practice piece for a beginner, and a mini-patchwork would make an unusual greetings card.

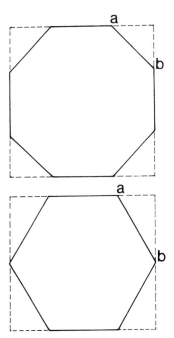

Fig. 14: *Templates for patchwork pictures.* Templates may be cut in any shape or size but must fit neatly together. A good hexagon or octagon can be cut from a square of thin card, $1\frac{1}{2}'' \times 1\frac{1}{2}''$ (4×4 cm). For the hexagon, mark a spot halfway down each side, i.e. $\frac{3}{4}''$ (18 mm). Mark $\frac{3}{8}''$ (9 mm) from each corner top and bottom and cut, a to b. Octagons can be cut from a $1\frac{1}{2}''$ square (4 cm square) card by measuring $\frac{1}{2}''$ (12 mm) from each corner. Cut off corners, a to b.

Opposite: A Patchwork Picture. Heirloom for tomorrow. A revived interest in patchwork has led to great activity in groups and classes, as well as visits to the fine American Museum outside Bath, where a memorable collection of American folk designs may be seen.

Paisley Shawl Border.
Fashion clings to the Paisley pine, in bedspreads, summer dresses, headscarves and cravats. Both men and women still wear this ancient design that Queen Victoria so successfully revived.

Paisley shawls and their design

The bulbous 'pine' motif that we associate with the Paisley shawl has its origin in Kashmir, in India. This curious curved figure, tightly packed with tiny flowers and leaves, which we have come to value in the design of carpets, curtain and bedspreads, as well as in ties and scarves, was used in patterns of shawls from the 1770s onwards, in England, Scotland and France. It appeared later in Germany and the Low Countries.

The famous shawls of Paisley, first known modestly and with truth as 'imitation Oriental shawls', by 1830 had become big business, enabling their producers to under-sell competitors in Edinburgh and Norwich and to earn for themselves the enviable and it would seem the undying name of 'the Paisley shawl'.

Weaving was already an important industry in Paisley in the seventeenth century and a large number of cottagers of that town were 'wabsters' or weavers. The earliest Paisley products were homespun linens and woollens but, with the development of the looms and the improvement of the yarn, cotton and silk were added, followed by a variety of lawns, muslins and gauzes. The history of the Paisley weaving industry may be traced in the street names still existing, such as Gauze, Silk, Incle (a kind of thread or yarn), Thread and so on.

The original Paisley shawl was woven on a white ground, the ends being decorated with a repeat motif of a single flower, with foliage and root. The motif developed, changed shape and filled out with smaller leaves and flowers, until it became what is now known as 'the Paisley pine'.

During the Franco-British hostilities in India, Kashmir shawls woven of goats' hair were brought home by soldiers as souvenirs. These beautiful, light yet warm wraps became so popular in Europe that, by 1790, they were being copied by the weavers of England, Scotland and France. The first of these shawls to be woven in Paisley appeared in 1805, although the 'pine' pattern was not introduced for another nine years. Black patterned shawls were worn following the death of Queen Charlotte in 1819, after which came red, orange and other bright colours.

The Jacquard loom had been invented in 1800 but it was not until 1840 that it began to be largely used in Paisley. The shawl finally moved from cottage to factory. The shawl boom was followed by a slump, leaving the weavers in a desperate plight. Queen Victoria attempted to improve their situation by purchasing a number of Paisley shawls in an effort to revive the fashion and the market improved. After the Great Exhibition of 1851, taste deteriorated and the pure vegetable dyes were 'improved' by the new acid greens, muddy crimsons and crude magentas so dear to the hearts of the affluent Victorians.

The reason for the basic design of this curly-topped, flower-packed pine having maintained its popularity for such a long period and over all other designs is not obvious. Cosy, warm, richly coloured and skilfully woven the shawls undoubtedly were, and many are of great value today, but the pine emblem cannot claim for itself any great elegance. However, a border or a corner worked out in tiny pressed flowers makes a charmingly nostalgic picture, resembling a sampler or a piece of treasured embroidery in a neat and narrow frame.

The design can be worked out in forget-me-nots, hawthorn flowers, wall ferns and whatever tiny growing things are available, providing you can find enough of each for a repeat pattern. It is a matter of patience rather than skill; once the pines are accurately spaced out the rest is simply infilling. A template of the pine can be cut and used to draw round or a tracing can be made. It is important that the spacing between each pine should be measured and marked. The background can be any light attractive colour and the picture made to any proportions. The one illustrated measures 9×19 in. (23×48 cm).

Arrange and finish the pines first, with each tiny flower firmly stuck down. Cover this with glass while the top border is settled and fixed, so that you have somewhere to rest your hand without disturbing the fragile flowers. Next, work the bottom border in the same manner. It is as well to have breaks between these operations, or the work will become tedious instead of enjoyable. Much time can be saved by putting minute dots of adhesive on to the mounting paper, several at a time, and then lightly pressing the flowers on to the dots but an accurate eye is needed for this method. One thing is certain, your labours will be appreciated and will result in a much loved picture of a cherished pattern.

Flowers in embroidery

The craft of embroidery was in itself an interwoven tapestry of church and state, for coloured silks and silver-gilt thread have shown through the centuries the proud histories of prelates and of kings. These frail threads have outlasted the men and women who wore them by countless years

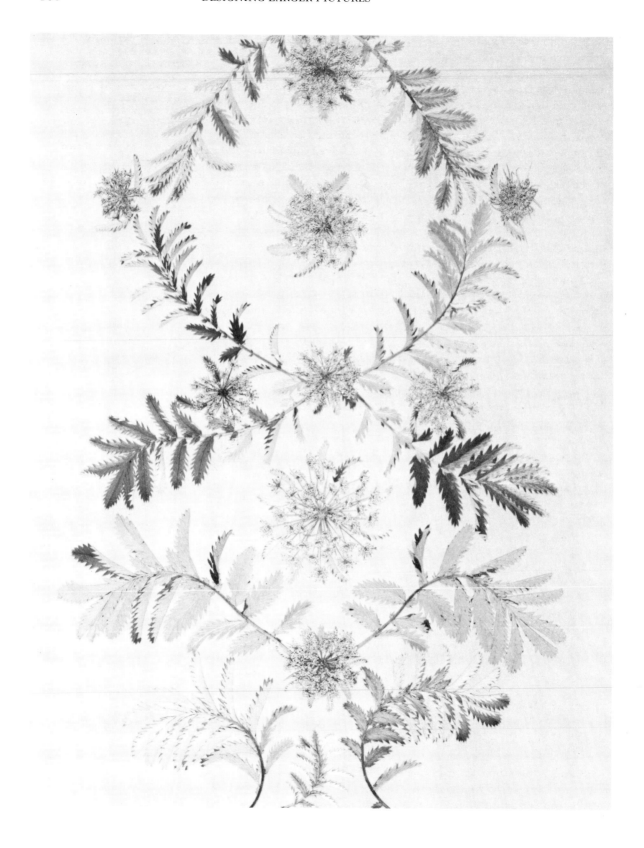

and the fine stitching of the early professional embroiderers has always been regarded as a priceless heritage.

With the coming of brocades and brocaded velvets, embroidery became less important and, during the fifteenth century, applied work, where embroidered motifs were sewn on to a silk or velvet ground, was found to be a quicker method of decoration. Secular embroideries, bearing the arms of the donor, or even embroidered portraits with, perhaps, the stitched request for a prayer, were given to the church. With the Reformation, the great tradition of ecclesiastical embroidery came to an end and the wealthier families began to turn their attention to the decoration of their own persons and property; most noble ladies occupied their spare time and that of their waiting-women with embroidery.

Amateur needlewomen of the Elizabethan age invented new and less difficult techniques. Some grew bold enough to work their names in proud acknowledgement of their employment, a thing no professional embroiderer had ever ventured to do. Flowers were copied in skilled stitching from contemporary herbals and a few embroidery instruction books began to appear. Black and white work became fashionable, since it was discovered to be a good way of copying designs from books.

A panel of black-sprayed ferns and lacy material, with small flowers, such as those used in the two fan designs (pages 129 and 132), would make a charmingly original pressed flower picture today. It would also be useful to have a stock of silver-sprayed flowers and leaves at hand to mix with the grey leaves which are so valuable in design. There are great possibilities in a pattern made with black, grey and silver leaves on a background of the palest grey paper or silk.

It was during the reign of Elizabeth I that embroidery on linen canvas became a pastime, one that is still with us. Flowers with petals raised by padding were wonderfully realistic but of little use to the flower presser, whose flowers must remain flat. Book-covers, gloves and little purses were charmingly embroidered; so were samplers but these, although of great appeal to the historian, were at the time regarded as severely technical exercises. Only later did samplers appear in the form of texts and alphabets bordered with flowers, framed and hung upon the parlour wall with more than Christian pride.

The eighteenth century saw ladies busy with flying needles, embroidering posies and sprays and knots of flowers for their bodices and petticoats and for the satin waistcoats and sleeves of their menfolk. Bouquets, baskets and cornucopias spilled over with flowers and butterflies of coloured silk and chenille, with the bright twinkle of sequins to echo the sun by day and the candles by night. Some were painstakingly copied from botanical illustrations; others were blossoms of pure fantasy.

Mrs Delany, who delighted in many skills, including embroidery, also enjoyed describing the fashions of the day, to earn our everlasting gratitude. She was present at the birthday party of the Prince of Wales in 1739 and describes the Duchess of Bedford's outfit thus: 'Her petticoat was green paduasoy [a grosgrain silk] embroidered very richly with gold and silver and a few colours; the pattern was festoons of shells, coral, corn, corn-flowers and sea-weeds; everything in different works of gold

Flowers in Embroidery. Detail from the front panel of a lady's petticoat, *c*.1750. These richly embroidered petticoats first made their appearance in the 1730s, and climbing plants, seaweeds, shells, urns of flowers and even, as Mrs Delany wrote, 'nothing at alls supported by pillars no better than posts', made their appearance in the candle-lit assembly-rooms of the eighteenth century.

and silver except the flowers and the coral; the body of the gown white satin with a mosaic pattern of gold facings, robings and train the same as the petticoat. The men were as fine as the ladies ... My Lord Baltimore was in light brown and silver, his coat lined quite thoroughout with ermine. His lady looked like a *frightened owl*, her locks strutted out and most furiously greased ....'

Ladies spent much of their leisure hours in the occupation of drizzling, which does not mean that they sat regarding the passers-by through a mist of tears. Costumes were worn so heavily embroidered in gold and silver thread, which, being almost indestructible, long outlasted the costumes themselves, that patient hours were spent in unpicking and rolling these valuable threads, which might be used again or sold for their intrinsic value. Special drizzle boxes were made for the purpose of drizzling, the work of unpicking. These contained two departments or drawers, one marked 'SILVER', and the other 'GOLD'.

Our design is derived from a detail of a silver-embroidered dress, *c.* 1750. The turquoise paper seems a suitable background for a pattern of silverweed and Queen Anne's lace. For a designer, silverweed has the virtue of sending out pliable stems of paired and toothed leaflets, usually grey with a silvery underside, which can be gracefully curved before pressing. The yellow buttercup-like flowers may or may not be used but one can hardly have too many of these curving silvery leaves. Their silveriness varies but, since they obligingly twist and turn and fold their leaflets, they show both sides to great advantage. They are found in damp and grassy places; the damper the situation, the taller they grow. There is another species, *Potentilla supina*, which is green and small, with leaflets more rounded at the top. These are worth pressing for small pictures but of far less general value. The heads of Queen Anne's lace, bordered with leaflets of the larger silverweed, *P. anserina*, make suitable embroidered medallions. The picture measures $16 \times 20\frac{1}{2}$ in. (40×52 cm).

As far as possible choose matching pairs of leaves, with smaller sizes for the top. Measure the extent of your design at the widest points and mark with a pencil where the outlying tips of the leaves will come. Mark the exact centre where the leaves will meet and the medallions be placed.

Working downwards, arrange the first pair of smaller leaves in a downward curve, with stems meeting at the top centre of the panel. The second pair, slightly larger, are placed a little wider, turning up to meet the first. Arrange the cut ends of the third pair centrally to meet the cut ends of the second pair. They should, if possible, have a little wider curve downwards. The fourth and largest should droop downwards with the top of their curve nearly meeting the third pair. The fifth and shorter pair at the bottom have a small leaf between them. After satisfying yourself at this point that the leaves are well placed, stick them down in the usual manner.

Lastly, measure again to make sure that the medallions you have chosen are accurately placed and that two will cover the two spots where the leaves join. Fasten the medallions down as before. Any faulty or damaged leaves may be replaced by perfect ones.

If all this sounds too complicated (it is not as complicated as it sounds),

Wallpaper as a Source of Design. A panel derived from a typical English wallpaper of the 1830s. The true-lovers' knot, an emblem known since 1575, began as the endless knot of love, a twisted ribbon that bore a message which could be read from any point. When, predictably, the ends were freed, the message lost its permanency, and the design became popular in textiles, jewellery and indeed anywhere that flowing and twisting lines could suitably be adapted to fill a given space.

get yourself a number of these lovely leaves and some background paper of a colour that pleases you and play around with them. The only really necessary thing is to mark the centre at top and bottom before you start. The silverweed will do the rest, or almost!

Wallpaper as a source of design

Another useful source of flower design is to be found in both old and modern wall coverings. The desire to create patterns and pictures of contemporary life was known among the early cave-dwellers; plant forms appeared with growing civilization in the form of mosaics, bas-reliefs and paintings. Tapestries in which slender ladies and handsome youths hunted or made polite love against a background of a myriad flowers adorned the chilly walls of mediaeval castles but the less well-to-do had to await the arrival of the paper-making and printing crafts and industries to decorate their homes.

Early wallpapers were often printed on the backs of old documents, which has helped to date them. The first printed papers used for the linings of boxes and luggage were printed in black only and bore a strong resemblance to the Tudor 'black work' embroidery, which was in turn frequently copied from printed illustrations in books. Later these papers were used to line chests and cupboards. This use of black work might appear of academic interest only to the pressed flower artist, until it is remembered that flowers and ferns of a lacy type, when sprayed with black, make the most striking designs and have the added advantage of being proof against fading.

A metallic dust was used in Nuremburg to produce an effect of gold or silver brocade on paper. This idea can be adapted for pictures made with seaweed, ferns and flowers, by means of silver and gold sprays.

One of the early developments was the making of flock wallpaper, which began to appear at the end of the sixteenth century, from a process that had been known in the Middle Ages. On a pattern already drawn or printed on canvas or coarse paper, the parts to be flocked were coated with varnish or glue; the flock, prepared from finely shredded wool, was sprinkled on the design while it was still tacky. The surplus was removed when dry and the colour added by stencil or by hand.

At that time, hand-coloured papers were fitted to battens; not until 1730 was the use of paste discovered and paper-hangers became paper-pasters, although we still know them by their original name. Still the wallpapers were made only in small pieces, about 14–16 × 11 in. (35–40 × 28 cm). By the beginning of the nineteenth century, the small pieces were joined and delivered in rolls.

Wood blocks were in common use by the end of the seventeenth century, although the difficulties of securing an accurate register were not overcome until the middle of the eighteenth century, when the 'patch-mark' on the selvedge was invented. By this time, painted cloth, embossed leather and tapestry were disappearing in favour of the cheaper wallpaper. All wallpapers were now taxed at one penny per square yard, in addition to the tax levied on plain paper, and had to be stamped by the

Excise Officer. This state of things remained until 1835, when the multi-coloured printing machine was introduced by Bumstead.

Flock papers returned to fashion about 1880, when they were made in silk instead of wool. They are still in use, although rather less popular at present.

The enthusiasm for everything Chinese, which swept English society in the early eighteenth century, brought with it some charming and elaborate landscape designs, which led to the golden age of the pictorial wallpapers. These were printed from engraved blocks and coloured by hand. They were sold in 12 ft (3·6 m) rolls, with a complete absence of repeats. Trees, shrubs and flowers, alive with birds and butterflies, were so accurately reproduced that Sir Joseph Banks claimed in his journal that they 'are better figured there than in the best botanical authors I have seen'. Later, human figures were added to these botanical scenes. So greatly were these papers valued and conserved that many are still to be seen in fine condition. Needless to say, Chinoiserie papers were soon imitated by English wallpaper manufacturers.

It was William Morris who was the first to design wallpapers especially for the purpose, instead of adapting from old embroideries and brocades; it is his name, together with that of Walter Crane, that is best known today, although there were many other accomplished designers at this time.

In the introduction to the catalogue of an exhibition of Historical and British Wallpapers in 1945, Sacheverell Sitwell, not an admirer of William Morris and the Pre-Raphaelites, describes wallpapers as 'visions on paper'. He admires the wallpaper designs of such great artists as Graham Sutherland but says that, for himself, he would like to see, adapted, 'the roses and castles of the barge pails and the winged horses of the merry-go-round. I should have asked of the caravan maker and the costermonger down in Lambeth Walk.'

Today, the Morris and Crane designs are as popular as they were a hundred years ago and they are now to be found as reproductions in the form of postcards and wallpaper books. Among these, the designs of William Morris are of the greatest value for reference, although they can only be adapted in a very much simplified form. A small collection of postcards and an outdated wallpaper book can be extremely useful to the student. It is impossible to copy exactly any drawn design with pressed flowers; the student is forced into originality by the nature of the material. Adapting from the skilled artist-craftsmen of the past is a great deal better then making faithful copies, even if it were possible. Variations on a theme often produce quite brilliant and original results. Last season's wallpaper books may often be obtained free of charge from decorator's shops, whose owners are only too happy to make room for their new season's books.

The true-lovers' knot design shown on page 109 is typical of the light and pretty patterns of English wallpaper of the 1830s. The ribbon bows are made of the cut petals of hydrangeas, alternately arranged front and back, to give a suggestion of light and shade. Tufted vetch and daisies give an effect of simplicity, and a repeat design is imagined.

The bows can be very lightly pencilled in and the petals stuck down, with the exception of the centre of the knot. This is left free until the daisies are arranged. The knot is then fastened down under and over the daisy stems and the tufted vetch added as a link between the bows. The panel measures $6\frac{3}{4} \times 17\frac{3}{4}$ in. (17×45 cm).

The Virgin's Bower

Jan Brueghel the Elder painted one of the best known and most charming flower wreaths ever to surround the figures of the Virgin and Child, when he thus adorned the work of Peter Paul Rubens. Brueghel's riot of roses, lilies, irises, columbines, marigolds, peonies, hawthorn and only he and heaven knew how many more, acts as a climbing frame for Rubens's deliciously pagan ballet of winged cupids, the most unangelic infants ever to be born of paint and brushes and to be allowed in so close a contact with the Holy Child.

Many other Madonna pictures were painted in bowers or garlands of flowers. They are usually the work of two artists, a portrait painter and a flower painter. Another portrait of the Holy Family by Rubens is surrounded by a garland which is the work of Daniel Seghers or Zeghers (1590–1661); although cherubs are lacking here, each blossom is vibrant with life and colour and on nearly every petal rests a minute insect.

Our *Virgin's Bower* must necessarily be a muted version, since we have no brilliant colours at our disposal. It is essential to start with a good reproduction of a painting of the Virgin and Child or a nativity scene. Well printed cards are to be found in most museums and galleries, or you may have Christmas cards that have been kept from year to year. A Mother and Child such as the one illustrated is a better choice than a card with a number of figures in it which may be lost among the flowers. Whatever is chosen, it may be placed centrally or to one side, leaving both narrow and wide borders to be filled.

The best background colour seems always to be a soft dark blue, although a surround of white *Hydrangea paniculata* petals on a gold background surrounding a circular picture has been successful. Whenever possible keep the flowers in the same colour range as the picture and of a suitable size, so that nothing makes a greater impact than the figures depicted. A few petals and leaves should be allowed to stray over the borders and the flowers should thin out and disappear towards the edge of the frame.

Insects may be contrived to imitate the work of the old masters, if not nature itself. The calices of rockroses make believable representations of the horny wings of flies and small petals serve for butterflies. The picture measures 11×14 in. (28×35 cm).

Trellis and treillage: its use in design

Trellis has been in use in gardens since classical times and is to be seen depicted on frescoes at Pompeii. It seems to have been employed for

The Virgin's Bower. In making this design, small flowers from field or garden may be freely used and there are no guide-lines or measurements that must be followed, except that the placing of the picture of the Madonna should be carefully studied and the flowers scattered more thinly towards the confines of the frame.

Trellis and Treillage. Making a trellis picture is an interesting and useful exercise, since it follows the method of most textile designers of working on squared paper. This ensures the accuracy of repeat patterns, and shows clearly how the parts of the design that escape from the bounds of one finished square are caught up and repeated in the adjacent pattern. The Trellis was one of the first and most famous wallpaper designs of William Morris.

fencing, screens and pergolas, as it is today, both for practical use and for garden decoration.

With the advance of the fifteenth century, when the necessity for defence of the home diminished, lattice-work fences became more general and climbing plants more ornamental. Trellis surrounded flower-beds as well as gardens and was often painted in the bright armorial colours of the owner.

By then, moats and high walls had been dispensed with; shelter and privacy were given by covered paths formed by climbing plants and pleached fruit trees trained on this carpenter's work, as it was called. Francis Bacon wrote, in his essay *On Gardens*, 'Because the alley will be long, and in great heat of the year, or day, you ought not to buy the shade in the garden by going in the sun through the green; therefore you are of either side the green to plant a covert alley, upon carpenter's work, about twelve foot in height, by which you may go in shade into the garden ...

The garden is best to be square, encompassed on all four sides with a stately arched hedge: the arches to be upon pillars of carpenter's work, of some ten foot high and six foot broad ... upon the upper hedge, over every arch, a little turret with a belly, enough to receive a cage of birds, and over every space between the arches some other little figure, with broad plates of round coloured glass, gilt, for the sun to play upon.'

Treillage was the architectural version of trellis work, sometimes in wood and sometimes in wrought iron. Having started as a support for vines and pleached fruit trees, to divide or wall-in gardens, it was later used by the wealthy for its own sake as background and for pavilions and gates. The 12-ft (3·6 m) high hedges, with pavilions at the corners, were so thickly grown that they formed a house of greenery within a garden. But stout and bellied hedges were not suitable for small country gardens and, in 1630, Sir Hugh Platt recommended that garden partitions 'should be made of laths or sticks, thinly placed, and after graced with dwarf apples and plomme trees, spread abroad upon the sticks'.

When landscape gardening took over in the eighteenth century and the practical gave way to the romantic, what remained of the formal garden, as well as the still necessary kitchen garden, was shut off from the controlled romantic scene with trellis.

Throughout this changing garden scene, artists never ceased to paint flowers and fruit against a lattice work, from the *Madonna in the Rose Bower*, painted by Martin Schongauer in 1473, to the jasmine trellis printed fabric of 1868–70 and the magnificent embroidered bed-curtains and valance of 1893, both designed by William Morris. The latter hung on Morris's bed at Kelmscott and were probably made by May Morris; the arrangement of birds and flowers against a trellis was almost certainly inspired by a design for wallpaper made by Morris and Philip Webb in 1862, one of the first wallpapers made by the famous firm of Morris and Co.

Students of design will no doubt be familiar with a sort of lattice work or grid of lines drawn on the paper on which a design is worked out and which serves as a guide-line for repeats. This bears a strong relation to the lattice on which flowers so gracefully arrange themselves and the study of natural curves in relation to the lines and spaces of lattice-work has considerable value.

Such antecedents should prove to the pressed flower artist that a flower-covered trellis is a valuable subject for their medium. Any climbing flower that is available and known to be reliable for colour may be tried.

The lattice shown in our picture is not graced with 'dwarf apples and plomme trees' but with passion flowers, an exotic which arrived in England in 1629. The curving stems and tendrils form their own arrangements most gracefully, although the flowers lose a lot of their beauty after pressing.

The picture, measuring $13 \times 16\frac{3}{4}$ in. (33×42 cm), is on green Canson paper, which has a suitably good thick texture. The laths of the lattice are cut from Japanese bark paper, although any brown paper will do; the rougher the texture, the better. The strips, about $\frac{3}{8}$ in. (1 cm) in width, are roughly cut and should not be ruled with straight edges, or realism will be lost. Four strips should be placed equidistantly and stuck down firmly top and bottom, leaving the rest of the length free. The five cross lengths should then be woven in and out; when accurately spaced, they can be fastened at both ends with adhesive.

The lattice work having had a short time to dry, the leaves and flowers of the passion flower or clematis or whatever suitable plant is available can be arranged and woven in and out where possible. When the design is settled, the sprays must be removed one at a time for the adhesive to be applied; they must then be gently restored and the leaves and tendrils carefully arranged. The flowers are put on last; in the case of these passion flowers, a second 'crown of thorns' has been added to the original one. This is because the anthers and stamens do not press well with the flower; even when separately pressed, they would give a cluttered look to the picture which does not appear in the living flower. The addition of a second 'crown' helps to reinforce the colour of the first.

Bryony presses well, although its flowers are small, and it would be best arranged with a second climber, such as pink jasmine.

Masters of tile making

Early in 1862, some tiles were needed for use at the Red House, Bexley Heath, the house designed by Philip Webb for William Morris at the time of his marriage. There were then no hand-painted tiles produced in England. Plain white tiles were imported from Holland and Morris, with Charles Faulkener, started experimenting with various glazes and enamels. Burne Jones furnished the earliest figure designs; these were outlined on the tiles, after which Morris filled in the flat surfaces with enamels. After the first firing, a soft glaze was applied. Morris designed conventional floral and diapered tiles to surround the figure subjects. Some of these may still be seen in Cambridge, at Peterhouse and Queen's College.

An interest in Morris's work caused William de Morgan to take up tile decoration. He worked for the firm of Morris and Company Art Workers Ltd for a time. De Morgan revived the beautiful Hispano-Moresque lustre and his colours were afterwards the only ones used by the firm.

By the 1880s, hand-painted tiles had become fashionable, not only for fireplaces, stairways and interiors but on art furniture. Between 1872 and 1882 de Morgan created some four hundred designs. Growing tired of the poor results of the firing of Wedgwood and other tiles bought from outside, he acquired clay to make his own. These were usually 6 in. (15 cm) square but he also worked in 8 in. (20 cm), 10 in. (25 cm) and 12 in. (30 cm) sizes. His strong palette was modelled on the Islamic tiles of the sixteenth century, using several blues, purple, green and yellow.

The best examples of William de Morgan's tile work may be seen in Debenham House, 8 Addison Road, London, (Richmond Fellowship), which was built in 1907 and incorporates all the remaining stock of the de Morgan Factory, which then closed. The brilliant blue tiling throughout the house was originally made for the Tsar of Russia's yacht but was

Daisy Tile Design. A much simplified daisy pattern based on a well-known set of hand-painted tiles by William Morris. Morris also used the daisy as a motif in wallpapers and wall-hangings, deriving his figure from a Froissart manuscript in the British Museum.

never delivered. He also made the panels for the P. & O. Line ships that sailed between London and the East but nothing remains of these since the ships were all sunk in the First World War. William de Morgan died in 1917.

Walter Crane also made many beautiful and highly individualistic tiles at this time, nearly all with classical or nursery-rhyme figures; the flowers are only incidental to the design. Many of these were used until 1938, twenty-three years after his death.

William Morris's Daisy and Rose tiles might well be studied and interpreted by pressed flower artists. A much simplified version of the Daisy tile, with one daisy plant confined to each tile (instead of four to a tile, two of which cross over the joins), may be seen on page 117. The pattern is made on squared blue paper, with a little blue and white ground chalk rubbed in with a small pad of cotton wool, to represent the contours of the slightly raised surface of the tiles. The backs of the flowers are used, since they present a more striking contrast than a front view would have done. This neat picture, tightly framed to keep out the moisture from steam, would make an attractive decoration for a kitchen or bathroom. The picture measures $11 \times 16\frac{1}{2}$ in. (28×42 cm).

Tulipomania

Second only to the rose, the tulip is the most important, romantic and fascinating flower in the world and of the greatest value to designers. Throughout the centuries, its graceful curves were adapted and formalized by painters, weavers, potters and metal-workers to suit their demands; the durability of the materials have left us with an inheritance of beauty, long after the fever of tulipomania flickered and died.

The small and slender-waisted Persian tulip grows wild in the fields. According to Persian legend, a little scarlet tulip sprang from the blood shed by Ferhad, who died for the love of Shirin, causing the flower to become the emblem of perfect lovers. Whoever these unhappy lovers may have been and however long ago they acted out their story, there was, even earlier, perhaps three thousand years ago, a Minoan craftsman who shaped a black pottery jar on which to incise a design of similarly pointed tulips. This is the earliest tulip portrait known.

Long ages were to pass before the tulip sat for her portrait again. A lily-like red flower was noticed in a Turkish garden by Augerius de Busbec, Ambassador from the Emperor Ferdinand I to Suleiman the Magnificant. Busbec brought seeds and possibly bulbs back to Vienna; his reference to the 'tulipam', from the Turkish name for a turban, which it was thought to resemble, was the first such reference in Western literature. Conrad Gesner, a Swiss naturalist, saw and recorded a similar red flower growing in a garden in Augsburg in 1559: the tulip's second portrait thus appeared in *De Hortis Germaniae Liber*, 1561. Gesner died of the plague in 1565, before his planned *Historia Plantarum* was finished, but the tulip was named in his honour, *Tulipa gesneriana*, and became the principal ancestor of today's garden tulips.

The tulipomania which swept through Holland like a mad gardener's dream and brought that usually sober country to disaster is another story. The Dutch, and the English, too, for that matter, have since learned to love these splendidly decorative blooms this side idolatry.

When the quiet beauty of the self-coloured flowers began magically, as it seemed, to break into feathers and flames of a previously unknown brilliance, the cultivation of tulips became big business. Varieties were divided into Roses, Bybloemens and Bizarres and the competition between florists became intense. In the Roses, deep scarlet and crimson,

Fig. 15: *Method of assembling Tulipomania.*
(a) Cut dark paper on board to size for background.
(b) Cut out and stick down paper vase.
(c) Arrange and stick down flowers in order as numbered.
(d) Fill in with leaves and add moths. (For method of making moths see page 46).

as well as rose, sprang from a white base. The Bybloemens, rising also from white, broke through shades of purple into black. In the Bizarres, the colours ranged from red, brownish-red and chestnut to maroon. In a feathered tulip, the colour was finely pencilled round the margin of the petals; the flamed varieties showed stripes of pure colour from the top of the petals towards the base. The self colours were now regarded only as breeders and many strange and doubtful methods were employed to cause them to 'break'.

In Holland, the breeding of these fantastic flowers led to buying and selling which became a gigantic gamble. The prices of rare bulbs were artificially forced up, like the tulips themselves, and soon everyone with a yard of ground to spare bred tulips. Clubs for tulip trading were set up and buying and exchanging became a fever. Tulipomania was at its height between 1634 and 1637, until the markets were flooded and sellers were more numerous than buyers. Then the great Tulip Bubble burst. In England, too, the enthusiasm for tulip trading was reaching danger point, until, in 1636, when bulbs were offered in the London Exchange, the dealers met with little success and it was discovered that the bottom had fallen out of the market.

Strangely, the passion for tulips did not seize the flower-loving Turkish people until the eighteenth century, long after the mania had died out in the West. In Turkey, a thousand pieces of gold might then be paid for a single Persian bulb, until the Sultan ordered the Commander of Constantinople to control the prices. Between 1703 and 1730, under Sultan Ahmed III, tulip fêtes became the rage of the court and the palace gardens contained more than half a million tulips. A Feast of Tulips was celebrated annually in the Grand Seigneur's seraglio, in which galleries, amphitheatres and pagodas were erected to house garlands of lights and crystal vases crowded with tulips. The banks on which the visitors reclined were covered with valuable carpets and a splended pavilion sheltered the Sultan while he and his nobles watched the circling of the dancing girls among the tulips.

Tulipomania (page 119) has the richly subdued colouring of a Dutch flower painting, largely because of the dark red background and the petals of the modern parrot tulip, 'Gay Presto', once a brilliant scarlet and white, now dried and pressed to soft crimson and fawn. Except for the purple-black parrot tulips, these flowers by their nature are bound to fade but, although their brilliance is lost in a day or two, the feathers and flames and blotches of colour will keep a different beauty for a long time.

The picture measures 15 × 19 in. (38 × 48 cm). In choosing the background, a warm dark colour is recommended both in order to suggest the beautiful Flemish and Dutch flower paintings and to provide a gentle softening for petals which will slowly change colour or fade. For the same reason, the vase should be cut from a dark patterned paper. The whole atmosphere of this flower piece, even if other large flowers are chosen to replace the tulips, should be of a subdued richness. You may wish to copy the outline of one of your own vases, filled with other flowers from your garden, but, whichever shape you choose, the vase should be lightly pasted down first, with a very small amount of adhesive, so that it dries perfectly flat, which it must be left to do under a large book.

When dried and completely smooth, arrange the central flower so that its lower petals, which should have been separately pressed, cover the rim of the vase. This may now be fixed, each petal having a few minute dabs of adhesive applied to the back, to avoid marking. A small sheet of glass or clean paper placed over this while you work on the flowers above will avoid damage.

It is preferable to make large flower pieces from a standing position, as when painting in oils, so that you can step back from time to time to judge distances. Unlike painting, however, the picture must be kept flat or it will be impossible to keep the flowers in place.

The rest of the work is careful infilling with leaves to avoid awkward gaps and mask the absence of stems. Let some of the leaves droop towards the two lower corners. The grey leaves of willow and the reverse side of

black poplar have been chosen as a cool contrast; the blackberry was chosen for its colour link between the flowers and the grey leaves. The centre of the opened flower in the middle of the composition is a small clematis. The making of the hovering moths is described on page 46.

English block printed cotton, *c.* 1775

Textile printing in England seems to have begun auspiciously enough in about 1676, in river areas around London, but the developing industry received a severe setback when, at the instigation of established wool and silk manufacturers, the use of all English and Indian cottons was prohibited in Britain. London printers were compelled to print for export only and then, later, for the home market, only under heavy excise duties, which were not withdrawn until 1831.

At first patterns were printed from wood-blocks, and followed the dyeing methods of traditional Indian chintzes. The dyes used were those already employed in Indian flower patterns, black, red, purple and brown, to which blue and yellow were later added.

This was followed by the introduction of engraved copper plates, which made possible the reproduction of a much more delicate draughtmanship. This was first used by the Irish in Dublin in 1752. Since 1732, textile printing had begun to flourish in Glasgow and the north of England, with the advantage of proximity to the weaving areas. Wood-block printing for furnishing and clothing continued with the northern firms, with a very high standard both of design and of printing. The London copper-plate printers were noted for their designs of large flowers and birds, as well as topical subjects, pastoral, mythological and theatrical scenes and, of course, Chinoiserie, when no English home of any standing could afford to be without its pagodas and temples and bamboos.

Rotary printing from engraved metal rollers radically changed the scene, not immediately for the better, with the inevitable early problems, but this does not concern us, for our design opposite is in the style of a late eighteenth-century block-printed textile.

The panel, which would be treated as repeatable, measures $9\frac{1}{2} \times 16$ in. (24×40 cm), and is a simple design of potentillas, white bryony flowers and fern leaves on a pale blue background. The pattern is as balanced as is possible with pressed flower material; the balance is the sole difficulty in an otherwise simple design. Other small flowers, such as primulas or primroses, can be substituted, to hold together the delicate fern-leaf framework, but daintiness is the main objective. The border is cut from wrapping paper, which is probably reproduced from a Persian design and has no connection, except that its warm pinks and reds take up the subtle colours of the potentillas.

*English Block-Printed Cotton, c.*1775. The plant material in this design could as easily be adapted to a border design, a corner, or the proportions of any small frame. Patterns of this kind settle more easily into old frames picked up at jumble sales than they do into modern frames.

Papier mâché, a forgotten craft

From the middle of the reign of George III, 'paper ware', as it was called, began to rival the lacquer that had been imported from the East. It was also being made in Germany, Austria and France; indeed, it was said that it had originated in Paris, where the quantity of paper collected nightly after the tearing-down of public notices that had served their one-day purpose suggested the idea of making use of waste paper by mashing it in water and, after drying, moulding it into small articles. However, although papier mâché was undoubtedly paper, it was not mâché but the name had been accepted and was to stay for its comparatively short life.

In England, the first trays were made by Henry Clay, a japanner of Birmingham in 1772. His patent gives minute details for the pasting of sheets of paper one over the other until a sufficient body resulted. After being stoved, the process was continued until a strong board, called a panel, was produced. It was the ornamenting of this panel that was of the greatest importance. Since the new craft was carried out by japanners, so called because the work was an imitation of Japanese lacquering, there was a strong oriental influence in its decoration at first.

The early decorations were the work of skilled artists but, as the work cheapened and was popularized, the decorating might be shared by three or four men. The first would cover the surface with sky and mountains or a lake or whatever background was required. Next a 'flower man' would paint a large urn or spray of flowers in the foreground, while a 'bird man' might supply a bird in the middle distance. The border was the work of a skilled 'gold-worker'.

The glossy black backgrounds frequently bordered with this gold made a splendid foil for temples, castles or pagodas, with rustic bridges and weeping willows, or, if the buyer should be patriotically inclined, for a triumphant Britannia, trident aloft, in a coach drawn by fiery steeds, heralded by a winged figure modestly draped in clouds.

The early colours were not pigments but were obtained by a process characteristic of contemporary japanned work. The various surfaces were made sticky by gold size, and powders mostly of a metallic origin were scattered on this preparation. Greenish-yellow and gold-bronze or a silvery-bronze-green were typical of this period but with time their colours faded.

The use of pearl shell ornamentation on papier mâché was patented in 1825. The earlier pearl ornament was in fairly large flakes or laminae. The larger flakes were usually coloured with transparent paint. The pearl was not the genuine mother-of-pearl but from the shell of a giant sea-snail or nautilus. The proof of good pearl-work was in the arrangement of the masses in such a way that the iridescence was taken into account and the grain and the way of the shell used to advantage.

Papier mâché was at its peak in the 1840s and '50s, until, by the end of the century, the craft cheapened and coarsened toward a decadence that ended in its death. No longer could the papier mâché shops of the early years fill their showrooms with elegant tea-trays and wine-trays, hand-screens, card-tables, card-trays and door-plates, opulent with full-blown roses and peonies, proud with peacocks or dignified with oriental potentates. Vanished were the gorgeous palaces, the cloud-capped towers. The magicians rolled down their sleeves, closed their pearl-lined boxes and with a bow departed, leaving only a shabby heap of papier mâché toys, won as prizes on the hoopla stalls, or sold for a penny at the fair. The show was over.

For pressed flower artists, however, the show is just beginning. The black background, gilded borders and generally burgeoning arrangements of fully opened blooms can be an interesting and exciting challenge. The pearly sheen that is miraculously present after drying and pressing flowers such as poppies, hollyhocks and Japanese windflowers shows to great advantage on a black background and disasters caused by damp in dark-petalled blooms, with a little skill and a lot of luck may be rectified. The fully-opened tulip in the centre of the *Papier Mâché Tray* (page 126), a victim of that disastrous spring of 1980 (see *Random Flight*, page 101), has been treated cosmetically with a single coat of green and blue waterproof ink. The metallic shine it has acquired is very suited to its purpose.

The beautifully veined hollyhock petals have been reassembled round the centre of an opium poppy, since the thickness of their own centres produces an unpleasant bulge. The hollyhock centre need not be discarded, however, for it might serve as a furry insect body in another picture. The gilded rim can be made of seaweeds or hydroids or of soft ferny leaves. Prepare one or two extra in case of disaster and spray each one lightly with a can of gold spray. The method of spraying is the same as that described for the fans (pages 129 and 132) and will be the same throughout.

The design, which measures about 12 × 15 in. (30 × 38 cm), can be cut out of black paper in the shape of a tray, in which case a smear of white chalk applied with the fingertip before starting will indicate the contours of the rim. If preferred, it can be arranged as an ordinary rectangular picture. In a wide frame, fitted with heat-proof glass, plywood backing and a handle on either side, it could be the tray that it resembles. It would be advisable, for this purpose, to strengthen the corners with angle irons, and to cover the underneath with green baize or Contact. The design could also be adapted for use in a glass-topped table.

Flowers as marquetry

There are certain flowers which, when dried and pressed, will turn to dull browns, greens and parchment shades. These make poor companions for others which keep more lively colourings. The beautiful hellebores belong to this group; *Helleborus niger*, the lovely snowy Christmas rose, so great a blessing in our winter gardens, turns a dull and lifeless brown. *Helleborus orientalis* exchanges its soft pink for strange greens and parchment colours, although the freckled varieties are saved from total dullness. *Helleborus corsicus* does no better. The foliage of all these, a splendidly rich feature in the garden, fades to a consistent lifeless green. The complete lack of silken or pearly sheen on these flowers gives them

Papier Mâché Tray, c.1850. The papier mâché tea tray was a familiar sight on our grandmother's table, both for the comfortable sit-down tea and in the drawing-room for more formal occasions. These handsome objects were superseded about the middle of Queen Victoria's reign by the invention of tin-plating, and by the electro-plating of base metals: a sad loss of a minor art of great charm

the appearance of old wood, and it is in this that their value lies from the flower artist's point of view.

Arranged on small panels of dark brown, light brown, soft green or silver birch Japanese bark paper they take on the appearance of marquetry. If framed in a narrow, dark brown stained wood, they would make fitting and unusual pictures in a study or hall or any room with panelling.

Marquetry is the craft of inlaying various coloured woods, which is so brilliantly exemplified in French, Dutch and English furniture. Tables, chairs, bookcases and china cabinets were often almost completely covered with intricate designs in many coloured fruit woods, some of which were ebonized, especially by the French, whose work in the late seventeenth century was superior to either Dutch or English. The English, however, learned much from the Huguenot refugees, from whom they were to learn so many skills in arts and crafts.

There is an overlapping of the veneering, marquetry and inlay processes. In veneering, a decorative figured over-lay is glued on to a base of plain wood. Inlay consists of gouging out shallow depressions of

various shapes, into which metal, ivory or other decorative woods are glued. Marquetry creates decorative patterns with woods of various colours and grains, set in a contrasting background; this may be achieved either by veneering or inlaying. Inlay is probably the oldest known of these related crafts; it has been found in Egyptian tomb furniture. The Romans used veneers and marquetry.

The finest period of floral marquetry follows the flower painting of the late seventeenth century. It is a translation of flower arrangements into wood, instead of oil paints or water-colours. A palette of differently coloured and contrastingly grained woods was used instead of pigments in a formal arrangement of flowers, an art requiring extreme skill. The saw-cut veneers were inserted into each other, or into a solid background, probably of ebony, by careful selection, with a sharp pointed knife. The flowers, as in the paintings, were arranged in classical vases or urns, or springing from acanthus scrolls, or tied into bunches with bows of twisted ribbon. The flowers thus treated were usually tulips, carnations and various types of daisy. Jasmine flowers were cut from ivory or bone, which, dyed green, were also used for leaves, buds and stems. Less

Flowers as Marquetry. A use of flowers under adverse conditions. Those beautiful snow-white and greenish-pink flowers, *Helleborus niger*, *Helleborus orientalis* and *Helleborus corsicus*, whose faultless complexions are the saving of our gardens during the harsh early months of the year, turn relentlessly to parchment and wood in old age. It is their fate, and could be our opportunity to keep them lovely.

frequently, roses, anemones, honeysuckle, rye and barley were used; birds, butterflies, and other insects were set in with ivory, bone or mother-of-pearl. In the best work, these flower patterns were also engraved. Marquetry flower patterns were more costly than the flower paintings of the period, which today would probably fetch many times as much.

A great name in English eighteenth-century cabinet work and marquetry was that of Pierre Langlois, although little is known of the man himself. His trade card announces that 'Peter Langlois, Cabinet-Maker in Tottenham Court Road, near Windmill Str. Makes all Sorts of Fine Cabinets and Commodes made and inlaid in the Politest manner with Brass or Tortoiseshell. . . .' Repeating the notice in French, Pierre Langlois, *Ebeniste*, adds, '*Meubles Inserulez de fleurs en Bois et Marqueteries.*' His marquetry work often takes the form of inlaid sprays of flowers, tied with ribbon bows, in various woods, in key pattern borders with rosewood surrounds.

After a time, the English, discarding floral patterns took to designing with seaweed and arabesques. Different seaweeds on panels of Japanese bark paper would be an interesting variation to try. Marquetry as a decoration for English furniture went out of fashion about 1715 but the Dutch continued to use it throughout the eighteenth century, making floral patterns almost exclusively.

At the beginning of the present century a pseudo-marquetry was popular as an amateur pastime in which picture frames, pipe racks, watch stands and small boxes were decorated with garlands of bay, laurel or olive tied with scrolled ribbon, in various greens, blue, brown and black stains, and afterwards French polished. Articles made of holly or sycamore wood already traced for colouring could be bought and the skill of the craft lay mostly in the patient and lengthy process of the French polishing.

Anyone possessing a stock of pressed flowers and leaves from which colours have more or less completely drained away, leaving only parchment shades and soft fawns, browns and greens, might find it extremely rewarding to recreate an urn or vase of dull silver, gold or marbled paper on a background of Japanese bark paper. The result could be unusually decorative, with roses, lilacs, hellebores and indeed any large cream flowers; it would have the added advantage of being more or less fade-proof. You could, in fact, become the innovator of a new craft.

The preparing and mounting of the plants for flower marquetry present no special problems but it is advisable to use flowers with good stamens and buds and it is important to mount them on wood-textured paper for a satisfactory result. In single groups they make effective panels. The picture illustrated (page 127) measures 10 × 14 in. (25 × 35 cm).

Hedgerow lace

The English countryside in high summer is still bordered with lace. Each narrow lane and many of its busy high roads have tiny frills of stitchwort and chickweed, goosegrass and woodruff, buried up to their petals in

grasses, or in unhappier surroundings defiantly powdered with dust. But the real glory of the roadsides lies with the *Umbelliferae*, knee high, waist high and sometimes more than man high; so many species that only botanists can tell them apart. To us it makes little difference; we refer to them alike as Queen Anne's lace. Of this we may be sure, however, that we need them all if we are going to make lace pictures. Only the giant hogweed needs handling with care, as it has an evil reputation with those who have sensitive skins. Most of the species have fernlike leaves, some with the added bonus of a red and purple transformation in late summer, and all press like a dream: leaves, flowers and even young seed-heads while still soft and when the petals have just fallen. We may pick as many as we like, because few are rare; even the despised ground elder comes into its own at last. Neighbours might even thank us for removing it from their gardens, though it would be wise not to transfer it to our own.

There is a wonderful range of possibilities in the making of lace pictures, for you can work with gold lace, silver lace, black lace or white, according to your need.

For example and for practice, why not make a design for a fan, by using various sizes of these florets? We have above a bridal fan of about 1860 and on page 132 a mourning fan of twenty years later. Taking the white fan first, an experiment was made here to ascertain whether it was possible to mount white flowers on a white background with good effect. For a bridal fan, a white ground seemed essential. The answer is that there are no such things as white pressed flowers but a white background makes a very good foil for the dull green, fawn, soft pink and cream that lace flowers acquire in their pressed state. Large white flowers would certainly look shabby if mounted on white but with lace flowers it can be an advantage. The background used here is from a roll of Chinese paper, obtainable from an address given at the end of the book and useful for

*Wedding Fan, c.*1860. In these days it is difficult to imagine what part was alloted to the wedding fan in the bridal ceremony. Fashion plates of the period show the bride holding flowers and/or a prayer book bound in white velvet, which she handed to the chief bridesmaid immediately before the ceremony. The addition of a fan, however charming, to these proceedings must surely have created problems, and indeed afterwards, at the reception, with handshakes and tearful embraces, followed by champagne and wedding cake, not once can the flutter of a fan have been called for. That bridal fans existed, we have proof, and it would seem therefore that their use was confined to the grand ball that followed.

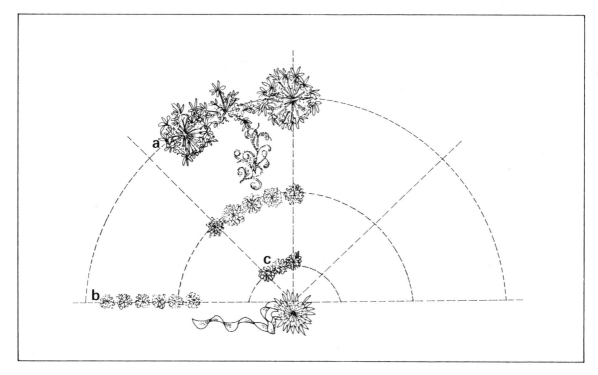

Fig. 16: *Method of assembling Wedding fan.* Mark the centre of the paper and measure equally either side, making clear the angle of the opening of the fan. Indicate the outer or guard sticks, and the inner sticks, which must each be the same length from the central point. For a fully opened fan the middle stick should be placed in the centre, and the others measured at equal distances from this. Next mark the upper and lower semicircles of the fan mount. The complete skeleton of the fan should now be indicated in light pencil. Mark the outside rim of the fan mount (a) with the largest lace flowers, starting top centre, working down to either end. Next cover guard sticks (b) with smaller flowers, and then the other supporting sticks. Outline the inner rim of the fan mount (c) with small flowers. Complete the infilling with small sprays, and finish with a bow of cut hydrangea petals, alternately light and dark.

other types of picture. It has a soft, slightly woolly surface, very sympathetic to tiny flower-heads, although a white silk might be even better.

Make careful measurements to place the fan centrally on the paper and make tiny pencil marks to indicate the distance between the outer rim of the fan and the central point of the handle. The lower semicircle of the fan mount must be measured and lightly marked, and a few guidelines indicated for the spacing of the sticks (fig. 16).

Start by using the largest florets for the lacy edge of the fan, each one connecting with its neighbour. Having done this, stick them down and then arrange the corresponding smaller flowers to outline the lower circle of the fan mount.

Next form the sticks as regularly as possible with yet smaller flowers and stick them down carefully, working from left to right. The infilling should be done now, with hydroids or fern leaves, and tiny heads or sprays of flowers between. The handle is now added; in this case, a single astrantia flower.

The ribbon bow is made of a few hydrangea petals cut in halves, using alternate sides to give an effect of light and shade to the ribbon. Framed in narrow gold, or gold and white, the bridal fan will look like a family heirloom.

For the mourning fan, the plant material chosen has first to be sprayed with black matt surface paint. The paint will dry almost immediately, and the plants should be pressed again for a few hours.

As a sign of half mourning a touch of purple, mauve or grey used to be introduced into the costume, as if human loss could thus be neatly regulated. The fan on page 132 is therefore a sign of half mourning; any small mauve flowers such as candytuft and *Spirea × bumalda* 'Anthony Waterer', which from pink dries to a suitable purple, may be introduced into the design.

Black fans of this period were usually mounted on tortoiseshell but here we make do with black-sprayed hydroids. The braid floating from the handle is made from the tassels of Japanese knotweed but in lace pictures there is great scope for inventiveness. Today a fan seems a symbol of light-hearted extravagance and flirtation and this mourning fan may be regarded as a peculiarly heartless frivolity to hide the tears of a young widow but we must remember that half-mourning was only allowed after twenty-one months of full black paramatta (a mixture of merino wool and silk) and crêpe, followed by three months of 'slighting' by way of a little jet jewellery and silk fringe, until the goal was reached when, for the next three months the widow might, by gradual degrees, break out into purple, violet, mauve, lavender and grey. No wonder she coveted a little black lace fan trimmed with mauve flowers to end her regulated gloom.

Once the spraying has been done, the mourning fan can be pictured fully expanded or half open, by the same method as the bridal fan. The measurements are all-important but, having marked these accurately, the rest is not difficult. Try a soft blue, pink or apricot-coloured background. If you have a fan, it helps to use it as a model and arrange it in different positions to see what best suits the plant material you have at your disposal.

Gold and silver lace is perhaps most suitable for borders, and for imitation jewellery (see *Tribute to Arcimboldo*, page 140). Before embarking on a lace picture of any kind, it is useful to build up a stock of lacy leaves and flowers and to have a session with your sprays – gold, silver, black or whatever you may need. Take as many sheets of white or coloured paper as you can spare (cheap papers will do for this purpose), fixing them one at a time on to a drawing board or sheet of cardboard or a piece of hardboard, using a double-sided adhesive tape to avoid pinholes at the corners, as these sprayed papers may be useful as backgrounds later.

Next impale a few leaves and flowers in random positions on the paper, by means of a single pin in the centre of each. Leave plenty of space between each specimen and thus you will not only get your material sprayed but, when carefully removed, both leaves and flowers will have imprinted a fascinating silhouette for future designs (page 133).

The spraying should be done in the garden on a still day or in a garage or an odd jobs room and it is advisable to wear an overall and rubber gloves. The spray should be vigorously shaken before use and then lightly wafted over the leaf or flower at a distance of about 12 in. (30 cm). Too vigorous spraying may dislodge the specimen and it will result in clogged flowers and runnels of paint on the paper. A lightly sprayed flower, even if it is underdone, is far more attractive than a heavy looking one and the background should still show plenty of its original colour. The result is at first attempt unpredictable but all the more exciting for that and you will

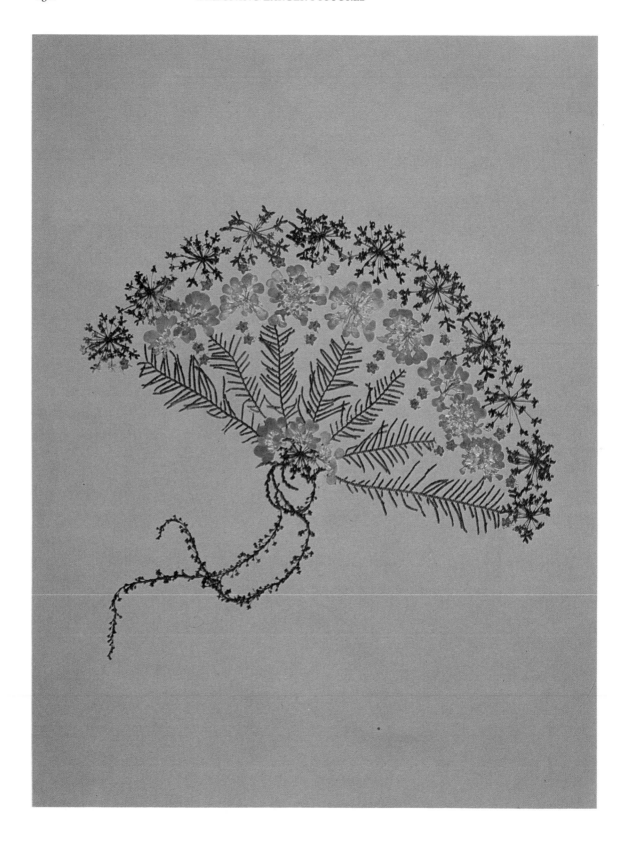

Above: *Sprayed Leaf Pattern*. Three white silhouettes from which the leaves have been lifted. On the outside are the actual leaves, sprayed black. They are mounted on an off-cut of a silver-sprayed card.

*Mourning fan, c.*1880. The introduction of mauve into the fan is an indication of the slow lifting of the clouds of grief – the widow has achieved half-mourning. Tailoring our emotions to fit a social calendar seems an incongruous custom today, but perhaps slow introductions of colour might have brought a little warmth back into a frozen heart.

Fig. 17: *Sprayed silhouettes*. Some pins, three leaves and a paint spray can produce many different designs for use on calendars, note-book covers and greetings cards. The impaled leaves, leaving a silhouette when lifted, can be re-arranged and stuck back on to the same design in different places, doubling the number of leaves.

find that a little practice will provide you with a lot of valuable backgrounds as well as plant material. Unsuccessfully sprayed paper can be left to dry for a few minutes and then reversed and sprayed on the other side.

The result of this double purpose spraying may be seen opposite, *The Night Has a Thousand Eyes*. This fantasy picture is the product of the method described and was prompted by the memory of an old song:

> The night has a thousand eyes,
> The day but one.
> But the light of the whole world dies
> With the setting sun.

It is a poetic thought, if not a very scientific one.

A few heads of Queen Anne's lace, several extra florets and one or two star-shaped calices of borage were pinned to a background of dark blue paper measuring 12 × 15 in. (30 × 38 cm). After a light spray of silver and a few minutes drying, these were removed. A number of dark blue cineraria blooms taken from an indoor pot-plant and previously pressed whole were fastened by their centres only to the centres of the silhouetted Queen Anne's lace and one and a half heads of African daisy, once white, now dried to cream and grey, were added in the same way. To complement the silhouettes of the borage stars, a silver-sprayed star is seen in the left lower corner and, to finish, a few scattered silver lace florets light the sky as well as the centres of the cinerarias. The dark blue of the flowers has not yet been tested and it is not expected to be lasting in this experimental picture; so the long term result is not known.

A picture such as this could not possibly be copied even if one wanted to. Its making is described in the hope that it will start you experimenting on your own account. This can be said for all the other pressed flower pictures in the book. They are there to spark off ideas which will give pleasure in the working out and not to be painstakingly copied.

The Night has a Thousand Eyes. A free illustration rather than a design. A line from a song or poem that stays in the memory could involve the use of pressed flowers suitable for a music cover or a record sleeve.

Mirror painting in the Italian style

A small paper booklet published in 1886, and written by Mrs H. M. E. Sharp-Ayres, who might have been a singing teacher if she had not taken up mirror painting, tells us that, 'The revival of Mirror Painting in the Italian style will doubtless stimulate many lady amateurs to master the few mysterious manipulations involved in the process'.

This it undoubtedly did, for, having filled all the available mantelpieces, glass-fronted cabinets, walls and whatnots with her works of art, there was nothing left for the Victorian and later the Edwardian lady to paint on. Ignoring the fact that mirrors have innate qualities and practical uses of their own, the fair sex must have straightened their bonnets and anxiously viewed their reflections in a setting of cranes, storks and bulrushes which, Italian or not, could have done little to assist them in the important matter in hand.

However, having convinced us of the desirability of this form of art, Mrs Sharp-Ayres gives able instruction in more than a few mysterious

A Mirror Painting, 1886. A prime example of gilding the lily, mirror painting was mercifully of short duration. While it lasted however, almost every known flower was portrayed, as well as long-legged bird life such as cranes, herons, flamingoes and swans, and a superabundance of bulrushes. Students were advised 'never to paint anything on glass which is ungraceful or verging on vulgarity'. Now rare, it may sometimes be found in attics and outhouses.

manipulations with rose madder, permanent blue and pale chrome and the new medium known as Sosicrystallograph, recently put on the market for the sole purpose of painting on mirrors. We are carefully taught how to deal with a number of favourite flowers, grasses and rushes, butterflies and even gadflies, although figure painting, saved up for a final treat, is to be approached with caution. No family portraits should be attempted, we gather, although cupids and fairies are permissible. No further mention is made of the Italian scene and we are left wondering if mirror painting is a revival of an old Roman custom or the art of modern Milan.

Since fairies and cupids are beyond our scope and bulrushes are not good pressers, we can try a simplified version of a lily pond, in the style that can be regarded as a *Mirror Painting*, c. 1880–1910 (opposite). This is done on the pale golden bark paper, although it might be thought nearer to reality on dull silver, such as Pantone by Letraset can provide. It measures 10 × 15 in. (25 × 38 cm).

The tall, almost black rushes that frame the pond were, a few months earlier, bright green iris leaves. The water-lilies were not so long since celandines and they rest on the leaves of snow-on-the-mountain (*Lepadina marginata*), although their own leaves would provide a fair substitute. The dragonfly, or if you prefer it, the gadfly, has wings of wild mallow flowers (*Malva sylvestris*), readily available on waste ground. The more distant insects are made of the trifoliate calyx of a rockrose, with one leaflet removed. Pond ripples are suggested by the reversed white petals of the African daisy (*dimorphotheca*), and the mossy verge, bright green when discovered, has settled down to quite a pleasant shade. Tucked into the moss on the left side is a totally unjustifiable tomato flower.

Art nouveau

After the solid imitations of Classical Baroque, Rococo and Gothic, well-made products of a flourishing industrialization, came the brilliant, exotic and entirely unexpected flowering of Art Nouveau. The rich blues and crimsons of Classical art had been vulgarized, to suit the taste of the newly affluent middle classes, into strident pinks, sharp yellows and greens of the Berlin wool era of the Victorian parlour. It was from this unpromising background that there arose, by way of William Morris and the Pre-Raphaelites, the New Art.

It was indeed an art that was entirely new, a sudden stirring of the creative spirit, an excitement and a dream. It was an art of flowing line and sinuous curve, of other-worldly women and other-worldly plant-forms, that followed the lines of hand-mirrors, lamps and pendants with ripples like those left on sand by an ebbing tide. For twenty years, architecture, furniture, ceramics and jewellery, even book-bindings and posters, were completely taken over by the new vision. It must have been a good time to be alive and young with a pencil or a brush at hand.

The corset and the bustle were abandoned for a soft line and Liberty print. Wax fruit under glass domes gave place to a single peacock feather in a tall vase. The strident pinks softened into old rose, sharp yellow to ochre and russet, and acid green became sage green. In the mysterious

Moonrose. Honesty seeds come into their own in Art Nouveau designs. In book-binding, vases, frames, wrought-iron and jewellery, these seed-cases, in their silver, green or brown stages, are already formalized by nature, seeming to dictate to, rather than obey, the designer.

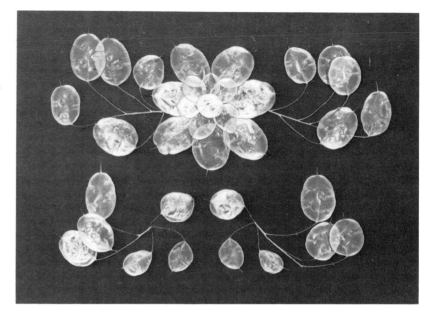

manner of fashion, buxom figures dissolved into the tall and willowy. Even complexions faded and short curls lengthened into heavy auburn tresses.

The flowering of Art Nouveau was of short duration, from about 1890 to 1910, but it was a period of the greatest importance to artists and craftsmen, bringing to fame the names of Beardsley, Crane, Tiffany, Lalique, Mucha and Munch, names that after a temporary eclipse between the two world wars have once again caught the imagination of a new generation.

By the turn of the century, the houses of the well-to-do resembled petrified forests of wrought iron and beaten copper, pewter plaques and pedestals. Clocks, mirrors, frames and vases became vehicles of the new art. Above all, so did jewellery. Brooches, pendants, bracelets and combs took the sinuous forms of snakes, and the glitter of insects, or became women with butterfly wings and flowers with women's faces.

The range of plant forms used was limited: acanthus, ivy, willow and the blooms of water lily, iris, poppy, pansy and sunflower, elongated in line and gentle in colour.

Inevitably, the new art, when not so new, lost its freshness and there were signs of anaemia in the over-crowded drawing-rooms. As usual, mass-production brought a memorable era to an untimely end but, between 1914 and 1918 and maybe for a generation to come, many a stiffly uniformed bridegroom and serious high-collared bride gazed into a bleak world from a silver photograph frame decorated with lotus flowers and other emblems of a fertility never more vital of achievement than at that time.

Today, this brilliant, short-lived period is undergoing a revival of interest. The art of pressed flower pictures, though not one of the manifestations of Art Nouveau, is nevertheless a suitable medium for reproducing its designs. The seed-pods of honesty (*Lunaria annua*), the moon plant, are ideal for this purpose, for, although no pattern of plants can ever be repeated, its shapes are regular enough to balance right and left of a central motif, as in the *Moonrose* pattern, silver on dark blue, pictured opposite.

Honesty seed-pods show an interesting variety of shape, from long and slender to full and almost circular, and each disc appears to have been fastened securely into its frame with large stitches, three or four on either side. This rigid outline, which could have been made with a sharply-pointed HB pencil, makes it a satisfying subject for decoration, especially on a dark background, and the silver discs dictate their own design. The adhesive must not be allowed to disfigure the pearl but should be run along the underside of each curved stem, with a small spot at either end of the disc. Immediate pressing is necessary, under a sheet of glass or a heavy book, for the dried plants are resilient, and will spring from the paper without firm control. The picture measures $8\frac{3}{4} \times 15\frac{1}{2}$ in. (22×39 cm).

Tribute to Arcimboldo, 1527–93

Pressed flower artists may perhaps shrink from this illustration but they can rest assured that this floral caricature has a respectable forerunner in the work of Guiseppi Arcimboldo, who was born in Milan in the sixteenth century.

Arcimboldo was made official portrait painter to Maximilian II, King of Bohemia, a position he also held with Rudolph II, Maximilian's successor. However, it is Arcimboldo's fantastic heads, compounded of flowers, fruit and vegetables, which are remembered today. The accuracy with which he reproduced his jigsaws of natural materials appealed to the wealthy collectors of his time; indeed, he is now regarded as one of the first surrealists and, as such, he has a following today.

The art of these vegetable-human forms was practised even earlier in the East and it was probably from Hindu painters that the fashion derived. Arcimboldo produced several series of the Four Seasons and he also personified the Elements: Fire composed of torch, lamp, flint, guns and tinder, with a bonfire on his head; Water, a figure of shells and fishes. His young male head of Spring is made completely of flowers; features and clothing are formed of peonies, roses, daisies and columbines, with an iris at his breast and on his cap a jaunty white lily. The shoulder knot on the leafy jacket is a cabbage, or it may be a lettuce. Summer is composed entirely of fruit and vegetables; Autumn of fruit and vine leaves; Winter of leafless wood, with ivy in his brittle, twiggy hair, and his lips two pallid tree-fungi, with a sparse, twiggy beard. As a jovial twist to this grim portrait, Arcimboldo adds a straw cloak, decorated with an orange and a lemon, living and juicy, to remind us of winter's harvest.

Whether the Emperor Rudolph or Arcimboldo was the stranger character, it is now too late to discover but, at the Emperor's request, the artist painted him in the character of Vertumnus, the Roman god of orchards and gardens. Rudolph, as Vertumnus, was painted with a pear

Opposite: *A tribute to Arcimboldo*, 1527–93. Mad or sane, Guiseppi Arcimboldo was a brilliant artist, and his composite portraits of the Seasons, the Elements and such promising subjects as Agriculture and Hunting have never been more appreciated than they are today. Arcimboldo's heads representing Cooking, by means of pots, pans and colanders, and Learning, composed of books and book-marks, give little lead to pressed flower artists, but his heads of the Seasons, especially Spring, are entirely suitable.

Comedy and Tragedy. The classical theatrical masks of Comedy and Tragedy may be seen in some form or other in nearly every theatre. Comedy comes from the Greek *Komē-ōdē*, meaning a village song, and refers to village merry-making and the comic songs that were part of the festivities. An ode was sung on these occasions, which became the foundation of Greek comedy. Tragedy derives from *Tragos-odē*, the goat song, the song that wins the goat as a prize, although even *The Oxford English Dictionary* admits the connection is obscure. The making of this theatrical mask is a useful exercise in the accurate placing of delicate petals.

for a nose, cherries for eyes, a water-melon for his bulging forehead, and a beard of prickly chestnuts, dressed in a robe of flowers and vegetables.

This pressed flower version of an unusual artist's work may appeal as an interesting challenge, giving scope for colour, design, imagination and a rare chance of caricature in a craft in which opportunities for wit are not too frequent.

It is often desirable to soften or change a little the colour of your mounting paper, by the application of powder colour or, in this case, chimney soot. A pastel crayon, ground to powder with a penknife or a fine kitchen grater and rubbed in with a wad of cotton wool, can produce all sorts of interesting effects of light and shade, or of age, which may be seen in the *Morris Tile* (page 117), *Pricksong-wort* (page 146), the *Chinese Willow* picture (page 151) and the *Balloon Race* (page 157). It is worth while experimenting with backgrounds for your work. For Arcimboldo, the only available paper was of too harsh a green and it has been improved with the 'antiquing' of a little soot.

The size of the head depends entirely on the petals available for the features, which must be concentrated on first, for the hat is merely a matter of massed small flowers and the jewellery is composed of flower-heads sprayed with gold. Smooth, flesh-coloured petals must be found for nose, chin and cheeks. Plan a left-facing profile, so that the hand can work away from that most important feature, the nose. Eye, eyebrow, nostril, lips and ear can be added later, when the shape of the head has been worked out in petals.

The head is composed of hollyhock petals of various shades, slightly overlapping. The thickened growing-point of each petal should have already been cut off before sticking down by the cut end only, leaving the rest of the petal free for adjustment. The overlapping should be minimal and yet no gaps must be allowed. Arrange the petals from left to right; nose first, followed by chin, forehead and then the cheek of a deeper rose colour, fading back to the hairline. Do not fasten any petal finally until you are certain that you have the effect that you are aiming at. The ear is indicated by an ear-ring formed of a conveniently curved hebe flower but a hanging fuchsia or a columbine would be as effective.

Having arranged the outline of the head to your satisfaction, it is important to stick the petals down before the features are added. It will be noticed that most of the petals are put on sideways, with the rounded outline to the left and the point to the right, until the hair-line is reached, when the petals are then reversed to make the rounded contour of the back of the head. If gaps do appear, they can be filled in with a petal or half a petal, taking care to avoid too much thickness.

Next, position the eye, eyebrow, nostril and lips, which may be chosen from any suitable flowers available. The space between the open lips can be gently cut away with curved scissors, after the lips are finally fastened into place. It is desirable now to cover the face with a small sheet of glass before starting the flowered hat, so that the delicate flowers are protected while you work above or below and yet the whole design can still be seen. The border is made of leaves, ferns, seaweeds or hydroids, sprayed with gold. The picture measures 14 × 19 in. (35 × 48 cm).

The Victorians had a liking for all sorts of pictorial jokes, such as rebus letters, where each word is a picture of objects whose name sounds like the word, with letters added or crossed out. They also indulged in reversible faces, like the well-known *Courtship and Marriage*, where the heads of a man and a woman, facing each other and smiling, stand for *Courtship* but, when reversed for *Marriage*, their expressions are quite ferocious. The joke would have been better had both been rather more attractive during the courtship stage.

Comedy and tragedy

In 1946, a book called *OHO!*, by the brothers Rex and Laurence Whistler, was published after the death of Rex in the Second World War. There are fifteen of these ingenious reversible faces, offering a challenge hard to resist.

The reversible *Comedy and Tragedy* mask is made by a method similar to that of *Tribute to Arcimboldo*. The double head is first built up with fifteen hollyhock petals, with the thick points already removed, fixed by that end only, the rest of the petals lying free. Shaded pink petals make up the smiling rosy mask of *Comedy*, and greenish-white the tortured face of *Tragedy*.

It is necessary that the double head is fastened down before the features are worked out, because of the extreme slipperiness of the petals. There is only one pair of eyes to serve for the two opposing characters, so, whatever material is chosen, the eyes must be large and situated half-way between the two heads. Various combinations of seeds and petals were tried before two centres of passion flowers were chosen largely because the thick black fringe suggests the heavily mascara-enhanced eyes of the actor.

The noses should be placed next, since the all-important expression of the mouths depends on this. Each nose is made from a single petal of a Japanese windflower (*Anemone japonica*). The smiling up-turned mouth of *Comedy* and the drooping lips of *Tragedy* should be made of the same material, to stress the contrasting expressions, but a greenish tinge in the bracts of leycesteria used for *Tragedy* emphasizes the greenish-white of the face. *Comedy*'s fern-leaf eyebrows form deep cuts under the eyes of *Tragedy*. *Tragedy*'s eyebrows, however, are made of unopened honeysuckle flowers, so that they follow the curves of *Comedy*'s chubby cheeks.

Only the nostrils remain to finish this pressed flower theatrical mask. It would make a suitable gift to celebrate a first night, or for a budding RADA student. It measures $8\frac{1}{4} \times 9$ in. (21 × 23 cm).

Illuminated mediaeval manuscripts

Illuminated manuscripts of the Middle Ages may be a source of inspiration to the pressed flower artist, for, although rare and beautiful breviaries, missals and psalters may be difficult of access, good

Design Derived From an Illuminated Manuscript. The tiny flower and leaves used here are in proportion to a page of a small book; the arrangement and colours have a more sharply enamelled quality than the soft masses of *The Virgin's Bower* of a later date.

reproductions in the form of postcards and Christmas cards are well printed and within reach of everyone.

Breviaries or Books of Hours, missals containing the Mass for the complete year and psalters containing the psalms were painstakingly lettered and faithfully painted and were usually the work of monks. They were men with a considerable knowledge of herbs and medicine; the flowers decorating the initial letters and margins were for the most part as accurate as the works of any of the later botanical illustrators. They worked on a fine vellum, very thin and yet strong enough to stand the test of time and the handling of many devout readers.

Pure colours had to be discovered and then ground and mixed; gold leaf had to be prepared and laid down with accuracy and skill. The work took long hours, sometimes months or even years of patient labour and a special part of the abbey called the *scriptorium* was laid aside for it, 'for the greater glory of God'. Sheets of religious music were often decorated too.

By the thirteenth century, the patronage had changed and books were commissioned by noblemen for their own private use. Guilds of illuminators were founded, with organized workshops and rates of payment. Decorations depicting agricultural life, scenes of battle, customs, sports and costumes of the people have become the sources of our knowledge of mediaeval life.

Brightly painted on backgrounds of rich blue or gold, the illuminations became less a work of devotion than a celebration of worldly pomp and circumstance, although never without a foreground of faith: man, with his widening horizons, seen through the wrong end of a telescope. Kings and queens and noble dukes commissioned such works to celebrate coronations or weddings; so greatly were they valued that many have been preserved and still keep their gem-like quality.

A Book of Hours was at this time a small, richly-bound prayer book adorned with miniatures, borders and decorative initials, used for private or family devotions. It contained prayers related to the liturgical hours of each day, hence its name. By the fifteenth century, secular workshops made Books of Hours available to a wider public but the invention of printing, bringing books of many kinds to many people, caused the art of illumination to come to an abrupt end.

The *Italian Madonna and Child*, known as the *Madonna della Quaglio*, is a reproduction of a painting by Pisanello, cut from a Christmas card, but the sparse arrangement of tiny flowers and leaves is reminiscent of a French illuminated manuscript of the fourteenth or fifteenth century. A purist would object to the introduction of the coral bells (*Heuchera sanguinea*), a native of the American continent, but the black, blue and gold of the picture seems to demand some touches of warm red and no other red flowers of a suitable size were available. Pressed flower artists, like flower painters, may have to choose between colour arrangement and botanical history, or even the patterns of the seasons, and the Dutch flower painters left us an example with their superb combinations of tulips, hyacinths, peonies and roses, to show where they set their values. Only those who prefer to study the picture on a seed-packet rather than a flower-piece by Rachel Ruysch can have any serious doubts.

The positioning of your card upon the mounting paper is of first importance, since the flowers used and the final balance depend upon it. Note that some small leaves and flowers have been allowed to stray on to the bottom left corner of the picture. The mounting paper, $7\frac{1}{2} \times 13$ in. (19×33 cm), is Pantone, a paper by Letraset, obtainable at commercial art shops. It is duller, richer and more antique looking than picture framer's gold board or gold wrapping paper, either of which could be used. Two hawthorn blossoms and a scarlet pimpernel have found a place on the card itself.

Pricksong-wort: a mediaeval music picture

Pricksong was ancient when Shakespeare wrote *Romeo and Juliet*. He knew it as a descant or accompanying melody to a plainsong, a simple theme, and he makes Mercutio, describing Tybalt's prowess as a duellist, say to Benvolio: 'He fights as you sing prick-song, keeps time, distance, and proportion; rests me his minim rest, one, two, and the third in your bosom.'

Musical notes were called pricks. It seems likely that the labour of writing music by hand and the making of as many copies as were required caused singers and players to prick the notes through on to prepared sheets underneath, so that several copies could be made at one time.

The plant that we now call honesty was known to Chaucer, Spenser and Drayton as Lunaria or Lunarie and, because of its moon-like seed-vessels, it was believed to possess supernatural powers. Seeing these seed-vessels in their undeveloped green state, musicians must have recognized their likeness to the notes of music and so Lunaria acquired the popular name of pricksong-wort, a name that was lost after the invention of printing.

As a decoration for a music-room, or a gift to a musician, a reproduction of an old sheet of pricksong, with young honesty seed-vessels in their undeveloped green state used as notes, causes considerable interest. A sheet of cream paper, suitably aged with a mixture of brown and black powdered pastel crayon or soot rubbed in around the edges and corners is simple to prepare; an illustration of some mediaeval figures or an ancient initial letter or a group of carollers cut from a Christmas card and mounted on gold paper makes the necessary decorative motif. The musical stave is best ruled in red.

If lettering presents any difficulty it can be traced. Opposite, some other ancient names of the plant, Lunaria, Judas-pence and the old French, *Monnaie du Pape*, have been used, although a line or two of some old carol, in smaller letters, would be equally appropriate. Letters can be black, red or gold, or a variety of all these. The 'notes' have been arranged at random, with the old clef made of an upright seed-vessel with a circle cut from it. An appropriate air might be achieved by the more knowledgeable.

Seed-pods picked at this early stage of their development may in time darken and go brown but this may be no disadvantage. The sheet should be no less than 14 × 19 in. (35 × 48 cm).

The thousand flowers

Strip cartoons in wool, heightened with gold and silver thread, bible stories, battle scenes, mysterious unicorns and unconsummated love, these tales are not to be abruptly ended by the turn of a switch, the push of a button. Tapestries were first made as a work of devotion and woven in the monasteries. The oldest known, fragments of which still survive, dates from the eleventh century. Early tapestries were woven only in wool and flax but later they were enriched by threads of silk, silver and gold.

By the fourteenth century, the technique had spread through Europe and local characteristics were beginning to strengthen. The age of travel, with all that it meant in the dissemination of crafts and skills, had commenced. The wealthy and adventurous were on the move and the result was, as far as the craft of tapestry was concerned, that what had started as an expression of faith developed into a flourishing secular industry. Tapestries grew smaller as well as larger and practical uses were discovered to enhance their decorative value.

Reliable dyes were few and weavers depended on those they knew they could trust. Their problem, in fact, was much the same as for pressed flower artists today, to find natural plant colours that were proof against fading. Woad was used for blue dyes, madder for red; kermes, a species of insect, gave red or purple dye and weld gave yellow. Oxide of iron and gall-nut supplied the blacks and greys. The judicious mixing of these dyes extended their range to about twenty colours, which were rarely exceeded at that time. Highlights were obtained when silk was introduced; this enlarged the palette, since it took the dyes differently and gave further tones to the design.

It was found that tapestries were not only useful for wall pictures and screens but that they helped to keep out the draughts and temper the chill of stone. They began to be used as canopies and bed-hangings or were draped over chairs and benches. Above all, they were appreciated as signs of social importance. In churches, they were not only dedicated to the glory of God but to the glory of the worshippers of God. Heraldic designs were blazoned in wool and silk. The end of the fifteenth century saw the peak of the activities of the tapestry weavers.

With the age of chivalry, chivalrous deeds were told in song, story and picture. Literary sources of some of the tapestries can be determined by the inscriptions which accompany each one. The famous *Floral Tapestry*, the *Millefiori* or *Thousand Flowers*, which bore the arms of Philip the Good, was woven in 1466. When his son, Charles the Bold, set off on a campaign against Louis XI of France, he took his tapestries with him, an ill-advised custom of the time. Charles fell in battle, and the *Thousand Flowers* was captured by his conquerors. It is now in the Historisches Museum, Berne.

The famous *Dame à la Licorne*, the mysterious *Lady With the Unicorn*, comes from a series woven in wool and silk, illustrating the five senses. A sixth tapestry, '*a mon seul desir*', is probably a dedication of the whole set by Le Viste, whose coat of arms the tapestries bear, to his fiancée. They were acquired by the Cluny Museum in 1882, from the Castle of Boussac in the Auvergne. There are many good reproductions of these mysterious tapestries and they have never been more popular than they are today. A set of postcards is available, from which charming pressed flower pictures can be devised from small details.

Tapestries were often woven in sets of six and matching bed-hangings were made. Much of the best work was done in Arras, so that Arras became a synonym for wall tapestries in general. These tapestries were hung free of the wall, and could be used as amusing or sinister hiding places. Such a tapestry was a fatal hiding place, as we know, for Polonius, killed by Hamlet with a rapier thrust through the arras, by this time demoted to a common noun with a small 'a': 'How now! a rat? Dead, for a ducat, dead!' We still sit on the edge of our seats, clutching our programmes, although we know what will happen.

These chamber tapestries, as they were called, often carried a romantic story, such as *The Offering of the Heart*, where we see a gallant presenting his lady with what a first glance appears to be a strawberry. The flowers in this series have a softer appeal, more of fairyland and less of botanical exactitude, but still the rabbits skip between the lovers. Even scenes of battle take place in flowery meads, where every petal remains happily undisturbed between the horses' hooves and a splash of red is only the red of a petal.

The woven bible stories, the fairy tales and the legends remain but the workshops gradually disappeared, until, between the eighteenth and the early nineteenth centuries, the last had gone. Tapestries, because of their cost and size, were essentially for church and aristocracy but today they remain for the people, records of historical importance.

Delightful pressed-flower pictures can be made by carefully examining a small and flowery area of one of these tapestries, reproduced in books or on cards. Tightly packed groups of plants, some botanically accurate,

The Thousand Flowers. Detail derived from *La Dame à la Licorne*, Brussels, c.1480–90. Divorced from the lovely lady with her heraldic lion and fairy unicorn, there is little of mystery left in this detail of a great tapestry. The rabbit, though an endearing creature, as an emblem is of no significance, but its inconsequence remains part of the charm of this remarkable series of wall-hangings.

others wildly imagined, occupy the base of many designs, although in
some the space between the figures is just as tightly packed with a
thousand flowers from top to bottom of the tapestry. In the verdure
gambol small beasts, some identifiable and others of heraldic or legendary
provenance; these can be introduced if petals and leaves and seeds to
make them are available.

The joy of these designs is the complete freedom of choice: nothing is
wrong that is pleasant to the eye. A day that is forever summer may be set
on a black background but what does it matter? The *Lady With the
Unicorn* holds a mirror to show the reflected image of her beautiful white
unicorn against a bright red setting. She is the emblem of sight. She, with
her two companions, the heraldic lion of Le Viste and the mysterious
unicorn, seem to soar in mid-air on a magic carpet, black and enamelled
with flowers and small animals and flanked by two black trees, an oak and
a holly.

The illustration on page 149 is devised from a small rabbit on the right
of the tapestry, surrounded by flowering plants, and bordered on the left
by a few black holly leaves. These have not been treated. The leaves were
pressed while they were young, causing them to blacken within a few
days. The contrasting grey-white holly leaves have been lightly sprayed
with white.

The rabbit's head and body are made of raspberry leaves in reverse, the
ears of a *Stachys lanata* and the paws of *Cineraria maritima*. The eye is
made of a flower bud that had gone brown while pressing. It is a pity that
the lithe alertness of the tapestry rabbit cannot be reproduced in our
medium but the angle of the head to the body and the small top leaflet to
the larger bottom one is important to give him the air of listening, which
the artist some five hundred years ago caught so marvellously.

In the light breeze the willow branches bend

The first Chinese paintings, it is believed, were frescoes. Legend tells that
they dated back to the mythical Yellow Emperor, twenty-seven centuries
before Christ.

A painting on silk of about the third century BC is the earliest example
of its kind known today. Four hundred years later the use of paper was
discovered and a technique was perfected that is still in use. The medium
was ink diluted in water. When the artist had finished his picture, it was
mounted on brocade or paper and kept in a box.

Under the influence of Taoism and Buddhism, Chinese artists learned
a great love of nature. They taught themselves to paint leafless trees and
rocks in an atmosphere of mist and desolation. They studied stormy
landscapes and driving rain and invented a symbolism of colour which
became standard.

The Emperor Hui-tsung (1082–1135) was a painter as well as a
collector of paintings and he became a great master of animal and flower
paintings. He painted the 'four noble plants, bamboo, plum blossom,
orchids and chrysanthemums'.

Wood-block printing was invented in China at least seven hundred

In the Light Breeze the Willow Branches Bend. A suggestion of movement, difficult to achieve in this medium, as well as an interpretation of Chinese art, is the object of this attempt at a bamboo pattern with willow leaves.

years before it appeared in Europe but there are no Chinese prints dating before the ninth century AD still in existence. The use of wood instead of stone gave a tremendous impetus to printing and, as later techniques were perfected, the craft of the engraver developed separately from that of the artist. Techniques reached their peak by the seventeenth century.

In *The Ten Bamboo Studio Album*, published between 1622 and 1633, there is an exquisite study of bamboos blowing in the wind against a wind-blown stream. The plate is printed in two colours, grey and blue. Since the willow is almost as greatly loved by Chinese artists as the bamboo, the illustration shown above is composed of the leaves of the English black willow, as nearly as is possible in the Chinese style.

Chang Ch'ao, a mid seventeenth-century poet, counts the willow among the four things in the universe which touch man's heart most profoundly. Our picture illustrates the lines of another poet, Liang

Ch'ing Piao: 'In the light breeze the willow branches bend.'

Here we do our best in another and less flexible medium to join two cultures and two periods. For this a sheet of light blue paper, measuring $13\frac{1}{2} \times 17\frac{3}{4}$ in. (34×45 cm), is treated with a powder made from ground blue pastel crayon, gently rubbed in with a small pad of cotton wool. Next, the stream is indicated in white Chinese paper, although other thin white papers would do, irregularly cut, lightly pasted at the edges and gently slanted from the top left. A few curving lines in charcoal or black pastel indicate the wind-blown water.

Continuity of line is most important when applying the willow leaves, as the use of branches or even stems is impossible. The endeavour must be to give the suggestion of a weeping willow blown by the wind and here the contrast between both sides of the leaves will give a hint of light and shade. The three insects, which do not appear in the Chinese bamboo print, are made of poppy petals and give a touch of colour to this cool design.

Japanese ink painting

Here is an impression of old Japan, in as near a Japanese style as we can manage with our materials.

The art of monochrome ink painting was brought from China to Japan by the Zen Buddhist monks and, for four centuries, by means of a solid stick of black ink, the Japanese expressed their love of their landscape. They became masters of empty space and atmosphere, mist-shrouded country, bamboo leaves trembling in the wind, gnarled and ancient pines on a grey background. Rivers, waterfalls, rocks and sand were all in black. Even for flowers, the use of colour was not thought necessary, although neither was it considered wrong to add small areas of colour if the artist wished to do so.

This controlled and sensitive landscape and flower painting was the work of intellectuals, the scholar-artists; their painting was usually on silk or on the bark of mulberry trees. The ink painters combined the naturalism of the scientific observer with the abstract virtue of the calligrapher, for calligraphy was often regarded as the most important part of the picture. The painting was directly by brush, for there were no pencils or pens, and the work was done on hand-scrolls or hanging scrolls, which would be unrolled for viewing only a little at a time.

In the ninth century, when the Japanese first dispensed with high tables and chairs and sat on the floor, it was realized that folding screens and sliding doors were necessary to keep out the draughts. A new and valuable surface was available for artists to work on.

In the thirteenth century, the screens were painted with brightly coloured flowers and, later, wealthy merchants began to order screens treated with gold and silver as background to consecutive paintings of bamboos and maples. Flowers painted in this pigment on to gold leaf glowed with an entirely artificial but none the less, atmospheric, sunshine.

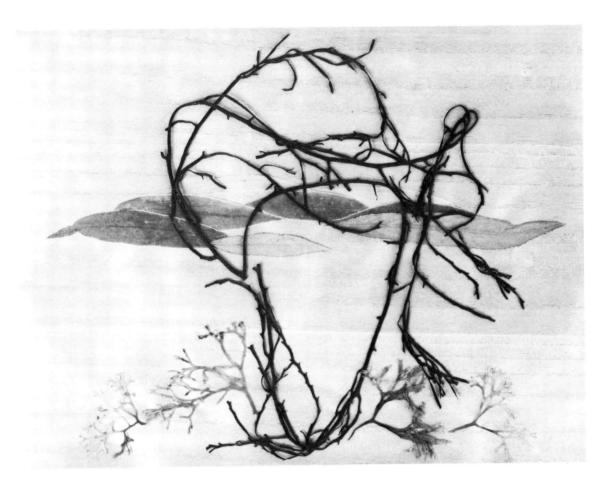

The Chinese and Japanese have always been regarded as the supreme painters of trees, flowers, birds and insects. Japanese flower paintings and wood-block prints might at times be confused with Chinese but never with Dutch, French or English.

Our scene is designed on silver birch bark paper, as suitable a background as may be, although lacking in the wonderful atmosphere of outdoors that marks the Japanese ink painting. The mountains are made of horizontal layers of narrow leaves, some in reverse to provide contrast. These must be laid down first, measured equally each way from a centre point marked on the paper. The view is seen through an arched silhouette of bare trees, in this case one complete branch of seaweed. Dried seaweed is tough but brittle and needs rather more adhesive than other materials.

On either side, some smaller, paler seaweed balances the picture, which is accompanied by a verse attributed to the Emperor Yuryaku (AD 148–179):

Japanese Scene. An endeavour to capture, without figures, the atmosphere of old Japan. A view of mountains through bare trees.

> O the mountains
> Of Hatsuse the hidden land,
> The lovely mountains
> That face me when I leave my house.

Bouquet for a white witch

The story is told (perhaps as an excuse for making a black and white flower picture; that is, of course, if any excuse were needed), that there lived in a certain village uncertainly long ago two black witches and a beautiful white witch.

Now, a white witch is as good as a black witch is evil; a white witch is as beautiful as a black witch is hideous. Both, from the herbs that grow around them, can mix love potions and cures. The white witch's love potions were made with lad's love, vervain and bridewort; the two black witches' with henbane, hellebore and mandrake, mixed with muffled curses. Those who drank the white witch's love potions lived happily ever after. You can guess what happened to those who partook of the black witches' love potions. There are examples of both to be seen to this day.

The jealousy of the two black witches knew no bounds. They plotted to send a splendid bouquet to the white witch. Each cast an evil eye after the bouquet to ensure that it reached her. Instead of henbane, hellebore and mandrake, which she would instantly have recognized, the bouquet was to contain a perfume which would cause the white witch to drop senseless, just as Snow White did after eating the poisoned apple.

All unsuspecting, the beautiful white witch took the flowers in her slender white hands, not seeing the two evil eyes that hovered in the background. . . . But we are wasting time. Let us see how to compose a bouquet suitable for a white witch, a magic bouquet, with or without two evil eyes.

Skeleton flowers, of course, we must have, and strange animal-ferns called hydroids, from the sea. Grasses are the common perks of any witch and the centres of two passion flowers make up the ominous arrangement. A slight spray of gold on the hydroids and silver on the grasses by way of disguise and the introduction of a spot of pink in the little group of stamens may be considered as cheating but it adds a little warmth to the otherwise malevolent chill.

First make sure that you have enough silver-sprayed grasses and gold-sprayed ferny materials available. If you have not, make this the time to start a collection or to replenish stocks of these invaluable items, for they will last indefinitely and add interest to many different types of picture. For spraying, refer to page 131. The skeleton hydrangeas should also have been prepared in advance and a collection made of these and other skeletonized plants for use when required (see page 46).

Having measured and prepared the black background, 16 × 13 in. (40 × 33 cm), mark the outlines of the bouquet with five leaves of *Cineraria maritima*, which will show up well and act as a guide to the rest. The silver-sprayed grasses are added next; these will require only a minute amount of adhesive along the backs of the stems to anchor them.

Next, place the hydrangeas to cover any unsightly stalks of leaves and grasses, sticking each one down with a central spot of adhesive. The infilling of the base depends on the stock you have to draw from. For those who are well supplied with materials, the picture takes very little time to make.

Bouquet for a White Witch. Witches or no, the proof of the magic power of this bouquet is that there is nothing to fade or even to change in this black and white, and silver and gold arrangement. Many different designs and sizes of picture can be made with this or similar material. The evil eyes can be dispensed with and a totally innocent picture will result, which will represent no particular difficulties in execution.

Balloon race – a celebration of 1784

'Do not wonder that we do not entirely attend to things of earth: Fashion has ascended to a higher element. All our views are directed to the air,' wrote Horace Walpole in 1783. 'Balloons occupy senators, philosophers, ladies, everybody.' Balloons also occupied fans and snuff-boxes, plates and dishes, pendants and prints, in materials varying from enamel, porcelain, leather and ivory to paper: a very pretty array of trophies were available to the collector of the day. Prints varied from the romantic to the ridiculous; mementoes ranged from delicate Sèvres tea-cups and saucers, gilt-edged and balloon-decorated, to fairground trifles.

Walpole was not impressed. 'Well! I hope these new mechanic meteors will prove only playthings for the learned and the idle, and not be converted into new engines of destruction to the human race,' he said with disapproval.

Six months later he was to see one for himself. 'I have, at last, seen an air-balloon,' he wrote. 'I was going last night to Lady Onslow at Richmond, and over Mr. Cambridge's field I saw a bundle in the air not bigger than the moon ... It seemed to light on Richmond Hill; but Mrs. Hobart was going by, and her *coiffure* prevented my seeing it alight.' So great a miracle to be obliterated by a lady's *coiffure*!

It was the beauty, as well as the danger, of these serenely floating bubbles that captured everyone's imagination but even the gay colours and fragile-looking baskets depending from them, it seemed, on silken threads, did not mollify the beauty-loving Horace: 'The papers say, that a balloon has been made at Paris representing the castle of Stockholm, in compliment to the King of Sweden; but that they are afraid to let it off; so, I suppose, it will be served up to him in a desert.'

The enthusiasm of the brothers Montgolfier, Joseph and Étienne, which had resulted in the first successful launching of a man into the sky, soon led to similar attempts in England. Several trial balloons had been sent up unmanned, or with animals as passengers, but it was left to a young attaché of the Neapolitan embassy, Vincent Lunardi, to make the first ascent from English soil. He rose from the Artillery Ground at Moorfields, on 15 September, 1784, taking with him a dog, a cat and a pigeon. They descended safely in a meadow near Ware in Hertfordshire, to the approval of the *hoi-polloi* no doubt but not that of Horace Walpole. 'So far from respecting him as a Jason, I was very angry with him: he had full right to venture his own neck, but not to risk the poor cat...'

In this, as in so many matters, Walpole chose to be in the minority. Most people never ceased, and probably never will cease, to marvel at the beauty and gaiety of these silently floating spheres. From London, John Constable wrote on 17 June, 1824, 'We had a full view of the balloon – which looked so near that I could see the divisions of coloured silk. On its rising higher we saw it on a clear blue sky looking like a golden egg – it then went into a thin white cloud – and then emerged from it with great beauty, one side so very bright – and the other so clear and dark.'

Balloon prints are now collectors' items and hard to come by but a pressed flower balloon collage might prove an attractive alternative. The

Balloon Race: A Celebration of 1784. One of the most exciting inventions of the eighteenth century, for scientists, travellers and painters, balloons were originally called Montgolfières after the brothers who first designed them. Today, many people are still fascinated with this other-worldly method of progress; the earth-bound can do nothing but gaze transfixed at these frail-looking spheres floating gracefully above the earth, seeming to miss the trees by a fraction of an inch. A combination of collage with flowers and leaves, this is an unusual subject for the pressed flower artist.

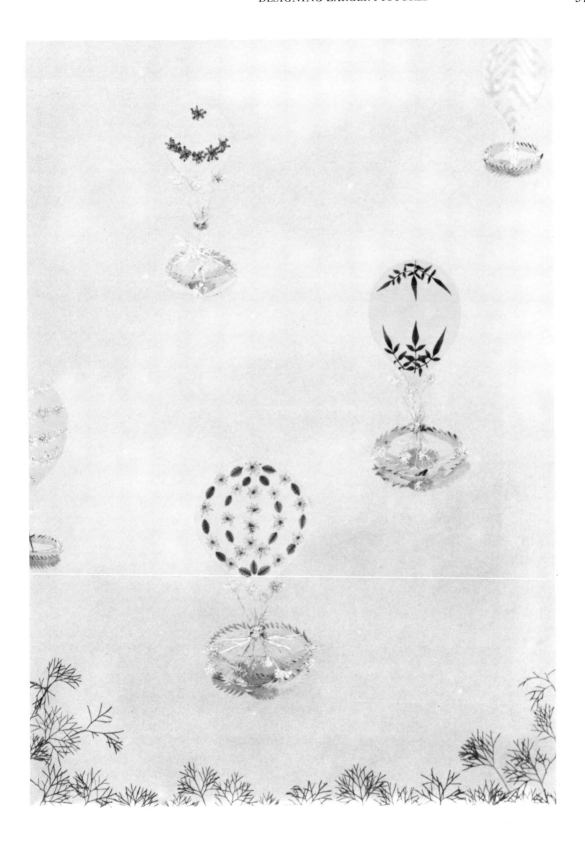

illustration on page 157 is made on a blue-grey paper, $15 \times 21\frac{1}{2}$ in. (38×55 cm), with a few fluffy clouds and some deep blue patches of sky, rubbed in with a cotton wool pad dipped in ground blue and white chalk or pastel colours. The method is the same as that used for the *Chinese Willows*, page 151.

A single balloon, or a group, can be cut out of small pieces of coloured paper and trimmed with bands or sprays of tiny flowers and leaves. It may be found more convenient to decorate the balloons before placing them on the background, so that they can be moved around and the effect considered. The simplest way of cutting out a balloon is to draw one half on a folded paper, so that when unfolded, each side is identical. This can be used as a template, or a tracing can be made. Distant balloons, of course, must be cut smaller.

When arranging groups before sticking, be sure you have left enough space to accommodate the hanging baskets and a little landscape below. A balloon arriving and another floating off the edge of the paper could give life to the scene. Distant balloons should be cut from lighter coloured paper. The baskets are made of the woven leaflets of silverweed or bracken, although bracken, being less pliable to use, would be best in its green state. Woven grasses would also be suitable. The ropes and decorations on the baskets are formed of single florets of Queen Anne's lace; the stems of the umbels are also used, sprayed with silver, although these look quite well in their natural colouring.

Design for a border on a two-coloured background

It can give a great lift to a design if more than one colour is introduced into the background.

The aim of the pressed flower artist should be to make the best possible use of flowers that may fade or have already faded or must be expected to change from the fresh bright beauty that was theirs for so short a time. This means giving them all the assistance within our means: flattery, if you like, but a little flattery hurts no one, not even a flower. If one colour can give them a little boost, why not two colours?

The only answer to this speculation is to try it and see. It is not easy and will require practice, so it would be as well to start with a very simple design. Take a piece of paper measuring say, 9×15 in. (23×38 cm), and a contrasting narrow piece of the same weight and texture, 5×15 in. (13×38 cm). Mount the two pieces side by side on a board or a sheet of good firm paper, so that they meet accurately. You will then have a two-colour background, measuring 14×15 in. (36×38 cm).

With the narrower side on your left, arrange a spray or a sheaf of flowers across the join with, perhaps, large flowers and leaves at the top, tapering down to a small bud at the bottom, or with a small flower at the top, with the design gradually widening towards the bottom. Whatever material you have chosen, you will find that both leaves and flowers will appear different on each of the colours, especially if you are contrasting dark with light.

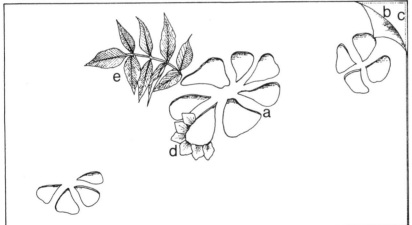

Above: *Design for a Border on a Two-colour Background.* Once freed from the restrictions of single background colour, the possibilities of pressed flower design are endless. Here a sheet of blue paper with three large flowers, outlined and cut as in a stencil, is placed over a peach-coloured sheet of identical size. The resulting pattern is outlined with small pressed petals and linked with leaves, to make a pressed flower brocade.

The border design, above, is the result of a more advanced technique, involving the use of two sheets of contrasting paper, $10\frac{3}{4} \times 20\frac{1}{2}$ in. (27×52 cm), used one on top of the other. A large, bold flower design is needed for this, such as may be found on a chintz or a wallpaper.

Choose a peony or a poppy or some fully-opened flower for the centre of the design, with a smaller flower or opened bud on either side. If you enjoy flower painting, you will also like making this pressed flower pattern, although the technique is different. If you do not paint, a tracing made from wallpaper or flowered material or a book illustration will be all you need to work from.

Left: Fig. 18.
(a) Cut stencil of petals on top sheet.
(b) Place over contrasting undersheet.
(c) Stick two sheets together along edges only.
(d) Outline stencil with cut hydrangea petals.
(e) Apply leaves, columbines and larkspurs to join stencils together.

Place the large flower centrally and draw or trace it on to the top sheet of paper only, with the smaller flowers each side. Now, you will need a sharp scalpel and a board, for the next step is to cut round the outlines of these three flowers. Leave a division between each petal, in the way that a stencil is cut. Keep this as simple as possible. The stencil having been cut, place this top sheet over the plain sheet (you will see the back sheet showing through the holes that have been cut) and stick the two sheets together lightly round the edges.

You will now have three stencilled flowers on a different-coloured background. Put the picture to dry under a heavy book, while you prepare the pressed flowers and leaves that are to compose the rest of the picture and that will form the outline of, and link between, the three cut-out flowers.

Hydrangea petals are used to outline the three stencilled flowers, since their colouring will be a link between the colours of the pattern so far. They are firmly textured and can be cut to fit your requirements. Outline the flowers and the divisions between the petals with cut hydrangeas, colour-graded and directioned according to the natural growth of each petal. Use varying widths, with larger pieces for the centre of the large flower. When you are satisfied with their arrangement, stick them down.

The dark leaves in this design are the young leaves of ash trees, chosen for their firm and beautiful outlines and the rich dark brown or even black that they finally achieve. Arrange them loosely to connect the flowers and to extend the outline of what should be regarded as one unit of a repeatable border pattern.

The stems of these young leaves are already firm and slightly twiggy and should be pared down at the growing end.

The gaps in the pattern have now to be filled in. The result depends on the stocks that are available and your ingenuity in their arrangement. Too many stems showing will look scratchy and thin; too many flowers may become stodgy. The final parts should be done standing up and regarding the whole design from a distance. Leave these decisions for a few hours or even days, before the final sticking down, but they must be covered and slightly weighted during this time. Ash leaves, especially, have an annoying habit of curling if left unattended for long.

Finally, if this seems too complicated a project, do not be put off. Try just one large flower, stencilled and arranged over a contrasting colour. Border it with cut petals; even tiny daisies will do for a start. It will give you a new interest and an extra exciting dimension.

The Autumn of the Green Man

We seldom see the Green Man in his own true colours. We know him to be lurking carved in wood or stone, a chilly and malevolent mask, boding us no good whatever from his leafy heights in roof bosses, capitals and corbels, his cold grey bulging eyes and petrified beard sending a chill to our hearts and an uncomfortable feeling that we are being watched. In the same cathedral or church, he may also be seen peering slyly at us from the lower levels of bench-ends and misericords, carved in wood, blackened with age but still bearded with leaves, or more often with leaves sprouting from his grinning mouth. Only rarely is he pictured in stained glass but there he loses his quality of watching and waiting, his torment and his evil.

Ancient as the Green Man seems to us, he comes from roots more ancient still, for his leafy ancestors appeared on a Roman temple dating from the first half of the third century AD.

The leaves from which he peers at us, at the same time seem to cause his own imprisonment. Although most frequently springing from his open mouth, they are also seen emerging from nostrils, chin or the centre of his forehead; sometimes, most horribly, they emerge from the pupils of his eyes. Often, they sprout all together in the same tortured head, as in a corbel still to be seen at Ottery St Mary, Devon. This terrible leafy martyrdom suggests that the Green Man is being sucked by nature itself back into the ancient stone from which the medieval mason once tried to free him, or into the dark heart of the tree from which he was carved.

By the thirteenth century, the acanthus and oak leaves that earlier had become almost a part of the Green Man himself became a little tamed in some English churches. The savage foliate masks became softened by the naturalistic carving of hawthorn, ivy, hops, bryony and other native plants and flowers; though still bizarre, he took on a more amiable appearance.

No longer did these strange heads give their former hint of imprisonment. Some would seem almost benign, although few could be described as jolly, as the eighteenth-century Jack-in-the-Green was jolly. There seems little but a covering of leaves to connect the chimney sweeps' Jack-o'-the-Green caperings in the old May Day festivals with the Medusa-like baleful glares of the early foliate masks. Neither does there seem any connection with the Green Man as an inn sign, for this Green Man presents a far more welcoming and hospitable figure. He, or rather his painted likeness, is said to refer to the collector of herbs and simples, who used to distil the volatile oils of mint and thyme and other herbs for sale to the apothecaries and would likely have set up his still at any nearby inn.

It is strange that, with all his leafy lineage, no-one seems to have thought of making a Green Man from what should be his natural composition, leaves.

With its lack of depth and therefore of shadow and mystery, a leaf mask takes on a savage and warlike appearance, although, perhaps, in another case, it might be given the more Bacchanalian mask of a publican's sign. What we have learnt, however, is that a Green Man made of leaves instead of stone will age with almost human predictability. Green is a fugitive colour. Dried and pressed green leaves will go on changing as nature meant them to do. Some greens will fade to fawn and yellow; others will darken to red or brown. If air is not completely excluded in the framing, an almost human wrinkle may appear.

This is what is happening to the *Green Man* opposite. Autumn has overtaken him since he was first conceived. Although his fierce expression has not softened, it would seem that, eventually, like Shakespeare's chimney sweepers, he must come to dust. That, we hope, will take a long time. Meanwhile, though we may not keep his memory green, we may keep it nearer to his natural colouring than did the mediaeval stone mason.

The mounting paper, with its grainy appearance, is inexpensive and suitable, although Japanese bark paper may be preferred. The size depends entirely on the material available for eyes, nose and mouth. It will be found more difficult, although perhaps more desirable, to compose a small Green Man than a large one. Our picture measures $16\frac{1}{2} \times 22\frac{3}{4}$ in. (42×58 cm). Having chosen satisfactory features for him, the mouth should be slit with a scalpel and a number of teeth cut from the pointed tips of any suitable white-backed leaves and inserted between the lips from behind, with a spot of adhesive on each and the reverse sides uppermost. Lack of suitable material made it impossible to allow large swathes of leaves to issue from the Green Man's mouth; these sharply-pointed teeth are used as an alternative. A grinning mouth can be made from a curved red leaf but this is more difficult to find.

Acanthus, bocconia and maple leaves make up the greater part of this mask, although choosing these is a simple matter and most gardens will supply whatever is needed. The eyes are made from the centres of passion flowers; the eyebrows and the contour lines of the cheeks are made of willow catkins.

It has to be admitted that our Green Man lacks the depth and brooding mystery of the mediaeval carvings; perhaps he bears more resemblance to an African mask or a Chinese devil. Even so, if one regards him as a Green Man in the autumn of his life, he is a figure to be reckoned with.

It would be just as fascinating to make a head of Bacchus of vine leaves and ivy, the antidote to drunkenness, by the same method. The head should be rounder in shape and the vine leaves from a black grape. These should be pressed in late summer, just as the leaves are turning but before they become dry and brittle, to lend a sufficiently vinous tint to his features. A curved red autumn leaf, with an entire absence of teeth, unlike the Green Man, would give him a jovial appearance. Leaves from a white grape keep their green and would not be suitable.

The Autumn of the Green Man. This fantastic foliate man may be sought and found in many parts of the world, leering, squinting, grinning or balefully glaring at human folly, as well he might, from his lofty eminence in cathedrals and churches. Large leaves pressed into curves and made to seem to spring from the mouth would add to the authenticity of this ancient folk figure.

A fanfare of flowers:
a design for embroidered silk

The origin of silk is wrapped in mystery or maybe in the silken threads produced by that mysterious worm, the caterpillar of a moth known to entomologists as *Bombyx mori*. Unless one traces the miracle to an even remoter source, the mulberry tree, it is this unattractive caterpillar that we must thank for the beauty and the wealth of a considerable part of the world. The continuous filament of fine thread which it spins around its body extends in an endless line from last year's eggs to early spring, when the mulberry trees begin to bud. In a week or so, tiny insects are hatched, which, like the rest of living things, are immediately in need of food.

A simple design of clematis and other leaves. The curved stems and tendrils of jackmanii and montana types are useful in composition with many other flowers, and give a firm and graceful structure on which to build.

Providing the mission is successful, the skin will be changed four times, in the usual manner of, but somewhat speedier than, baby-grow outfits.

Food and not beauty, nor even love, is the sole interest of this creature; when at last it is satisfied, it spins the vital cocoon. It ejects from an opening in its head a viscous solution which solidifies under tension to form a pair of endless filaments, closely bound together by a gummy substance called sericin, which enables the caterpillar to weave its thread into a solid structure, wall upon wall, in a sort of figure of eight. It will never be seen again, for, inside this cocoon, the caterpillar becomes a chrysalis and the chrysalis a moth.

When the moth is ready to emerge, it emits a solution that dissolves the sericin, to make an exit to the world outside. Strangest of this strange story, there will now be two sexes, a male moth and a female, whose short-lived duty is to mate and produce the eggs which must hibernate until the spring, when the continuous performance will begin again.

It is to China, as well as to this unattractive worm, that we owe the marvellous fabrics, silks, satins, taffetas, grosgrains and moirés, the brocades and damasks and velvets and all the other fabulous materials that have come and gone with changing fashion. Not that the Chinese were very forthcoming about their wonderful discovery, for these inscrutable orientals managed to maintain their monopoly for something like three thousand years, in spite of the desperate attempts of other nations to discover the secret. Throughout this time, a highly satisfactory trade, from the Chinese point of view, was carried on with the outside world. Silk fabrics journeyed by caravan across Central Asia to the Pamir Mountains, where Persian merchants bartered them for commodities of the Western world.

Like most of the skills of China, the secret of silk-making was finally learnt by the Japanese, then by the Indians, and, finally, secreted in a hollow cane (that legendary story, shared by the smuggling of saffron to Saffron Walden), silkworms' eggs reached the Emperor Justinian in Constantinople.

The rest of the world was no better off, for Justinian forthwith proclaimed silk an imperial monopoly and proceeded to raise prices even higher than had the Chinese merchants. But sericulture spread by way of the Arabs to Spain, to Sicily and so to Italy; it was the Renaissance that stimulated the culture and the use of silk throughout Europe.

By the second half of the fourteenth century, Italy had developed her own methods of silk weaving. Early motifs included birds and animals, followed in the fifteenth and early sixteenth centuries by a variety of plant designs. The Italians created every kind of damask, tissue and brocade, often combined with gold and silver. The pictures of Renaissance painters show figures dressed in gorgeous fabrics. This was the gateway through which silk weaving entered Europe. In England, James I issued a circular to all counties advising the planting of mulberry trees but met with no more success than with his exhortations against 'that pernicious and offensive weed, tobacco'. He was even less successful on both counts with his colonists in Virginia.

A Fanfare of Flowers (page 166) represents an eighteenth-century silk

A Fanfare of Flowers. There
is a close relationship
between the texture of silk
and the texture of petals,
which makes the design for
silk embroidery a natural
development. Not only the
colour-range but the subtle
differences between dull silk
and the sheen of satin should
be considered.

embroidery. It was designed for the coming-of-age of a grand-daughter, a Fanfare of Flowers for a girl reaching maturity today but also a tribute to a woman who designed in silk and wool, in cotton, shells and paper two hundred years ago. That lady embroidered and painted flowers and cut their likenesses in paper with botanical truth, calling them her paper mosaics. There is no record that she worked with pressed flowers but this picture is designed as nearly as possible to represent her work with silk embroidered flowers. Her name was Mary Delany.

A Fanfare of Flowers is the largest picture reproduced in this book. It measures 20 × 26 in. (50 × 65 cm), and it would be unwise to try anything larger. There is a greater risk of petals wrinkling and background paper warping in a work of this size; with the light-weight Japanese paper used, the risk is even greater.

The colours of tulips and salpiglossis will change but the lines are there and it is hoped that enough of the grace of flowers will remain. The curving lines of the stems on either side should be laid down first, to get a settled and dependable outline; next, the large tulips. At this point it would be safe to stick the petals lightly down, using a firm and continuous line of adhesive along the backs of the stems. These are tough and resilient; it may be necessary to cover them with a heavy book until the adhesive has dried. The infilling and flower centres present no great difficulty.

The bird of love and peace, a pressed flower emblem

The dove, symbol today of Innocence, Gentleness and Peace, has a pre-Christian history as a bird of Love, pre-dating Aphrodite, who inherited the bird from her ancestors, the love-goddesses of the Middle East and the Phoenician cities.

In the Near East, doves fluttered round the temples of Astarte, holy birds that must be neither killed nor eaten nor even touched. Atargatis of Askalon, a Cypriot love goddess, fish-tailed like a mermaid, was brought to birth by the warmth of her sacred doves, just as, later, Venus was said by the Romans to have been dropped from the sky into the Euphrates in an egg, which was rolled by fish on to the river bank and warmed and hatched out by doves.

Clay doves associated with fertility goddesses have been found in Crete and statuettes carrying doves or with doves perched on their heads survive from the late second millennium BC. Cypriot coins show doves perched on Aphrodite's temple at Paphos. A terracotta plaque of 460 BC pictures the goddess riding from the sea in a car drawn by Iris, the Rainbow goddess, and Zephros, the West Wind, who carries a dove in his right hand. Zeus was brought ambrosia by doves and Aeneas was led by two doves to the dark vale to find the Golden Bough, the mistletoe. Inside Aphrodite's temples, domesticated doves fluttered and cooed; outside they were on sale in cages, to be sacrificed in the cause of love.

Atargatis, Astarte, the Greek Aphrodite and Roman Venus: the dove was associated with them all. With the coming of Christianity, it

The Bird of Love and Peace.
Symbol of the human soul
and of the Holy Ghost; bird
of pagan love and of the
Annunciation; Aphrodite's
gentle messenger and yet a
blood sacrifice: an enigmatic
bird.

For her rose and for her ring
Venus bids her bird to sing:
　He, in modesty, puts on
The sober vestment of a nun.
　　　　ANTHONY RYE,
from 'The Inn of the Birds'.

obediently settled into the outstretched hand of the Virgin Mary. In Christian art, the dove symbolizes the Holy Ghost. Sometimes, in church windows, seven rays can be seen proceeding from a dove; these rays indicate the seven gifts of the Holy Ghost: Counsel, Fear of the Lord, Fortitude, Piety, Understanding, Wisdom and Knowledge. This gentle bird is also the emblem of the human soul. It is believed to come out of the mouths of saints at death.

The dove is best known as Noah's bird: 'And it came to pass at the end of forty days, that Noah opened the window of the ark that he had made ... Also he sent forth a dove from him, to see if the waters were dried up from off the earth; But the dove found no rest for the sole of her foot. ...' and Noah 'pulled her in unto him into the ark.' After seven more days Noah sent the dove out again: 'And the dove came in to him in the evening; and, lo, in her mouth was an olive leaf plucked off.' So the dove, as well as Traveller and Guide, became associated with the olive branch as a messenger of Peace.

To make this *Bird of Love and Peace*, the pressed flower artist has a narrow choice of materials, for the leaves may only be white and silver-grey. Here both body and head are made from two leaflets from a raspberry spray, shown on reverse. The wings and tail are made of silverweed. Beak and nearly hidden feet are portions of passion flower stamens, with the yellow side uppermost for the beak and the brownish reverse for the feet. The eye is a small flattened seed.

It is very useful, indeed almost a necessity, for the designer to have pressed a good stock of paired leaves such as vetches or one of the innumerable evergreen shrubs that are to be found in nearly every garden. When representing laurel leaves or bays, for example, miniature reproductions must be found for these largish leathery leaves. The garland of olive leaves surrounding the Dove of Peace was made in this way, of an evergreen shrub whose leaflets resembled olive leaves in their narrow pointed form. To give light and shade to the circle, they are used in reverse on the light side. They will need to be cut into small sections to get a circular effect. The silver knot at the bottom of the garland is formed of a circle cut from a silver-sprayed centre of a passion flower.

The dove is mounted on dark grey paper, cut round a plate measuring 8 in. (20 cm) in diameter. That, in turn, is fastened on to a paper or card with only one or two small spots of adhesive, to avoid buckling. The leaves are then applied in sections, so that the stem covers the perimeter of the circle, with the light underleaves on the left and the dark leaves on the right.

4 Preserving and Using Unpressed Flowers and Foliage

Jean Lorimer

Methods of Preserving

The beauty of preserved foliage and flowers takes on a new dimension when immortalized by means other than pressing which, of necessity, must flatten the natural contours of the material.

There are few varieties of flowers, ferns, foliage, grasses and seed-heads (those not suitable for preservation by pressing) which will not respond willingly to the opportunity of prolonging their natural decorative span of life if given the right treatment at the right time, such exceptions as there are being the few with very fine textured flowers, such as sweet peas and poppies. Captured in their prime, nearly all nature's gifts can be persuaded to retain a new and lasting beauty.

All too often, many of us leave it to one short season to collect the material we are seeking for preservation. Undoubtedly, the late summer into early autumn months are the most productive but, if an open 'seeing' eye is kept throughout the year, a wonderfully wide collection of plant life of varying textures and colours can be harvested.

No one method can be guaranteed to be absolutely foolproof in achieving success in preserving different types of material. Success depends not only on the extraction of absolutely all moisture but also on the moment chosen for gathering, the temperature at the time and the humidity. With all the forethought and care in the world, a few disappointments are inevitable.

According to the nature of the plant material you are working with and what you hope to achieve, you have, in addition to the traditional ways of pressing detailed in previous chapters, the choice of five different methods:

1 Preserving by air.
2 Preserving in water with the help of salt and glycerine.
3 Preserving with the help of a desiccant (a drying agent such as silica gel or borax).
4 Preserving with varnish spray.
5 Preserving with egg white and sugar for culinary use.

An arrangement of tall bluebell and nipplewort seedstems, wild grasses, larger bromas grass, helichrysums, honesty, pressed oak leaves and field sycamore leaves, cones, dried hypericum berries.

Whichever method is to be followed, certain guide lines remain constant: all material must be cut cleanly and at an angle with a really sharp knife or secateurs (picking by hand can too easily result in a damaged stem, even a damaged plant); cutting should be avoided until after the morning dew has evaporated, after rainfall, and in the heat of the midday sun (these are the times when all plant material is at its most vulnerable); flowers should be cut just before they are about to come into full bloom (tight buds seldom develop their full potential beauty indoors); long spikes of flowers like foxgloves, larkspur, delphiniums and lupins should be gathered when the lower buds are in flower, the top ones just about to burst; all material you hope to preserve must be chosen with special care (imperfections become more obvious after preservation).

Last but not least, it is important to care for your dried material after it has settled down in its final arrangement. There are few things less attractive in a home than an arrangement of preserved flowers and foliage which has remained in the same position un-dusted and un-cared-for throughout the year. An occasional change of position in the room, the addition of a living pot plant and a few fresh flowers now and again or, alternately, a branch or two of some evergreen leaves like *Elaeagnus pungens maculata*, variegated privet or ivy, each will help to keep up the alive and healthy appearance of your arrangement.

Preserving by air

This is the simplest of all methods, requiring the minimum amount of time, effort and equipment and it is successful for many varieties of flowers, grasses and seed-heads.

As the words 'preserving by air' imply, long life is given by a simple method of dehydration, all moisture being removed by exposure to warm, dry, circulating air.

Paradoxically, this can mean drying by water for hydrangeas. Flower heads such as these, as well as the seed pods of the Iris and Lilium family, are most successfully 'dried' when kept in a vase with a little water in a warm room. However, these are the exceptions which may be taken to 'prove the rule'.

Nature herself illustrates the simplicity of preserving in this way, for a walk in the country can produce seed-heads, oak apples, lichen-laced twigs with their lace-like overlay of silvery-green, graceful ropes of hops to be gleaned when the hop pickers leave the fields and branches of larch and sloe thick with tiny cones of varying shapes and sizes, all of which require no further treatment to ensure long life provided they are gathered before becoming damaged by rain or frost.

Teazles and sea holly ask for no more than the removal of all leaves and, if gathered at different times of the year, will give a wide variety of pleasing colour effects. Magnolia leaves, already rich in colour, their beautiful shape unblemished by weather and age can be found on the ground under trees in garden or parkland. Mounted on wire and attached to a well-shaped bare branch, these are an enviable asset to any home flower artist and much sought after.

Under pine trees there are always cones to be found, each one so intricately sculptured by nature as to resemble the wood carver's art; and in fields and hedgerows, there are grasses to be harvested before they begin to go to seed.

All these have been preserved by nature's own process of dehydration and in many cases need no further treatment apart from the removal of dust and dirt. When this has been done, they are ready to be used as part of your decorative design, without losing any of their subtle variations in colour.

The preservation of flowers and foliage, wild or cultivated, is different. The delicacy of flowers demands more specialized care to maintain individual characteristics of colour, shape and size, while foliage needs a substitute for the moisture which is to be extracted if it is to remain pliable, its leaves supple and soft to the touch.

From the foregoing, it will be apparent that the plant materials which respond most readily to dehydration by air fall into the following categories:

1 Flowers (see chart on pages 213–14).
2 Herbs.
3 Gourds and grasses.
4 Seed-heads and cereals

The orthodox way to give nature a helping hand in prolonging the life of any of the above is to tie the material you wish to preserve in small bunches at the base of the stems and hang these, heads down, in a dry, well ventilated, preferably dark, place. If flower-heads intermingle when tied in this way, each stem must be hung separately.

Light steals colour; therefore, the darker the space chosen for drying, the more vivid the resultant colours are likely to be. Again, the warmer the ventilation, the speedier the drying time but this will also be governed by texture (the more fleshy the material to be dried, the longer it will take).

Drying is always speeded up by the removal of all superfluous foliage immediately after picking. This not only increases the strength of the stem but, as leaves become brittle and powdery when dehydrated in this way, it is also the practical thing to do. The exceptions, of course, are herbs for culinary use, which should be gathered just before flowering, when the flavour concentrate is at its highest.

With this method of preservation by drying and with preserving with the help of desiccants, the total loss of moisture causes many stems to wither; flower-heads become too heavy and may break off altogether if not given support. This can be done in one of two ways, either by the insertion of a short length of florists' wire into the flower-head *before drying* or by using a hollow stemmed straw (the stem of a cereal can prove to be a very adequate substitute for the real thing) into which the weakened natural stem is pushed after drying and held firm with florists' wire or a little clear adhesive.

If strengthening is to be done *before* drying, first choose the length of

Left: On the wall, this swag of naturally coloured maize is known as 'squaw corn'. Limonium (statice), poppy heads, wheat, oats, skeletonized lime leaves and opened corn cobs have been arranged in a wicker-covered wine jar.

Opposite: An arrangement of preserved tall astilbe seedstems, dogwood twigs, astrantia, umbels of parsley and fennel, woodroses (ipomea seedpods) and camellia leaves.

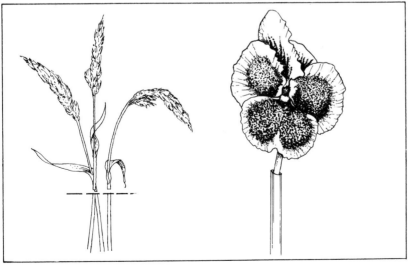

Fig. 19: *Lengthening stems*. Harvest grass or cereals immediately they have flowered. Thoroughly dehydrate them. Cut to required lengths. Use by inserting short natural stem into the hollow tube of dried grass or cereal.

wire you require for the stem and bend one end of this into a small hook. The straight end of the wire is then very gently inserted into the heart of the flower and pulled through the flower in the spot where the natural stem is growing. When this little hook is safely and invisibly embedded in the flower-head, the natural stem can be discarded and, when preservation is complete, the substitute stem can be covered with the plastic tape used by florists. This should be wound from the base of the flower face, twisting the tape as you work down the length of the stem. When cut, you will find this tape seals itself.

One advantage of using this method of strengthening the stem is that, when the preserving process is complete, the stem acquires a new flexibility and can be bent and curved to flow over the rim of the display container, always an advantage when the visual effect of the final arrangement is being considered.

Giving special strength *after* drying entails the use of a hollow-stemmed grass or straw as a substitute for the natural stem (fig. 19). It helps if the flower-head has sufficient stem of its own for this to be inserted into the hollow recess of its supporter. A spot of adhesive will hold real and false stems together, or a fine wire twisted round immediately and invisibly under the flower-head.

All natural stems shrink to some extent as dehydration takes place and nothing is more disappointing than to find some of your most prized possessions lying on the floor when you are using the 'hanging upside down' method of preservation by air. The possibility of this can be avoided if, when tying the bunches together before hanging, you use something like pipe cleaners or closure wires instead of twine, the advantage being that, should you at any time suspect there is danger of one or more of your bunches coming apart, you have simply to give an extra twist and so tighten your hold.

Unfortunately, even with this method of preservation, much of your plant material will lose some of its natural flexibility and grace of movement. The only way to avoid this is to dry the material upright in a tall, 'straight' container, each single stem supported and kept apart by the use of mesh wire netting. Grasses and cereals respond particularly well to this treatment, retaining much of their natural, fluid grace which is too often lost in the inevitable straightening out process of being dried hanging upside down.

In the preservation of plant life, flowers are the principal source of colour. The grasses, gourds, ferns and foliage provide background; seed-heads, driftwood, gourds and cones add the essential contrast in shape and texture.

In providing us with examples of the beauties of flowers during the barren months of the year and as an inspiration to us all to evolve our own methods of preservation, nature is co-operative in providing us with the Immortelles (the so-called Everlastings) which ask the minimum of care and respond well to the simple method of preservation by air.

The Everlastings have been used in dried-flower arrangements since Victorian days but the typical Victorian arrangement (often no more than a dust-trapping collection of Immortelles, grasses and ferns) has, largely due to the inspiration and creative genius of the late Constance Spry, been replaced by a totally new outlook embracing both modern and classically styled design. Old favourites still have their place but are now intermingled not only with exotic dried material imported by florists from all parts of the globe but also with living material in the shape of fresh flowers, pot plants, evergreens, fruits and vegetables.

Among those old favourites that have survived the test of time in spite of their somewhat quaint, old-fashioned look, are the Helichrysus family, easily recognized by the papery texture of the rather stiff incurled bracts which produce a bloom measuring 2–3 in. (5–8 cm) across when fully open and which remain colour true in all their vibrant shades of pink, red, purplish, violet, yellow, orange, crimson, golden brown and white. Gathered before pollination, these flowers of the Helichrysus family retain the shape and colour of the flower-heads without help and, bunched together boldly, can prove useful in giving a solid splash of vibrant colouring in a neutral arrangement of ferns, foliage and grasses.

Of the many varieties of Helichrysum (all of which have a contribution to make to the flower artist's craft), the most popular are ammobrium, with its domed yellow centre surrounded by silvery white bracts; helipterum, with tiny star-like flowers of golden yellow; statice or sea lavender, with brightly blue spikes of tiny funnel shaped flowers; xeranthemum, which, with its long, spiky petals in shades of rose, pink and purple, provides such an excellent contrast to those of circular

A mass of helipterum (acroclinium).

contours; and the many variations of yarrow (*Achillea*): 'Cloth of Gold' (golden yellow), 'Fire King' (pinkish red) and sneezewort (pure white double florets). The straight, stiff stems of all these make them particularly useful in any decorative arrangement.

In addition to all these, we have *Lunaria annua*, a charming, old-fashioned plant which we commonly call honesty. When the white and purple blossoms disappear, they leave behind flat, silvery seed pods.

However, it takes a lot more than the Everlastings and other plant materials so generously and freely preserved for us by nature's own process to satisfy the true flower artist's aspirations. The contributions of nature simply open up and demonstrate the possibilities.

The chart on pages 213 and 214 gives a few examples of the types of plant material most likely to be successfully preserved by this easiest-of-all method of preservation. It will be seen that nearly all herbs, grasses and seed-heads respond well. A few have been singled out for individual mention because of the importance of the colour they contribute to all displays of dried and preserved material. Most of the flowers, however, give happier results when preserved by desiccants (as described on page 187).

Plant material easy to dry by air

GRASSES

Ideally, these should be harvested at flowering time, usually in May or early June. They give a wide variety of texture, shape and contour line and in all their soft, neutral shades, provide a natural background and foil for colour.

Among the most decorative of grasses are wild oat (*Avena fatue*), with its erect stem bearing clusters of green spikelets enclosing tufts of brown bristles; barren brome (*Bromus sterilia*), with 2-ft (60 cm) high stems bearing green drooping spikelets often tinged with purple; cloud grass (*Agrostis nebulosa*), with graceful feathery flower-heads; meadow fescue (*Festuca pratensis*), similar in appearance to barren brome, with nodding, spike-like seed-heads; wall barley (*Hordeum murinum*), resembling cereal barley and easily recognizable by its spreading hair-like husks, so rough to the touch; common cat's tail (*Phleum pratense*), its closely packed, spike-like head giving a dense, cylindrical effect in marked contrast to other grasses; common reed (*Phragmites communis*), similar in all but colour to cultivated pampas grass and an asset for the flower arranger working on large display groups; and, prettiest of all, hare's tail cotton grass (*Erioporum vaginatum*), with its snow-white head, soft and fluffy to the touch and with a lovely silken sheen.

GOURDS

These come in many varied and wonderful shapes and sizes: apple shape, marrow, pear and round. Their creamy beige, yellow and orange colourings harmonize well with stylized arrangements of dried grasses, cereals, cones and with leaves and flowers with autumnal tints. They must be completely ripe before harvesting and, to make sure they are

A delicately arranged
assortment of round
seedheads of onion, senecio
buds, leaves from a tulip tree
and wild grasses.

Physalis, achillea, honesty
and helipterum
(acroclinium) hanging to dry
overlook this wheelbarrow
of mixed gourds.

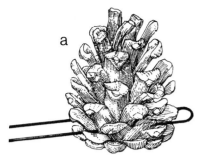

Fig. 20: *Pine cones and other stemless subjects.*
Pine cones and other stemless, scaly or rough-textured subjects can be given stems as follows:
(a) Insert a length of florists' wire between the lower scales. Pull the legs of the wire down and under.
(b) Twist one end of the wire round the other and bring both ends down to where the stem would normally be.

Opposite: A pretty arrangement of larch cones, wild clematis seedheads, with holly and ivy.

absolutely dried out, they should be laid on folds of newspaper at room temperature until, on tapping, you find the outside skin as hard as wood. It is only then that you may be certain of complete dehydration.

Gourds need no further treatment for a long life and may be used in their natural state with a matt surface or, if preferred, rubbed with linseed oil or given a shine with an all-over spray of clear varnish. They can be threaded with wire in order to make them suitable for a high-standing arrangement.

CONES

These may be found not only in many different shapes and sizes but also in many varying shades of brown, the depth of colour change most frequently depending on age. Cones become darker as they mature but, when completely dehydrated, often revert to a bleached-out shade of milky chocolate which harmonizes so well with all the tints of autumn.

Probably the most beautiful in design of all the cones used by the home flower artist and, fortunately, freely available in many parts of the British Isles are those of the larch and the alder which thickly adorn the twigs we collect to establish the outline and structure of many an arrangement. These cones are tiny and most delicately sculptured, particularly those of the larch, on which the cone loses its traditionally accepted shape and more closely resembles a rosette, skilfully carved out of wood.

SEED-HEADS

Here again, nature has been more than generous in providing us with so many seed-heads of individual appeal. It would be impossible to mention them all.

Unlike flowers, upon which we rely to provide the colour for an arrangement, seed-heads, like gourds, give textural value.

Generally, seed-heads come under the following descriptive headings: round, spiky, panicles and plumes. Under each of these headings, it is possible to find both cultivated and wild seed-heads.

Probably the largest of the seed-heads to be found in this country are the globe artichoke and the cardoon (similar in form to the artichoke but slightly smaller). Both these should be gathered as the flower is fading, for it is at its best only after being preserved by air for several weeks when the flower petals have withered, leaving a hard and dry centre, which, after a further week or two being thoroughly dehydrated, will be found to be surrounded by an attractive ring of golden hairy whorls which must be handled very delicately. Indeed, it may at times be necessary to use a little clear adhesive round the base in order to ensure that these whorls, which are particularly attractive, remain intact.

In contrast to such large seed-heads as the globe artichoke and the cardoon are those of iberis and nigella. Those of nigella are always useful when doing small arrangements; if gathered soon after they are formed, the beautiful mauve and green colouring of the pods can be retained by air preservation.

Spiky seed-heads include aquilegia, with seed cases similar in shape to those of the delphinium; grape hyacinth (*Muscari*), which gives short

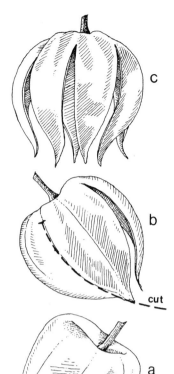

Fig. 21: *Physalis*.
Colourful physalis lanterns
are given a new look when
the dried petals are divided
and allowed to open out like
an exotic flower.
(a) Cut the clearly defined
veins of the lanterns using
sharp scissors.
(b) Separate the individual
'petals' rolling them gently
between the thumb and
forefinger.
(c) The 'petals' or segments
open out like an exotic
flower.

spikes of seed capsules; oenothera (evening primrose), which, gathered
early, will retain its distinctive markings.

More dramatic are the brilliantly coloured vivid rose hips, which can
be preserved for a limited time if rubbed with linseed oil to help maintain
the high gloss image; bells of Ireland (*Molucella laevis*), with the
unending fascination of its tiny shell-like sheaths of soft lime green
growing in whorls and spirals around a single stem; and *Allium
albopilosum*, a spectacular addition to any arrangement of preserved
material. Such treasures as these are all freely available in Great Britain.
It is also well worth searching for lesser known grasses, gourds and seed-
heads which come to us from so many different parts of the world.

Preserving in water with glycerine

This is the method which has proved to be the most successful in the
preservation of foliage and, by using this method, it is possible to obtain
many varying shades of colour from a single species of tree, shrub or
plant. The early autumn foliage of deciduous trees such as the oak, elm,
beech, lime and eucalyptus can all be preserved in this way, whilst many
of the evergreens like holly, spruce and bay will dry green on their own
without outside help.

One of the great advantages of preserving material in water with
glycerine is that, in contrast to drying by air or by pressing or with the
help of a desiccant, leaves will not become brittle and will remain pliable
without losing individual characteristics.

The final depth of colour may be controlled and many interesting colour
tones achieved by careful time immersion, first in a salt solution (solution
No. 1) and, later, after twenty-four hours, in glycerine and water
(solution No. 2). Hot water is always used in making up these solutions,
for this is absorbed more readily than cold water, with the result that the
glycerine is carried up to the tip of the topmost leaves in the shortest
possible time, thus preventing curling at the tips.

Apart from your foliage (suggestions as to your choice of this are given
in the table on page 215) you will need:

> Hot water
> Kitchen salt
> Commercial glycerine (or anti-freeze)
> Permanganate of potash
> Bleach

Solution No. 1 is prepared by dissolving one tablespoon of kitchen salt
in one gallon of hot water. This must be stirred really thoroughly to
ensure that every grain of salt is dissolved. Carefully inspect those sprays
and branches you want to preserve, wipe clean of any dust and select only
those which are perfectly shaped and without blemish of any kind. Crush
or split the ends and leave these in Solution No. 1 up to a depth of
approximately 3 in. (8 cm) for twenty-four hours. All leaves which come
under the level of the water must be removed.

Solution No. 2 is prepared the following day by the addition of one part commercial glycerine to two parts of very hot water. If commercial glycerine is difficult to find and proves to be too expensive, anti-freeze is an adequate substitute. If anti-freeze is used, it must be mixed in equal quantities with very hot water and given a vigorous shaking in a tightly stoppered bottle. Glycerine and anti-freeze are both heavier than water, so this vigorous shaking is absolutely essential to ensure a good, even, mix; stirring alone is not sufficient to do the job efficiently.

The container you use for preserving foliage with glycerine should not be unnecessarily wide for, if it is, it will be unnecessarily extravagant (fig. 22). Instead, you should choose one that is tall and narrow (a pickle jar or one that is made to store macaroni and spaghetti is often just the right size) and this should be placed in a bucket or wider mouthed receptacle weighted with damp sand to prevent the possibility of the foliage over-balancing, a sad event all too likely to happen when tall sprays are put into a wide mouthed container with no more than some 3 in. (8 cm) of liquid to give weight and stability.

The leaves should be left in the glycerine solution in a dry, cool, well-ventilated place until the colour results you are hoping for can be seen. It is wise to check the container at frequent intervals to make sure no 'topping up' of the solution is necessary.

The time taken for a permanent colour change will vary according to the material; for example, a branch of small leaves will frequently absorb all the solution it needs for preservation within a few days, whereas leaves of a tougher, fleshier, texture can take ten to twelve days or even longer.

Beautiful rich colourings can be encouraged by keeping the material in bright light whilst in the solution and, later, by exposing it to sunlight. It is also possible to deepen colour still further by adding half a teaspoonful of permanganate of potash to the solution, or, alternately, to lighten colour by adding one tablespoonful of bleach to every pint of solution.

Leaves are fully processed when the undersides are shiny and damp. If the foliage is allowed to absorb too much of the glycerine, there will always be the danger that any leaves which touch a wall will leave an oily mark almost impossible to remove. To avoid any possibility of this, wipe off as much of the sticky residue as possible, swish the leaves through clean, warm water and pat gently dry. This will remove any feeling of sliminess and will not harm the leaves provided they are kept in a warm place until completely dry and any residual moisture has completely evaporated.

Small sprays of tiny leaves and individual leaves of special interest by reason of colour or shape, are best preserved by total immersion in the glycerine solution. This is a more demanding process of preservation and is used only when rather precious and unusual specimens demand specialized, individual, treatment by reason of some individual characteristic of shape and texture.

Leaves which are to be completely immersed in the glycerine solution must not overlap. Use a large, flat container (there are Pyrex pie dishes that might have been specially designed for this). Arrange your leaves carefully and cover with the glycerine solution. Incidentally, in the name

Fig. 22.
To economize on the use of glycerine stand the branches of foliage in a small pot of the glycerine mixture inside a larger container which will support the foliage.

Rushes and honesty, both dried, with fresh ferns, mahonia, thuja, lonicera, lupin and London pride foliage.

Opposite, left: Fig. 23. Single soft leaves can be given new flexibility and strength if they are backed with self-adhesive transparent material such as Fablon.

Opposite, right: Fig. 24: *Lengthening stems.*
(a) Take a hairpin or length of wire bent into a loop of the required length.
(b) Lay the loop against the short end of the stem. Hold it in position firmly between finger and thumb. Take the long end of the pin or wire and twist it so that it passes tightly around the stem taking in the short leg. Press together and down to create a continuation of the natural stem.

Strengthening leaves.
Stitch soft leaves with fine wire *before* pressing or drying but after preserving.
(c) Use silver (or fuse) wire to make fine stitches through the leaf from the back. Twist the ends of the wire together to give a single stem, enclosing a small piece of the natural stem or the base of the leaf itself.

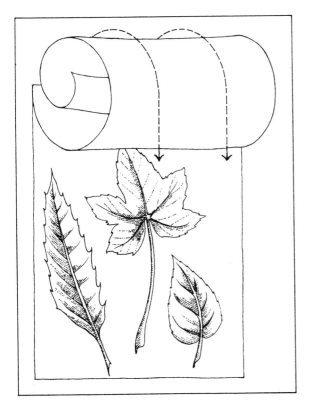

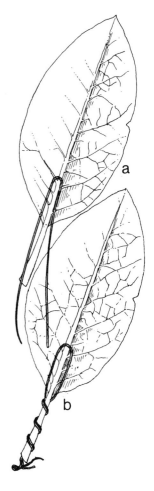

of economy, it is good to remember this solution may be used many times. It simply needs straining and should then be kept in an airtight bottle until the moment comes for a further adventure in preservation.

If the leaves you are preserving show an inclination to float, they must be weighted down, for total immersion is essential. Preserved in this way, you will find leaves take very much longer to acquire depth of colour but they can be removed at any time once you are sure sufficient solution has been absorbed and they will lighten further if kept in sunlight.

Individual leaves preserved by total immersion are often rather limp and may well need strengthening. There are several ways of doing this (see figures 23 and 24) but one of the easiest and most successful is to place each leaf (thoroughly cleansed of any suspicion of sliminess or oil) face down on a sheet of paper. Holding a length of fine wire firmly in position following the natural spine of the leaf, the leaf is completely covered with a clear, transparent, adhesive plastic. When you first attempt this, you may find some difficulty in persuading the leaf to remain in place but this can be achieved if a tiny drop of clear adhesive, applied with a matchstick, is put on one or two strategic places to hold the leaf. Once in position, the backing is pressed down smoothly and firmly with particular care around the edges, making sure the wire remains in position correctly following the line of the leaf's natural middle rib, where it is unlikely to be noticeable once the leaf is cut out. The leaf will then have acquired a new strength and, with the flexibility of the wire 'spine', may be used at any angle or be attached to an otherwise bare but beautiful branch or twig.

Beech, oak, sycamore, hornbeam and sweet chestnut all take on a new lease of life after immersion in the glycerine solution; eucalyptus, both the variety with round leaves and the one with sickle-shaped leaves, is particularly co-operative, responding well to just forty-eight hours in the glycerine solution, which is usually long enough to fix and perpetuate the shape and the lovely soft, blue-grey colour of the leaves.

This is also the most successful method when the leaves and 'fruits' of a shrub or tree are to be preserved together. These may need a little pre-preservation care; for instance, the acorns of the oak, the fruits of the Spanish chestnut in their hard prickly covers and the nuts of the beech should be removed from their cradles and secured back in position with a little clear adhesive before being put in the glycerine solution.

Blackberries can give exciting results and shrink only slightly if harvested at exactly the right moment, when they will shine like black velvet. The red berries of mountain ash, hips and haws and the red and yellow holly berries all need a light spray of clear varnish or ordinary hair spray if they are to retain their high gloss. If bulrushes are given the same treatment, you will avoid the possibility of those giant seed pods bursting in the home and scattering a multitude of seeds in all directions.

The late summer and early autumn are the most productive times for the preservation of plant material, for it is then, with thoughts of the approaching winter months, that we start seriously to think of prolonging for as long a period of time as possible the beauty of the garden, the parkland and the hedgerow, but the early months of the year also provide many opportunities for those with 'seeing' eyes, when those trees which produce exciting flowers or florets before the leaves appear (the wych elm, with its trusses of bright, green heads; acers, with apricot-coloured buds; and Norway maple, with vivid green flower-like sprays on coal black branches) have their own dramatic beauty to contribute. Picked in the early months of the year and before the sharp onslaught of April rains, three to four days in the glycerine solution are often sufficient to preserve this young foliage. It must be watched carefully for some varieties react so much more quickly than others. Immediately there is a soft, moist and silky feeling, the foliage must be removed from the solution, swished through warm water and slowly and thoroughly dried.

Young growth, such as this, will give a wonderfully varied range of colour tones, from biscuit gradually darkening to a lovely creamy beige.

It is the beech tree which provides us with the preserved foliage most commonly seen in providing the outline for dried arrangements. If it is the autumnal tints that attract you, the time to pick your leaves is when you see the first tints of changing colour. You must choose your foliage from those branches still in verdant leaf, for it is only in this part of the tree that you will be able to find the leaves which will be preserved most successfully. The rising sap is slowing down but it is sufficiently active in these parts of the tree to carry the preserving solution through. Success is only assured when the glycerine solution can be absorbed through the branches, right up to the topmost leaves.

It is always tempting to try to preserve one or two choice specimens of exotic foliage imported from faraway places, when these are seen at the nursery or florist. Success cannot be guaranteed but there is always a reasonable possibility that it will come about so long as the leaves will absorb water readily.

To find out what the possibilities are, split the stem upward to a height of some 2–3 in. (5–8 cm) as soon as you reach home and plunge the branches immediately into a deep bucket containing 3–4 in. (8–10 cm) of boiling water. Leave them overnight, after which, if water is not being sufficiently absorbed right up into the leaves, there will be early signs of curling and withering.

If this happens, you must forget any hope of preserving these leaves for any length of time. It might, however, be well worth while immersing a few of the leaves singly in the glycerine solution and keeping a daily watch on their reaction. They may be rather limp at the end of this treatment. If so, swish them round in warm water and pat them dry. Then, placing each leaf separately between pieces of waxed paper, press firmly with a warm iron.

Though ideal for the preservation of foliage, ferns and other forms of plant life, this method of preservation is not normally outstandingly successful with flowers which respond more happily to drying by desiccant. Among the few that generally respond well are :

Flowers	Time for successful preservation
Alchemilla	When the large clusters of minute star-like florets are about to break into full bloom.
Christmas rose (*Helleborus niger*)	These lovely wax-like flowers preserve well but they absorb any moisture there may be in the atmosphere and should be checked frequently.
Garrya	Early in the year, when the pendulous catkins are fully developed and the shrub is in full leaf.
Lily of the valley (*Convallaria majalis*)	Flowers and leaves should be completely submerged in solution.
Love lies bleeding (*Amaranthus caudatus*)	In late summer or early autumn, when the long drooping tassels, blood red in colour, are at their best.
Spurge	Late summer, when the branched heads of tiny yellow-green bracts appear.

Ferns

Ferns are seldom disappointing when preserved by the glycerine method, which, in contrast to drying by air (or by pressing), keeps the material soft and pliable and avoids brittle withering. It is well worth while experimenting with ferns during different seasons of the year, as these are always valuable when planning small arrangements.

In the spring, the slow unfurling of each one of the fronds which make up the whole plant is exceptionally beautiful and this exciting moment of growth is one which should be captured if possible by means of the glycerine method of preservation to add the interest of contrast when fully mature fronds are preserved in the same way later in the year.

Ferns that are evergreen may be harvested and preserved at any time of the year. New fronds may be expected to appear around April or May but, once this period of growth is over, the ferns should not be harvested until they reach full maturity towards the end of August. This is the ideal time to gather bracken fern (*Pterifium aquilinum*), and lady fern (*Athyrium filix-femina*).

Drying by Desiccant

Preservation by glycerine is generally accepted as an excellent way of prolonging the life of foliage but drying by desiccant is undoubtedly the most satisfactory way of preserving the colour and delicacy of flowers. It helps them to retain much of their natural beauty from bud to maturity, for it is only with the help of a desiccant that sufficiently rapid dehydration can be stimulated to ensure that the shape, structure and colour of the natural flower is perpetuated.

Stems, however, are liable to suffer from such drastic and rapid loss of moisture and should be shortened to a length of not more than 3 in. (8 cm). A further length of stem can always be added artificially before or after drying in the manner illustrated on page 175. It is also permissible to give extra staying power to those stems which you suspect may have an inclination to shatter when dried by painting the base of the petals with gum arabic before they are buried in the desiccant.

The two desiccants most commonly used by the home flower artist are household borax and silica gel. About 1 lb (0·45 kg) will dry eight to ten open-faced flowers.

Borax is probably the cheaper of the two to buy in quantity but there are advantages in using silica gel. It will absorb some fifty per cent of its own weight of moisture before feeling wet and can be used over and over again provided it is thoroughly dried in a low temperature oven after use and stored in an air-tight container, sealed with self-adhesive tape.

Borax, being a fine powder, is more easily sprinkled into and through the petals of a flower than silica gel and can generally be loosened with a fine hair paint-brush without difficulty and shaken gently away when preservation is complete.

The granules of silica gel, being so much coarser, are more likely to damage a delicate petal but, on the other hand, are less likely to stick to the dried flower. Moreover, they provide an added interest by giving the opportunity of seeing the rate of dehydration as it takes place. The blue crystals among the granules change colour from blue to pale pink, indicating that moisture is being absorbed.

From the foregoing, you will see that, whether you decide to use borax or silica gel, it is entirely a matter of personal choice, for each has its own characteristic advantages. Whichever one you decide to use, successful preservation will demand the same care as any other method of prolonging nature's natural life.

All materials chosen must be completely free of surface moisture and in perfect condition. The tiniest flaw is immediately highlighted by dehydration. The container used must be of suitable size and, when silica gel is the chosen drying agent, must be fitted with an air-tight lid.

If space in a warm cupboard is limited in your home, silica gel has the advantage of needing no heat whereas, when borax is used, the container must be stored in a warm, well-ventilated place with an even temperature.

The type of container you choose must, therefore, depend on which one of the two recommended desiccants you decide to use. Cardboard boxes are not recommended for any drying out process or for the storing of material which has been successfully dehydrated, as cardboard tends to absorb moisture from the air. The important thing is that the container should be the right size for the material you plan to dry and with silica gel it must be absolutely air-tight.

In preparing the container, it is necessary that the bottom should first be covered with a layer of desiccant to a depth of approximately 3 in. (8 cm). Flowers of one type only should be preserved in one box and it is of the utmost importance that great care is taken in positioning these on the bed of desiccant so that no two flowers overlap or even touch each other. A petal crumpled at this stage will remain crumpled and special care taken now will pay worthwhile dividends later. Ultimate success depends on the most delicate handling at all times throughout the whole process of preservation and, later, when arranged for display.

The shortened stems of the flowers to be preserved are pushed into the bed of desiccant with flower faces upright. If using borax, the powder must be sieved through a fine sieve between the petals until the flower head is completely buried.

With trumpet shaped flowers, it is necessary to fill the 'trumpet' with the desiccant right up to overflowing before placing it on the bed of the container. Then, supporting each flower head between first and second fingers, the stem is bedded and the desiccant sieved or gently sprinkled over and around until the flower is completely covered.

Since the granules of silica gel are too coarse to be passed through the fine sieve that may be used when applying borax, extra special care has to be used to ensure these are sifted between two fingers over the flower face with a very light touch. If this is done with a heavy hand, irreparable damage can be done.

The time it takes a flower to lose all its moisture content depends on the nature of the material but is generally between one and five days. For example, cornflowers and open-faced flowers of this kind and the individual florets of delphinium and larkspur will dry more quickly than flowers of a more fleshy texture. For small single flowers, the time taken to dry out can be as short as one day.

With this method of rapid dehydration, many stems are inclined to wither; flower-heads then become too heavy and may break off altogether if not given support. The method of dealing with this problem has been described on page 176, where the same problem occurs when preserving by air.

Containers, Vases and Arrangements

The day of the traditional vase is by no means past but many people enjoy using a wider range of containers. The choice is a personal one, influenced by the atmosphere and colour of one's surroundings. Shallow bowls or dishes for short-stemmed blooms; a modern tureen or a Victorian vegetable dish for marigolds, larkspurs and zinnias; a copper kettle filled with beech leaves; a country bunch in an old teapot; or perhaps a salt cellar for a tiny posy. Any of these and many others will present themselves when you are searching for containers around the house.

At jumble sales and in antique markets it is often possible to find an old copper kettle that leaks and is therefore useless for the purpose for which it was created, a preserving pan long past its days as a culinary asset or a beautifully shaped tureen now minus a handle or a lid. Such finds should be treasured.

Glass is currently out of favour, possibly because of the difficulty of avoiding stains, hiding stems and disguising the wire mesh netting used to balance the display. In fact, all these little problems can be overcome very effectively with dried moss or with solid glass marbles which are pretty and colourful and help to provide some essential weight.

If you are tempted to use a glass vase, do not fill this with wire mesh as you might do with an opaque container. Instead, measure the circumference of the top of your vase, cut out the wire netting 1 in. (2·5 cm) larger in diameter, bend the cut ends of the wire over the edge of the vase and tie this firmly in position. With dried material, some extra weight must be provided to give balance and this can be done most easily by filling the vase with solid glass marbles.

A successful arrangement is always designed as an integral part of its setting, emphasizing rather than overwhelming surrounding colours and character of furnishing. White and palely painted walls can be relied upon to display flowers in sharp relief, whereas patterned walls can present difficulties. Mirrors and mirror-lined alcoves always provide an attractive background.

With the decision of placement made, it is time to concentrate on the container of your choice and the overall shape of the final arrangement.

The most popular shapes for the display of preserved flowers and their accessories (leaves, ferns, grasses, gourds and seed-heads) are:

1 Fan shaped, front facing, planned to be viewed principally from the front.

2 All round, a much more symmetrical design to be viewed from all angles.

3 Cascade, normally planned for a pedestal where trailing stems of flowers, berries and foliage can be seen to best advantage falling gracefully over the rim of the container.

4 Byzantine pyramid cone and similar foam shapes, to be used as the

Tall delphiniums, alchemilla (bright yellow) gnaphalium, (blue) hydrangea, (pale yellow) helichrysum species and heather make up this plentiful arrangement.

Fig. 25.
Three important steps in the construction of one of the most popular of preserved material arrangements.

foundation for many varieties of close work where short stemmed flowers, ferns, foliage, fruits (even vegetables) are intermingled to completely cover a shaped block of foam bought from the florist or made up to your own design with wire mesh packed with sphagnum moss.

Whatever the shape decided upon, perfection in overall structure and balance is always a challenge and this can be achieved only on an absolutely firm foundation. To have spent a lot of thought and time in creating an arrangement and then to see it collapse by over-balancing is heart-breaking. The only way to ensure against this is to prepare your container in the proper, painstaking manner; this may be time consuming but the time is well spent.

To ensure your material stays in position, it must be strongly supported by 2-in. (5-cm) wire netting (pliable 19-gauge) fitted into the container. To do this, cut the netting about twice the size of the container's base and crumple this in several layers into a U-shape. Push the folded end into the container, keeping the cut edges uppermost to be individually looped over the rim of the container, holding the netting firm. The holes should be made to overlap in several layers because, if holes are too large, flowers may tend to slip through; they are held more securely if gripped by the netting in more than one place.

If you are planning to have some of your material (a spray of flowers, a bunch of grapes, a trailing twig or cluster of cherries) hanging down over the rim of the container, it can be secured by pushing the stem through two or three of the holes or by hooking an end of the wire round the stem where it will not show. Once firmly held in this way, a little gentle pressure will enable you to bend the spray or bunch of grapes into the exact position you want.

From the above, it will be obvious that it is absolutely essential the wire netting is immovable and so firmly anchored in position that it will not be disturbed when the arrangement is moved.

Once you are satisfied that your foundation work is well and properly done, you must decide on shape and the angles from which your arrangement will finally be seen.

Fan shaped, front facing

Opposite below: Fig. 26: *The fan shape.*
This is probably the most popular of all designs for floral display and is designed to be seen only from the front and sides.
(a) It is usual for the tallest central stem to be one-and-a-half times the total height of the container.
(b) Main side stems should extend in approximately the same portion as the central stem; forword stems to be about a third of this length.
(c) Fill in with stems of varying length.

Begin by positioning the background and work forwards toward you (fig. 26). The tallest stems are used to outline height and width; the placing and firm hold of the central spine of this arrangement is absolutely essential. Stems should be approximately one-and-a-half times the height of the container and must be fixed in position some two-thirds of the way back to ensure that all stems inserted later will appear to flow out from one central point, some curving slightly backward and downward to soften the appearance at the sides. The fourth 'balancing' stem to be placed is the forward flowing stem, which should be inserted almost at right angles to the central stem in a near-horizontal position facing towards you as you work and curving slightly downward. On the firm and skilful placement of these background and outline stems will depend ultimate success.

When filling in, choose stems of varying lengths to avoid a stylized effect; short stems between taller ones give body but it is important to ensure stems are not seen to cross one over another. Those which are planned to spill out over the rim of the container should be approximately one-and-a-half times the height of the container and should be inserted through the wire mesh netting into the Oasis block some two-thirds of the distance towards the back of the container. This ensures that all stems inserted later will appear to flow out from a central point, leaning slightly backward in order to soften the effect from the sides.

The all-round arrangement

With this type of arrangement, whether oblong, trough-shape or round, the same basic principles apply, of outlining shape first; the height and width of the finished display is an individual decision based on the size of the container being used and the position it is to occupy (fig. 27). The all-round arrangement is most generally seen on the dining table or on a central table in the living room.

On the dining table, it has the advantage of height; this should not be more than 12 in. (30 cm) in order to avoid any possibility of your arrangement creating a barrier between those who sit opposite each other. The length of the lateral stems will be governed by the length and shape of the table but one-and-a-half times the length of the container may be taken as a guide line.

In establishing outline, one stem (the central spine) is placed absolutely upright in the middle of the container with four additional stems of the same height at right angles to this as if to mark the four points of the compass. With four more stems, slightly shorter in length, inserted between the triangles thus created, the foundation framework is complete. Side stems can now be inserted to define width. These may be as narrow or wide as desired, provided all intermediate stems are kept within an imaginery line drawn from the top to the side stems' furthermost point. Any dominant flowers being used should be made a focal point by being leant slightly forward; short sprays of foliage should

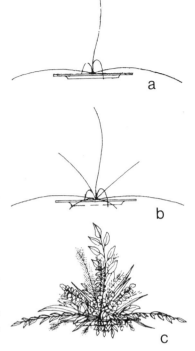

Above: Fig. 27: *The all-round design.*
(a) First define height. Make sure the top of the central stem is above the centre of the base of the container. Insert four side stems.
(b) Insert four shorter stems.
(c) Insert further material to fill out the design.

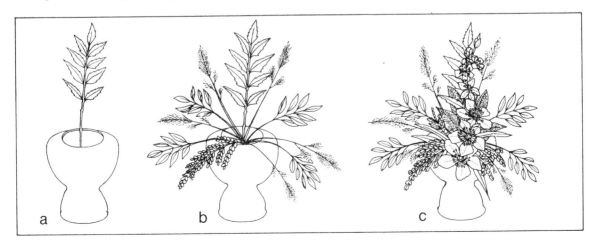

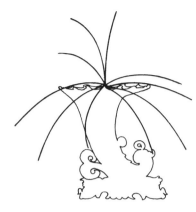

Fig. 28: *The cascade*.
The cascade style of arrangement is first outlined with foliage and then filled in with flowers. The final effect should resemble a fountain, every stem emerging from a central point which should appear to carry the whole weight of the arrangement before allowing it to flow over the sides of the container.

Right: A selection of aids to flower arrangement, consisting of pinholders, candlecup, plasticine, wire-netting, foamed plastic in specially designed holders, galvanized netting (the other is plastic covered), and an essential part of many arrangements, candles.

Opposite: The cone on the left is made of poppy seed capsules interspersed with tiny glixia flowers, the one in the centre is made of small helichrysums and variegated holly and the third is of helipterum and some glixia.

be used to flow over the rim of the container and to give extra body.

The choice of container for the all-round display is so wide that it is not possible to do more than generalize. In any case, the container is nearly always completely hidden from view by the flowers and short-stemmed sprays of leaves allowed to spill out over the rim. It may be an oblong trough, a vegetable dish or even one of those shallow plastic dishes in which so much is now served up at the supermarkets and into which a block of Oasis can be a perfect fit. All these might provide an adequate container for an attractive display. Whatever you decide to use, because of the angles at which many of the stems used will be placed, it is advisable to cover the Oasis with wire netting and secure it still further with a pin holder, itself anchored to the container with a spot of florists' clay or plasticine.

Here again you start with the central, vertical stem firmly embedded through the Oasis on to the pin holder. If you have chosen as your tallest

upright stem one measuring 10 in. (25 cm), then the four lateral stems should be of the same length and inserted at right angles to the upright. In this way, four triangles are formed and into each of these triangles four more stems are placed horizontally. This completes your framework for you have established both height and width and all that remains to be done is to give body by filling in with shorter stems of uneven lengths. According to the dried material you are using, an attractive base can be created with fir cones, gourds, sea shells picked up on the beach or pleasingly shaped and colourful fruit or vegetables.

The same principles are, of course, followed should you be using the trough shape for your all-round display.

The Cascade and the cone, or Byzantine

The Cascade, both as a large display which is planned to be seen to best advantage mounted on a pedestal above eye level and as a miniature when a long stemmed goblet, a figurine type of vase or an elaborate candelabra may be the container, is one of the most eye catching and decorative of all displays and, certainly, when successfully accomplished, one of the most satisfying to do (fig. 28).

Fig. 29: *The Byzantine design.*
Pyramid cones are ideal for combining short stemmed flowers, sprays of small leaves and ferns, with small fruits and vegetables. Prepare the cone by wiring it into a container of modified pedestal design before inserting the material.

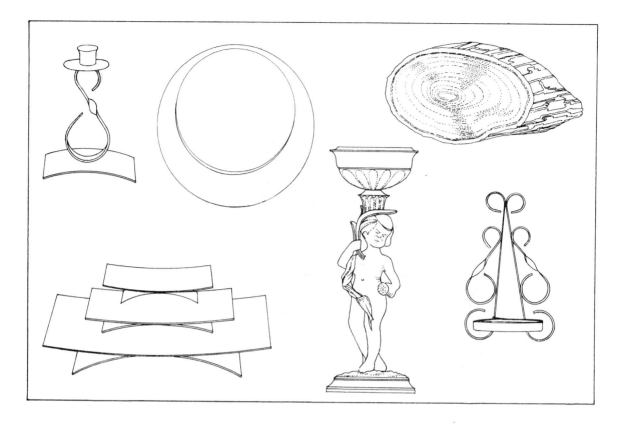

Fig. 30: *Display accessories*.
A tremendous variety of
these is now available at
florists' accessory shops.
They can be used most
effectively in the creation of
new and exciting displays.
Most of these are available in
varying shapes and sizes.

The principles of setting up the structure of the cascade display are
much the same, in their preliminary stages, as those which apply to the
front-facing fan shape arrangement. The balance of height and width
must first be created. With this done, the main difference lies in the wide
variety of preserved material which may be selected. This is the time
when you can make full use of all those long trailing stems such as old
man's beard, hops, ivy and the curving branches of brilliantly colourful
hips and haws which will together create the appearance of a cascade of
flowers, fruits and foliage.

If a candelabra is to be used, it will be necessary to get some small metal
candle-cups, which you will find are stocked by most florists. These are
inserted into the candleholders and tied to the candelabra with silver wire
or fuse wire to avoid any possibility of tilting when a lighted candle may
be in position.

With the Byzantine or pyramid cone type of arrangement, you are not
concerned with outline (fig. 29). This is provided by the shape of the cone
itself, which makes an ideal basis for combining short stemmed flowers,
sprays of small leaves and miniature ferns with fruits and vegetables.
These last must, of course, be reasonably light in weight (crab apples, red
currants, blackcurrants, grapes and baby tomatoes). There is no reason
why artificial fruits, which are so realistic these days, should not be
introduced. Whatever you use, both real and artificial fruits can be easily
held in position by running a hairpin or piece of wire bent in the shape of a

hairpin through the fruit. The beautiful complementary effect of the rich bloom on fruit and on the softer textures of flowers has intrigued artists for centuries and is no less effective today than it was in the days of the great Dutch and Flemish artists.

Whether you buy the plastic foam cone foundation at the florist or make up one of your own to the exact size you want with wire netting packed with sphagnum moss is a personal decision.

Natural containers

With the basic principles of creating 'shape' mastered (and, undoubtedly, increased skills come from repetition), there is little doubt that containers of unusual shapes and sizes will stimulate attempts to create original designs of your own.

You will be able to see, instantly, the beauty of the discarded bark of an ageing tree, a log of wood, hollowed out by time and the ravages of weather, a 'slice' of polished wood and the weird and wonderful shapes of driftwood which can so often be picked up on the seashore, mahogany coloured with age or bleached white by salt and sun.

Such things as these, which could never be used for thirsty fresh flowers, make unexpectedly beautiful settings for dried arrangements and frequently do not even require any sort of container lining. A block of Oasis, cut to fit and fixed in position with plasticine is all that is necessary to provide you with an exciting and original container.

These plastic foam stem-holders, such as Oasis and other similar products already on the market, are invaluable to the novice home flower artist; they simplify so many of the difficulties of displaying both fresh and preserved materials to their best advantage. The texture is soft, sponge-like and unresistant, accepting stems of all sizes readily and holding them firm whilst retaining its shape without crumbling.

Because, like dried material, Oasis is light in weight, it is always wise, if a shallow container is being used, to anchor the Oasis in position with a pin holder, a heavy metal disc with closely packed vertical spikes, available in many sizes. These pin holders can, of course, be used effectively in many arrangements of both fresh and preserved material without Oasis but, although woody stems, cut at a slant, can be impaled at almost any angle, the metal spikes do undoubtedly restrict the easy flowing lines so much to be desired, simply because the spikes, being all at the same angle, are inclined to give a somewhat stiff, stylized effect. With preserved material, they are of special value in giving weight and can be easily secured in position with a little florists' clay or plasticine.

Driftwood is another valuable accessory to all home floral artists. Bleached and weathered by fair winds and foul, this is often sculptured by nature into fascinating shapes, which can be used to establish the perfect focal point for many different types of display and help to make the most of very few flowers when these are in short supply.

To use driftwood successfully, it must first be mounted securely on to a firm, flat base (fig. 31). According to its size and weight, this can be done with a strong, clear adhesive, anchoring the driftwood to a flat wooden

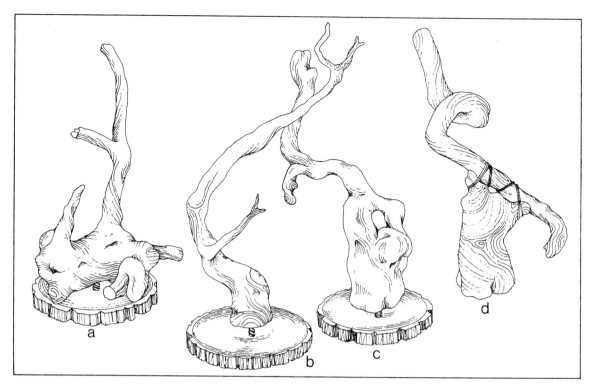

Fig. 31: *Driftwood.*
Driftwood or bark must be thoroughly cleaned before it is used in the home. Soak it in a bath of water with detergent or disinfectant to loosen debris and dirt and kill off insects. After it has thoroughly dried, brush it with a stiff or wire brush, and scrape out crevices with a sharp knife.

One way of using driftwood with security is to screw it to a 'log slice', which may be found at a timber merchant's. This is shown in a, b and c.

(d) A simpler method of securing driftwood. A length of wire is twisted round a convenient part of the driftwood, the ends are twisted and left sufficiently long to anchor the wood to the container.

base or, alternately, for greater and more permanent strength a screw through the bottom of the base into the driftwood will give a really firm hold. You will then have a permanent structural outline lending itself to many different types of display throughout the year, giving pleasure for a long time and enabling you to create many a spectacular display in the shortest possible time and with the minimum of preserved material.

Light and colour

Finding the right place in your home to show off to advantage such an original display as this depends on home surroundings, the character and atmosphere of the home, the decor and the predominant furnishing colours. The available lighting as well as colour contrasts must be taken into consideration.

Broadly speaking, colour comes in two distinct categories: advancing tones and receding shades. Advancing colours are yellow, orange, red, bright pink, salmon, white and lime; receding ones are blue, mauve, grey, green, brown and black.

It is helpful to remember several things, when planning an arrangement of preserved flowers and foliage for a particular room:

1 Blues and mauves are bad lighting-up colours; they tend to go grey at night. These colours should be reserved for those places where there is strong light or the display is to be positioned directly under a lamp.

2 White shows up wonderfully well even in a poor light.

3 Golden yellow gives a mystic, moonlight quality when combined with the more subtle shades of pink, whereas hard yellow tones create a cheerful atmosphere and an illusion of warmth, particularly when combined within their own colour range of orange and copper.

4 Pinks and red tones are splendid companions provided they have the same basic tonal value.

5 Silver and green have magical qualities of their own and, used skilfully, never fail to give additional interest.

6 Leaves with a matt surface absorb light and show to advantage with direct lighting, whilst those with a shiny surface reflect light and are more effectively displayed against light.

Colourful ingredients for a rose pot-pourri; roses, rose petals, orange and lemon with dried, powdered citrus skins, and, in the jars, vanilla pods, orris root and cinnamon.

7 Generally, a floral display is at its best when lit from above. Little more than outline will show up when the lighting comes from below and, in fact, both texture and colour values may be almost completely lost. If overhead lighting is not practical, the next best thing is to use full frontal lighting.

Experience soon teaches the different effects that can be achieved by placing one colour in close proximity to another and the effect lighting has on any display. For example, it will be immediately obvious that whereas ordinary electric light bulbs are apt to enhance such colours as reds and pinks, which have blue undertones, fluorescent lighting has the opposite effect and appears to drain away all colour, leaving an almost drab effect.

Pot-pourri

The natural development of an interest in preserving flowers is the making of pot-pourri. Apart from anything else, this provides an ever ready receptacle into which can be put those petals which inadvertently crumble in the process of preservation. Hopefully, these will be few and far between and, for the bulk of the material you will need in order to recapture and hold the sweet scents of a summer garden, you must collect flowers, fallen petals, scented leaves, herbs (such as thyme, marjoram and mint) and roots such as orris and angelica as each reaches peak condition for fragrance throughout the year.

Dried, scented leaves of all kinds, fragrant petals and colourful miniature flowers all have an equally important contribution to make to pot-pourri and, if you wish to be really successful, it is well worth while searching for the most highly scented varieties of these. It is not unusual to find that a flower which has little or nothing to contribute in the way of long-lasting fragrance is surrounded by leaves that have a delicious perfume of their own.

To test fragrance value, dry a small sample of the flower, leaf or herb you would like to add to your pot-pourri mixture quickly in the oven. When this becomes brittle, crumble it between the fingers, then smell not only the residue but your fingers as well.

The word 'pot-pourri' can be interpreted in many different ways and there are an infinite number of variations and family favourite recipes handed down from one generation to another.

Traditional ones that appear to remain the most popular are lavender-scented pot-pourri, rose-scented pot-pourri and herbal pot-pourri. The recipes given here for making these should be taken simply as guidelines (not hard and fast rules), for there will be some years when material of all kinds is readily available and other years when certain varieties are scarce but this is unlikely to affect the pleasure given by the final result.

Lavender pot-pourri is a deliciously pungent mixture made by adding $\frac{1}{2}$ lb (227 g) lavender florets to $\frac{1}{2}$ oz (14 g) dried thyme, $\frac{1}{2}$ oz (14 g) scented mint leaves, 1 oz (28 g) coarse kitchen salt, $\frac{1}{4}$ oz (7 g) powdered cloves and $\frac{1}{4}$ oz (7 g) powdered caraway seed. But, again, I would emphasize this should be regarded as little more than a reliable guideline. Of the many thousands of enthusiasts who make lavender-scented pot-pourri each year, there are few who do not have their own individual preference for one 'secret' additive or another.

Much of the same applies to rose-scented pot-pourri. Here as a standard guideline, try adding a quart (1.14 l) of dried rose petals to $\frac{1}{2}$ pt (0.14 l) of dried flowers and leaves of marjoram, lemon thyme (or lemon verbena), rosemary and lavender, 1 heaped teaspoon powdered citrus peel, 6 bay leaves, $\frac{1}{2}$ oz (14 g) cloves, 1 teaspoon all spice, 2 oz (56 g) coarse kitchen salt.

With fingertips, as if mixing butter, with flour, loosely intermingle all the ingredients, then put them in an air-tight container with a sprinkling of salt between each layer. This mixture should be allowed to mature for at least one month, after which time the fragrance should have stabilized and you will be able to pack the mixture into pot-pourri jars and in sachets.

Many people give an extra 'zing' to this particular rose pot-pourri recipe with an ounce of ground nutmeg and a teaspoon of powdered cinnamon and by the addition of two or three vanilla pods which are placed upright in the container so that the scent of the vanilla is evenly distributed throughout whilst the mixture matures.

A successful pot-pourri mixture is the result of many weeks, perhaps months, of collecting and preserving different varieties of fragrant flowers and leaves, as these develop. As flowers are collected, strip the florets from the stems and detach the petals of larger flowers from the calyx. Spread these out on newspaper in a warm, dry place out of draughts and direct sunlight, stirring them up once a day until finally you find them as crisp and crackly as tissue paper.

Herbs are best dried tied up in bunches and hung, upside down, in a dry, warm, well-ventilated place until the leaves may be removed from the stems without crumbling into powder.

It is not essential to choose every flower and leaf for its scent alone. There is always room for those of purely decorative value, a particularly beautiful shape or an outstanding colour.

The visual effect of any pot-pourri, when seen finally in its presentation pack, is greatly enhanced if whole, complete pressed flowers are used decoratively. Flat-faced flowers like the Everlastings, pansies, dog roses and such like, having been dried and preserved by the desiccant method, are laid on top of the pot-pourri mixture and immediately give a professional looking finish to any container. Petals which become detached from the calyx in the process of drying can, with a delicate touch, be put together again with the tiniest spot of clear adhesive applied on the end of a matchstick.

If you are seeking to achieve a particular colour effect with your pot-pourri, divide your material, according to colour, as you collect it and store in separate air-tight containers or tightly-sealed polythene bags. If blue is to predominate, the florets of delphinium, borage and larkspur and

A large swag flanked by four smaller ones, all made of preserved material including grasses, cones, seed-heads, acroclinium and beech foliage.

the petals of the cornflower will be invaluable; if you are concentrating on 'all the pinks' then, apart from the florets of hyacinth and stock, you have the wonderful world of roses from which to make your selection.

You can add more flowers and leaves of sympathetic colourings as these become available through the year and, when you find you have a mixture varied and colourful enough and sufficient for your purpose, the time will have come to 'fix' the fragrance. The more fixative you use, the longer will the fragrance last. Probably the simplest way to do this is to use one of the commercial preparations manufactured for the purpose and follow the directions given. Normally this will entail no more than putting the dried petals, herbs and leaves in a polythene bag, adding the commercial composition and shaking thoroughly. Left to mature for a minimum period of some two to three weeks, your pot-pourri will be ready to be packed for display.

Before the arrival of commercial fixatives, the traditional method of preserving and prolonging the fragrance of flowers entailed a great deal more effort but, in its own way, it is still the most satisfying and effective to use, particularly the centuries-old way with roses:

To five handfuls of dried rose petals, add four handfuls of coarse kitchen salt. Stir the mixture at least twice a day for a week. After that time, add five more handfuls of flowers, petals and leaves.

The fixative is prepared by putting 4 oz (113 g) powdered orris root into a bowl and, gradually, drop by drop, adding 1 oz (28 g) of a flower oil such as lavender, rosemary, geranium or other flower oil according to personal preference. After stirring well, 1 oz (28 g) ground coriander, 1 oz (28 g) ground nutmeg, 1 oz (28 g) crushed cloves and 2 sticks of powdered cinnamon are added. This mixture must be stirred frequently and very thoroughly to ensure that every petal and every leaf comes into close contact with the fixative paste; it should be stored in an air-tight container and left to mature for at least four weeks, being shaken and stirred once a week without fail.

A simpler way of fixing the fragrance lies in the use of citrus peel and in fragrant roots such as orris and angelica. There is, indeed, one very old recipe which asks for no more than salt; it maintains that rose petals well rubbed into one quarter of their own weight in salt and kept in an air-tight container, will keep their fragrance for years.

With citrus fruit (orange, lemon and tangerine), the peel is pared finely and dried slowly in a warm oven, then ground to a powder in an electric blender. Roots, once thoroughly dried, have to be pounded into powder. Of these, probably orris, which is scentless when fresh but gives off a fragrance reminiscent of violets as it ages, is the better known, followed closely by angelica, where roots are at their fragrant best after the plant has flowered.

To prepare roots such as these for use in pot-pourri, they must be washed and sliced as finely as possible and then dried very slowly in a warm oven. They will gradually become brittle and can then be pounded and ground; the resultant powder should be stored in air-tight jars.

If you are an enthusiastic pot-pourri maker, it is a good idea to keep some of this 'fixative' powder always in store, together with the spices

mentioned here, which contribute so much to the life of fragrance.

A well-stocked pot-pourri store cupboard would contain cloves, cinnamon, nutmeg, coriander, citrus peel and vanilla pods.

Such a store cupboard is necessary only for the professional and dedicated expert. Do not be afraid of experimenting. Successful pot-pourri has been, and is being, made with no more than the addition of powdered citrus peel and kitchen salt.

The Decorative Value of Preserved Flowers

Many of the most decorative uses to which preserved flowers and foliage can be put are overlooked. They are still regarded chiefly as an effective and colourful way of displaying floral display arrangements in the home throughout the year and particularly during those months when gardens and hedgerows are bare. As such, they inspire a lot of interest and provide the most fascinating of hobbies but when artifice joins forces with nature's art, the results can be surprising.

Candles, for example, make a charming gift at any time of the year. Choose plain, simple candles (fat, stubby ones are the easiest for the beginner to work with). The advantage of working with a white candle is that any preserved flower you already have will be shown up in sharp relief and give you the opportunity of seeing for yourself how very effective this treatment can be. In fact, there is no reason why you should not choose candles of any colour provided these will give an harmonious background to the preserved material you are using for the montage.

If you do not like the results of your first attempt, just dip the candle in hot water. The heat will float away the flower (or flowers) you may have used and you will be ready to start again.

You need an old saucepan (a double boiler is best), some melted wax (the ends of old white candles will do) and a child's paint-brush.

Melt the wax. While this is happening, prepare the flower (or flowers) you are going to use and rough out your design. I find a tiny spot of adhesive, just enough to hold the design in position on the candle for a few minutes, is a great help in ensuring the decoration does not slip and go awry as the liquid wax is applied.

With quick, positive strokes, to get as fine and transparent a covering as possible, paint over the material to be 'appliquéd' to the candle. This will be sealed in position immediately as the wax sets on impact with the cold surface of the candle. If there are any little blobs, these are easily flicked away with a fingernail.

Poppies, pansies, daisies, cornflowers, in fact, all the flat-faced flowers that preserve so well in a desiccant, lend themselves to this treatment, as do the delicate sprays of ferns, particularly a variety like maidenhair. Do not overdo it: simplicity is essential to success.

One charming idea for a dinner party is to use individual night lights, one for each guest. Select flowers and leaves in scale or snip off a few florets and separate petals and appliqué these with the molten wax to the night lights, which should be displayed (fixed with a little plasticine) on plain wooden coasters.

It is at All Hallows and at Christmas time that candles come into their own and inspire many an original way of presenting the dried and preserved materials collected and stored during the previous months. There is no end to the variety of container chosen at this time of year, ranging from wine bottles (fig. 32) to cleverly cut-out fruits and

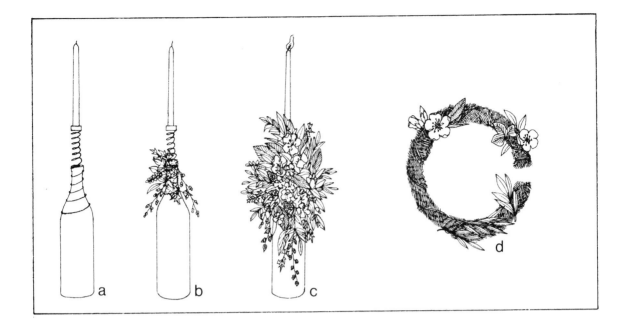

vegetables and there are few displays which are not enhanced by the addition of a candle here and there, whether it is to be lit up or not. If candles are to be lit, they must be placed well out of any direct contact with dry materials and, ideally, should be lit up only when used with water-soaked plastic stem holders.

Of all our Christmas traditions, the three most firmly established as a part of home decoration at this time of year are the tree, the kissing ring and the welcome wreath (or garland). It is from these that we automatically take our colour guide for the season: the red of the holly berry, white of the mistletoe and green of the pine.

The basic cone shape of the Christmas tree seems a natural shape for this time of year. With the help of the plastic foam cone shapes of many sizes so freely available, this is the easiest of all decorations and the most effective way of intermingling mixed snippets of evergreens, cones, small fruits and flowers.

In homes where space is limited, it is possible to create the illusion of the three-dimensional Christmas tree against any wall or flat surface. To do this, a well-shaped branch of spruce or fir, resembling as near as possible the outline of a tree, is fixed to a backcloth (a piece of plywood covered with red or green felt) and used as a wall-hanging. With an angel or shining star at the apex and a mass of colourful, glittering baubles interspersed with pine cones and coloured candles along the branches, and here and there a small bunch of artificial holly berries, the eye is easily deceived.

The kissing ring should, by tradition, be made by members of the family. One way of doing this is to buy four wire rings from the lampshade department of any big store. Three of these are bound together in one place; then, with one inside the others, the rings are

Fig. 32: *Using wine bottles.* A quick and easy way of making table or buffet decorations is to use attractive wine bottles. Fill the bottles with water or wet sand so they are well weighted and there will be no danger of over-balancing. (a) With the candle in position in the candlecup (which is filled with wet Oasis) the top of the bottle is covered with moss, bound in position round the neck of the bottle with wire or twine. (b) Short stemmed flowers, foliage and fruits are inserted through the wire into the moss. (c) Small bunches of fruits like grapes and/or currants are attached with hairpins into the moss, a few of the tiny bunches being allowed to spill down the sides of the bottle. (d) A floral ring round the base of the bottle is a pretty finishing touch. The ends are not joined so that it is easy to fit into position. This broken ring is made of wire covered with moss, held in position with twine. It is made slightly larger than the base of the bottle and small flowers and sprays of foliage are inserted into it.

These assorted foamed plastic shapes are used for mounting or sticking dried flowers.

Opposite: Backed by thuja fronds, this garland is made of acorns, lupin pods, beechmast cups, sweet chestnut burrs, pine and larch cones and holly berries.

spread into the shape of a skeleton ball and tied firmly together at cross over points. The fourth ring is now forced round the others and wired where they meet to ensure they remain evenly spaced in the shape of a ball. Cover all wire with moss bound round the wire with green twine and the ring is now ready for its final decoration.

Sprigs of greenery (fir, spruce, privet, cotoneaster, plain and variegated holly) are bound, one at a time, with wire until each ring is completely covered with greenery and ready for the finishing touches of colour. There was a time when tradition demanded three red apples should be hung inside the ring but nowadays it is more likely to be baubles or cones, gilded with gold or silver varnish spray and glittering with sequins. Large red ribbon bows at top and bottom and a sprig of mistletoe caught up in the bottom bow will transform those very ordinary-looking wire rings you started with into a spectacular symbol of Christmas.

With the low ceilings of many modern buildings, the traditional kissing ring may be too ambitious and over-powering. A very simple version can be created with a globe of non-absorbic foam bought at the florist's. Covered with moss and then with wire mesh to give security of tenure to the medley of dried flowers, leaves, cones, berries, baubles and bells with which it is to be disguised, this can be a successful substitute.

You will find an astonishing amount of preserved materials and evergreens can be used up if the foundation foam globe you choose is a large one, in which case you may have to trim your ideas still further and content yourself with something far simpler but quite effective.

In this case, the first thing to do is to spray the foam globe with gold or silver varnish and, when dry, divide it into eight equal segments with gold or silver ribbon, tying the ribbon in bows at the centre top and centre bottom and securing these bows with a little clear adhesive. The exposed segments of the globe can now be dotted with sequins of many colours if you want a kaleidoscopic effect, limiting yourself to one colour of sequin such as gold or silver if you are seeking greater elegance. A few dried flowers, ferns and tiny sprays of leaves are bunched in with the ribbon bows top and bottom, with a couple of Christmas bells or a sprig of mistletoe to give extra weight at the bottom.

Apart from the spray varnish which can so easily be used to add glitter to all kinds of preserved material and to evergreen ferns and leaves, there is probably nothing more useful than sequins for festive decorations. There seems to be no end to the number of occasions when these can be used effectively to give nature an extra special sparkle.

The transparent, papery moons of honesty, with sequins stuck to both sides, or big seed-heads like the ornamental onion, sequin tipped, have a fairy-like, irresistible beauty but sequins are slippery things to handle. The best way to do it is to use a knitting needle to transfer the tiniest drop of adhesive to the leaf, flower or seed-head you wish to decorate. Lift the sequin with tweezers and very gently slide it into place, holding it for a second or two with your fingertip until it has stuck fast.

As an alternative to the Christmas wreath, the Christmas garland gains in popularity with each succeeding year. Any type of evergreen and preserved material can be used for this.

The first thing is to make your base. This can be done with rolls of newspaper, which will make a soft and flexible base. If using newspaper, take three sheets and fold these together lengthwise to make a 2–3 in. (5–8 cm) wide roll. Work on one side of the roll at a time and start a few inches from the end of the roll to enable another length of newspaper to be overlapped and joined when the total length of the garland is achieved.

When this has been covered with red or green crêpe paper (an insurance against possible giveaway gaps in the finished garland) each sprig of foliage, approximately 3 in. (8 cm) in length, is bound separately into position with green twine, the twine being worked in a figure of eight once over the stem and once under, to make sure there will be a firm hold.

Small cones of larch can be interspersed between the foliage by running a stub wire or hairpin round the bottom scales of the cone; acorns in their cups and seed-heads of different shapes, sizes and colourings add their own special contribution and, if nature's red and yellow berries are in short supply, small artificial bunches of these will give a natural effect.

Because of its light weight, the finished garland can be draped over the front door, its two ends of unequal lengths hanging down at each side and held in position with Sellotape. It also provides a rather grand and effective decoration for a Christmas mantelpiece.

A different version of the garland can be seen in the wall plaques which are designed to hang on the wall. These have a foundation of thick cardboard or plywood cut to the size and shape the finished plaque is to be. Oasis, approximately 2 in. (5 cm) thick is firmly glued to this and covered with wire mesh to provide a firm hold for the flowers, foliage and fruits which will provide the final decorative effect. The cut ends of the wire mesh should be bent over the cardboard base, a light covering of adhesive glue applied and the whole covered with felt or hessian to avoid the possibility of marking the wall.

When making this type of preserved decoration, it is easiest to start in the middle, the focal point of the plaque at this, its widest point, and to fill in, working upward and downward simultaneously to maintain some continuity of design.

Choose well-shaped, tapering twigs for top and bottom. When fruit such as grapes and apples is to be introduced, intermingled with the dried flowers and foliage in the manner of Grinling Gibbons's wood carvings, it should be artificial to keep weight at its minimum.

The great thing about all these designs, created with such a wide choice of short-stemmed materials, is that complete freedom is given in the filling-in process. Small cones, gilded acorns in their cups, individual physalis lanterns, ivy berries, ribbon loops, seed-heads and colourful baubles and artificial berries all have the opportunity of being seen at their decorative best.

Crystallized Flowers

It is sad that so many of the old traditional ways of preserving flowers and the individual petals of flowers for culinary use in the kitchen are now almost forgotten.

Centuries before flowers were cultivated for their fragrance and beauty, they would be given growing space only if they could contribute something to the common good. They were used for jams, jellies and chutneys, for puddings and desserts, for summer drinks and tisanes and in confectionery.

Now we have gone to the opposite extreme and seldom take into account the nutritional value of flowers and their decorative use in transforming rather dull looking dishes into those that look exciting and appetizing. Instead, all our efforts are concentrated on producing bigger and more colourful blooms for visual effect.

Flower sugars are seldom found in a modern kitchen, yet, these, together with candied flowers, are one of the most economical ways of adding a touch of professional-looking luxury to simple cakes, ice creams and desserts. Violets, roses, primroses, daisies, cowslips, lavender, jasmine and apple blossom, to name but a few, are all edible. Avoid any flower grown from a bulb; this can be poisonous.

Making flower sugars is a simple operation; it entails no more effort than pounding together the petals of the chosen flower with icing sugar. How many flower petals? How much sugar? The proportions will depend on the density of colour you are looking for and must be the result of trial and error. As a guide, however, I have found that twenty-four violets mixed with two tablespoons of icing sugar result in a pale violet powdered candy and that lavender florets, well pounded with something like three times their own weight in icing sugar, will result in a conserve of lovely lavender blue.

Flower sugars, kept in an air-tight container will last well (many will keep for a year or more) and there are likely to be many occasions when they will justify their place in your store cupboard, giving a professional and appetizing topping to ice cream and a new look to iced buns. They can also be used for confectionery. Rose sugar lends itself particularly well to this.

A teaspoonful of lemon juice is beaten into the white of an egg until it stands in peaks when tested. Sifted rose sugar is now added and the mixture beaten till smooth. As a finishing touch a few rose petals (not candied) are blended in to the paste and this is turned out on to greaseproof paper, well dusted with icing sugar and rolled out thinly. When absolutely dry, this can be cut into 'peppermint cream' shapes and stored between sheets of greaseproof paper in an air-tight container.

The simplicity of making flower sugars is all the encouragement needed to progress to candied flowers. There are several schools of thought about the best way of doing this but probably the simplest is to beat up the white of an egg with a pinch of salt and two or three drops of water until stiff. Dip the petals in this, then coat each one with plenty of

icing sugar. Using tweezers for this operation is a great help, for the petal can be turned around in the beaten egg and then immediately transferred to a bowl of sugar. Each sugared petal must be thoroughly dried on greaseproof or wax paper in a slightly warm oven and, when dry, can be stored between sheets of paper in an air-tight container.

Rose petals, icing sugar, egg white, a pinch of salt and water are all you need to make candied flowers.

A slightly more complicated operation is that which involves boiling. Three-quarters of a cup of water and two cups of sugar are put into a preserving pan with a few flowers. Once this comes to the boil, the flowers are removed with a draining spoon and the liquid is allowed to continue to boil until the sugar begins to crystallize and turn white.

Put the flowers back in the preserving pan for one minute only, then lift them out with a draining spoon and place each one gently on a wire rack in a warm, dry part of the kitchen. When completely dry, these are sprinkled generously with icing sugar, shaking off any excess.

As with all crystallized and candied flowers, these should be stored without touching each other, between sheets of greaseproof or wax paper in an air-tight container.

Should any of the flowers disintegrate in the process of being preserved, the petals can be candied individually and re-arranged very effectively when the time comes for them to be used as a part of a decoration. A tiny piece of angelica makes a very realistic centre and stem.

Angelica has many uses and, fortunately, it is easy to grow and luxuriant in growth. Stems should be cut when young, washed and trimmed to equal lengths and cooked in boiling water until tender. Remove the stems from the boiling water, strip off the outer skin, then return to the pan and simmer until deep green in colour. Remove from the pan and spread out on kitchen paper. Pat dry.

The stems should now be weighed and spread over the base of a shallow dish covered with icing sugar, the amount of sugar used being at least equal in weight to the weight of the angelica stems. After two days in a covered container, stems and sugar are returned to the preserving pan and again brought to the boil. Once more the stems are removed from the heat and, after adding a further 2 oz (56 g) of sugar, the syrup is again allowed to boil. Put the stems back in the boiling syrup and allow to boil for a further five minutes.

The angelica can now be lifted out of the pan with a draining spoon, spread out on a baking tray, dried in a cool oven and stored in air-tight containers.

As a last minute emergency stand-by when guests arrive unexpectedly, it is possible to decorate a plain cake (or cakes) straight from the garden. Any of the edible flowers and leaves like mint can be lightly brushed over with egg white, then dipped in sugar. When dry, with angelica for stems and candied mint for leaves, they give a wonderfully professional looking finish to the homeliest of cakes.

Flowers that respond to dehydration by air	Best time for harvesting	Final colour to be expected
Acanthus	When lower florets are mature	White, purple
Acroclinum	Flowers half open	White, rose
African lily (Agapanthus)	When seed-heads have formed	Biscuit, cream
Alchemilla mollis	Fully mature	Green
Ammobium	All stages of growth, tiny buds to fully developed blooms	Silvery white
Anaphalis	Fully mature	White
Artemisia	As soon as flowers are fully open	Yellow flowers, silvery foliage
Beetroot (Beta)	After formation of seed-head	Mauve, purple, blue
Cape gooseberry (Physalis)	As turning bright orange	Bright orange
Cupid's dart (Catananche caerulea)	After formation of seed-head	Mauve, purple, blue
Eranthemum	When clusters of brilliantly coloured florets are in evidence	Silvery pink, mauve, white
Helichrysum bracteatum	July/August, when flowers are fully open	Red, apricot, yellow, orange, wine
Helipterum manglesii	Tiny star-like florets to be harvested midsummer	Yellow, white, purple
Helipterum roseum	When flowers partly open	White, pink, red
Hollyhock (Althaea)	When seed-heads have formed	Pink, red, white
Honesty (Lunaria annua)	As flowers begin to change colour, to avoid delicate seed pods being damaged	When papery covering is rubbed off the silvery heads are disclosed
Laburnum	Late spring, early summer as flowers begin to open fully	The pretty lemon colour when first harvested, matures to a dark cream

Flowers that respond to dehydration by air	Best time for harvesting	Final colour to be expected
Love in a mist (*Nigella*)	When fully mature	Silvery blue, blue
Love lies bleeding (*Amaranthus caudatus*)	Dries successfully if picked when fully ripe	Blood red
Lupin (*Lupinus polyphyllus*)	When lower florets are in full bloom	White, pink, yellow
Mignonette (*Reseda odorata*)	When seed-heads are fully formed (August)	Green, pink, white
Monkshood (*Aconitum napellis*)	When seed-heads have formed in early autumn	Violet, white, violet-blue
Sea lavender (*Limonium sinuatum*)	When brilliantly coloured clusters of florets are in evidence	Brightly blue spikes of tiny funnel shaped flowers
Sweet scabious, the pincushion flower (*Scabiosa atropurpurea*)	July/August	Dark crimson, white, lilac
Stock (*Matthiola incana*)	Late spring/early summer when fully open	Rose, pink, purple
Xeranthemum	When composite, bracted flower-heads are fully open	Long spiky petals in shades of rose, pink and purple
Yarrow (*Achillea*)	As soon as florets open	Golden yellow, pinkish red, white

Trees and foliage: Preserving with glycerine	Time for successful preservation
Australian gum (*Eucalyptus*)	At any time when leaves are in good condition
Barberry (*Berberis*)	Autumn, when berries are at their best
Bells of Ireland (*Molucella laevis*)	When flowers are in full bloom
Cotoneaster horizontalis	Autumn and early winter, when berries are at their best
Fig leaf tree (*Fatsia japonica*)	Autumn
Ivy (*Hedera*)	When berries are well formed
Lime tree (*Tilia*)	When sweetly-scented flowers are at their best and 'wings' of palest green are maturing
Magnolia	At any time when leaves are in good condition
Old man's beard (*Clematis*)	Before the seed-head is too fluffy and covered with dust
Parlour palm (*Aspidistra lurida*)	Any time: once preserved will last for years. May be rolled and tied up loosely scroll-wise; when dry and uncurled, leaves resume their natural curves. Will eventually be creamy-beige in colour
Solomon's seal (*Polygonatum*)	After flowering
Spindle tree (*Euonymous*)	Autumn
Sweet chestnut (*Castanea sativa*)	Individual leaves at any time

Bibliography

Allan, Mea, *The Tradescants* (London, 1964)

Anderson, A. W., *The Coming of Flowers* (London, 1951)

Armstrong, Nancy, *The Book of the Fan* (USA, 1978)

Basford, Kathleen, *The Green Man* (Ipswich, 1978)

Bazin, Gemain, *A Gallery of Flowers* (London, 1960)

Blunt, Wilfrid, *Tulipomania* (London, 1950)

Brimley, Johnson, R., *Mrs Delany* (London, 1925)

Brooke, Rupert, *Selected Poems* (London, 1923)

Brower and Miner, *Japanese Court Poetry* (London, 1962)

Coats, Alice, *Flowers and their Histories* (London, 1956)

Colby, Averil, *Patchwork* (London, 1958)

Coley, Hilda M., *The Romance of Garden Flowers* (London, 1945)

Dickensen, George, *Papier Mâché* (London, 1925)

Digby, G. W., *French Tapestries* (London, 1951)

Ellis, E. A., Perring, F. and Randall, R. E., *Britain's Rarest Plants* (Norwich, 1977)

Entwisle, E. A., *The Book of Wallpaper* (London, 1951)

Exhibition of Historical and British Wallpapers (London, 1945)

Floud, Peter, (compiler), *English Printed Textiles* (Victoria & Albert Museum, London, 1960)

Geijer, Agnes, *A History of Textile Art* (USA, 1979)

Grigson, Geoffrey, *The Goddess of Love* (London, 1978)

Grigson, G. and J., *Shapes and Stories* (London, 1964)

Hay, Roy and Synge, Patrick M., *The Dictionary of Garden Plants* (Royal Horticultural Society, London, 1969)

Hogg, Thomas, *A Treatise on the Growth and Cultivation of the Carnation*, etc. (London, 1824)

Hulton and Smith, *Flowers in Art From East and West* (British Museum, London, 1979)

Keim, Jean A., *Chinese Art* (London, 1961)

Kotewall and Smith, *The Penguin Book of Chinese Verse* (London, 1962)

McClintock, D., Perring, F. and Randall, R. E., *Picking Wild Flowers* (Norwich, 1977)

Mitchell, Sabrina, *Medieval Manuscript* (USA, 1965)

Phillips, Henry, *Flora Historica* (London, 1824)

Reeves, James (ed.), *Selected Poems of John Donne* (London, 1967)

Rock, C. H., *Paisley Shawls* (Scotland, 1966)

Salinger, Margaretta, *Flowers in European Painting* (USA, 1949)

Sharp-Ayres, H. M. E., *Mirror Painting in the Italian Style* (London, 1886)

Silberrad and Lyell, *Dutch Bulbs and Gardens* (London, 1909)

Silk Book, The (London, 1951)

Silver Studio Collection, The (London, 1980)

Sitwell, Sacheverell, *Old Fashioned Flowers* (London, 1948)

Sterling, A. M. W., *William De Morgan and His Wife* (New York, 1922)

Titley, Norah, *Plants and Gardens in Persian, Mughal and Turkish Art* (British Library, 1970)

Vallance, Aymer, *William Morris* (London, 1897)

Vedlich, Joseph, *The Ten Bamboo Studio* (USA, *c.* 1979)

Viale, Mercedes, *Tapestries* (London, 1966)

Walpole, Horace, *Letters* (London, *c.* 1926)

Wardle, Patricia, *English Embroidery* (Victoria & Albert Museum, London, 1970)

Whistler, Lawrence, *Rex Whistler, his Life and his Drawings* (London, 1948)

Whittle, M. Tyler, *Common or Garden* (London, 1969)

Suppliers of Materials for Pressed Flower Work

Peter Bates, Ltd, 1, West Street, Titchfield, Hants, PO14 4DH.
    Paperweights
Flora Products, Stanley Gibbons Magazine, Ltd, Drury House, Russell
    Street, London, WC2B 5HD.
    Paperweights
Framecraft, M. and M. Marketing, 83, Hamstead Hall Road,
    Handsworth Wood, Birmingham, B20 1JA.
    Frames, paperweights, boxes, dressing-table sets, etc.
Impress, Slough Farm, Westhall, Halesworth, Suffolk, IP9 8RN.
    Greetings card blanks, gift tags, reinforced ribbon book-marks,
    transparent-front bags, spray-on glue, etc.
Libro Frames, 5/8 Hart Street Bridge, Southport, Merseyside,
    Box frames
Paperchase Products Ltd, 213, Tottenham Court Road, London, W1;
    167, Fulham Road, London SW3.
    Japanese bark paper
Perpetua, The Firs, Stourton, Shipston-on-Stour, Warwickshire.
    Pressed flower kits
Paul Wu, Ltd, 64, Long Acre, Covent Garden, London WC2E 9JH.
    Chinese paper

Acknowledgements

The authors would like to thank Mr Neville Guille for the loan of the *Flowers from Jerusalem*, Miss Mea Allan for the Elder John Tradescant's recipe for glue and Mrs Constance Rye for permission to quote 'The Ring Dove' from *The Inn of the Birds* by Anthony Rye.

The authors and publishers would like to thank the following for supplying illustrations: Giolitto, Wrigley and Couch 46, 66, 68, 73, 86, 120, 130, 133, 159, 180, 183, 196, 205; Leslie Johns 7, 8, 10, 11, 170, 174, 175, 177, 179, 181, 184, 191, 194, 195, 199, 206, 207, 211: the Royal Society for Nature Conservation 54/5: Paul Wrigley 15, 20, 40, 50, 62, 70, 78, 175, 176, 185, 191, 193, 195, 198.

Index

Unpressed flowers and foliage